STUDIES OF THE RUSSIAN INSTITUTE
COLUMBIA UNIVERSITY

WEIMAR GERMANY AND SOVIET RUSSIA 1926–1933

A STUDY IN DIPLOMATIC INSTABILITY

WEIMAR GERMANY & SOVIET RUSSIA
1926-1933

A STUDY IN DIPLOMATIC INSTABILITY

By

Harvey Leonard Dyck

COLUMBIA UNIVERSITY

Columbia University Press

NEW YORK

The transliteration system used in this series is based on the Library of Congress system with some modifications.

THE RUSSIAN INSTITUTE OF COLUMBIA UNIVERSITY

The Russian Institute of Columbia University sponsors the STUDIES OF THE RUSSIAN INSTITUTE in the belief that their publication contributes to scholarly research and public understanding. In this way the Institute, while not necessarily endorsing their conclusions, is pleased to make available the results of some of the research conducted under its auspices.

Library of Congress Catalog Number 66–14594

Printed in Great Britain

For my Parents

CONTENTS

'Can two walk together, except they be agreed?'

AMOS 3: 3.

Can two walk together, except they be agreed?

Amos 3. 3

PREFACE

My purpose in writing this book has been to describe and explain two distinguishing features of German-Soviet diplomatic relations in the years 1926 to 1933 – their chronic instability and remarkable longevity. This aim has also largely determined the main focus of my study. In preference to a biographical approach, which would tend to subordinate considerations of policy to those of personality, my attention has been directed to policy questions: the manner in which policy makers framed issues of external relations and perceived spectra of political choice, the criteria they applied in choosing from among alternative programs, and, finally, the techniques they used to test, implement, reappraise, and revise those programs. The perspective of this book is partly inherent in the principal sources used: the records of the Reich Chancellery, the Wilhelmstrasse, and the German Embassy in Moscow. Although I have broadened my angle of vision by using additional German and Soviet printed materials, the vicissitudes of German-Soviet relations are nevertheless seen chiefly from the vantage point of the German Foreign Ministry.

The research and writing of this study was facilitated by a Ford Foundation Fellowship from 1960 to 1962 and a summer grant from the Russian Institute at Columbia University in 1965. My research was also greatly aided by the help of Hermann Teske and Wolfgang Mommsen of the Bundesarchiv, Koblenz; the staff of the Library of the Foreign Ministry, Bonn; and Fritz Epstein, Erich Hagewald, Ernst Georg Lange, Johannes Ullrich, Norbert Wagner, and especially the late and much lamented Joachim Lampe of the Political Archives of the Foreign Ministry, Bonn. A special word of appreciation is due Henry L. Roberts and Fritz Stern of Columbia University for encouragement and assistance in the early stages of my work. In the later stages I am much indebted to my friends Pierre L. van den Berghe, Boheslav B. Kymlicka, Peter Novick, and George H. Stein for reading the manuscript and for their criticisms, both of style and content. The final manuscript was typed with care by Sarah MacMillan and the secretarial staff of the Russian Institute at Columbia headed by Lyn Taheri.

Finally, I want to thank my beloved wife, Anne Konrad Dyck, for support at all stages of the preparation.

Harvey L. Dyck

New York City
August 1965

Part One

PROMISE AND PERILS, 1926

1. THE TREATY OF BERLIN

ON April 24, 1926, German Foreign Minister Gustav Stresemann and Soviet Ambassador Nikolai Krestinskii signed a bilateral agreement known as the treaty of Berlin. Its purpose was to stabilize the German-Soviet partnership that had been unsettled for the past eighteen months. Consisting of five articles and an exchange of notes, the treaty recognized the Rapallo accord of 1922 as the cornerstone of the relationship and bound the signatories to consult on all questions of common interest. The hard core of the agreement was a promise by Germany and the Soviet Union that they would maintain scrupulous neutrality in any conflict stemming from an unprovoked attack on one of them by another state. The signatories further promised that in the event of such a crisis they would not participate in economic or financial measures against each other. Appended was an exchange of notes in which the German government affirmed that its membership in the League of Nations would not conflict with a policy of friendship towards the USSR and promised that it would 'energetically oppose' anti-Soviet machinations at Geneva. The treaty had a life span of five years from the date of its ratification and contained no secret clauses.[1]

A study of the origins of the agreement suggests that the German-Soviet partnership was unstable and considerably more complex than a recitation of its terms might indicate. Indeed one can argue that the Berlin treaty was inherently unstable because of the partly conflicting diplomatic systems of its signatories. Instability was a new condition in German-Soviet diplomacy, for

[1] League of Nations, Secretariat, *Treaty Series* (Lausanne 1926), LIII, no. 1268, 387–96.

earlier the diplomatic interests of the two states had run parallel. In 1922, at Rapallo, they had joined a defensive partnership that was intended to end their shared weakness and isolation.[1] During the subsequent years, 1922–4, the acute friction in German-Soviet relations had originated less in diplomacy than in the turmoil of Germany's internal politics and the drive of revolutionary Communism.[2]

From late 1924, however, the diplomatic interests of the Rapallo partners began to diverge—ironically at a time when the stabilization of Germany's politics was removing one formidable obstacle to German-Soviet concord. It is questionable whether this divergence can be explained simply in terms of the variety of new diplomatic alignments that these years opened to Berlin and Moscow. Both states, to be sure, participated in the quickened diplomatic pace of international relations after 1923. But it was of critical importance to their later relations that they participated unequally.

German diplomacy of the mid-1920s was crowned with the success of Locarno; Soviet diplomacy, however, must be judged a failure when its record is contrasted with the sensitive goal set for it by the Soviet government. That goal, to carry through a diplomatic holding action in Europe while far-ranging anti-colonialist and revolutionary objectives were being pursued in Asia, was part

[1] See: W. von Blücher, *Deutschlands Weg nach Rapallo* (Wiesbaden: Limes Verlag, 1951); E. H. Carr, *The Bolshevik Revolution, 1919–1923* (New York: Macmillan, 1953), III, 339–82; Gerald Freund, *Unholy Alliance* (London: Chatto and Windus, 1957); Gustav Hilger and A. G. Meyer, *The Incompatible Allies: German-Soviet Relations, 1918–1941* (New York: Macmillan, 1953), 1–83; Golo Mann, 'Rapallo: The Vanishing Dream', *Survey* (October 1962), 74–88; Paul Noack, 'Rapallo—Wunsch und Wirklichkeit', *Politische Studien*, II (1960), 31–43; Kurt Rosenbaum, *Community of Fate: German-Soviet Diplomatic Relations, 1922–1928* (Syracuse: University Press, 1965), 1–48; T. Schieder, *Die Probleme des Rapallo Vertrags: Eine Studie über die deutsch-russischen Beziehungen, 1922–1926* (Köln: Westdeutscher Verlag, 1956). For a useful East German account with much new material from archives of the DDR see, Günther Rosenfeld, *Sowjetrussland und Deutschland, 1917–1922* (Berlin: Akademie Verlag, 1960). For a Soviet interpretation see, I. K. Kobliakov, *Ot Bresta do Rapallo* (Moscow: IMO, 1954).

[2] For the period 1922 to 1926 see: Alfred Anderle, *Die Deutsche Rapallo-Politik* (Berlin: Rütten u. Loening, 1962), 53–199; E. H. Carr, *Socialism in One Country, 1924–1926* (London: Macmillan, 1964), III, Part 1, 47–69; Freund, op. cit.; Hans W. Gatzke, 'Von Rapallo nach Berlin: Stresemann und die deutsche Russlandpolitik', *Vierteljahrshefte für Zeitgeschichte*, IV (January 1956), 1–29; Hilger and Meyer, op. cit., 84–164; Rosenbaum, op. cit., 49–187.

of a new strategic design that had evolved in 1924–5 with the shift in focus of Soviet activities from Europe to Asia. The abortive German 'October' in 1923[1] and the precipitate decline in Anglo-Soviet relations after 1924[2] had plunged the Soviet leadership into gloom about the susceptibility of the west to its revolutionary and diplomatic prowess. This pessimism, coupled with the meteoric rise of national revolutionary movements in China and nearby colonial areas, induced the Politburo to pin its hopes for the near future on the spread of Bolshevik influence in Asia.

At the heart of this shift of emphasis in Soviet policy was a political strategy whose principal target was Britain—the chief capitalist and colonial power in the area. The Soviet Commissar of Foreign Affairs, Chicherin, spoke candidly of the change in Soviet policy to Count Ulrich von Brockdorff-Rantzau, the German Ambassador in Moscow. 'It can be assumed', he told him in March 1925, 'that the development here will take a different course from what it has until now. At present the Soviet Union finds herself compelled to become active in Asia and her interests in the first instance point towards the east where she finds herself colliding everywhere with English interests.'[3]

In the four or five years after 1924 no consideration influenced Moscow's diplomacy quite so much as the presumption of British enmity. Soviet leaders reasoned that the geographical remoteness of their possessions in the Far East would impel the British to seek a European base from which to organize economic or perhaps even military action against the USSR. Consequently, the strategic purpose of Soviet diplomacy was to keep the states of central and western Europe out of the sphere of Britain's machinations by reaching a *détente* with them. The prior Politburo decision on a forward course in Asia dictated a cautious policy of winning prestige in Europe and creating an impression of political strength.

In the event Soviet diplomacy was only marginally successful. The Soviet Union's promising harvest of diplomatic recognitions

[1] Werner T. Angress, *Stillborn Revolution: The Communist Bid for Power* (Princeton: University Press, 1963); E. H. Carr, *The Interregnum, 1923–1924* (New York: Macmillan, 1954), 201–42.

[2] See E. H. Carr, *Socialism in One Country, 1924–1926*, III, Part 1, 21–34. For a Soviet interpretation, see F. D. Volkov, *Anglo-sovetskie otnosheniia, 1924–1929 gg.* (Moscow: Gospolitizdat, 1958), 79–111.

[3] Rantzau to Stresemann, March 9, 1925, L337/L100564–8.

in 1924 hardly led beyond legal formalities, and except for her close ties with Germany she was still comparatively isolated in Europe in 1926. Soviet officials were shaken by their string of failures and Germany's diplomatic triumphs, and in the eighteen months before the signature of the Berlin treaty assumed that Germany's rapprochement with their chief adversary, Britain, might terminate in an attack on the Soviet Union by a united capitalist world.[1]

So as to forestall such a perilous development Foreign Commissariat (Narkomindel) officials again, as in 1922, concentrated their diplomatic efforts on Berlin, using two approaches. In late 1924 they tried to turn Germany's rapprochement with France and England from a germ of future alliance against the USSR into a bridge on which Russia could enter a larger grouping herself. What Moscow had in mind was the imaginative yet far-fetched idea of enlarging the German-Soviet combination of Rapallo into a *continental bloc* including France and directed against England.

In December 1924, Chicherin proposed such a three-nation grouping to Rantzau, suggesting it would constitute the 'surest guarantee of the maintenance of peace'.[2] The initiative, however, was barren of results. In his reply Rantzau confined himself to two observations that were as brief as they were devastating. The French, he warned, were only interested in eliciting from Russia a guarantee of the humiliating conditions of the Versailles settlement and would not permit Moscow to engage them in a tandem agreement with Berlin. Equally important, Germany could not permit herself to be drawn into a combination antagonistic to Britain.

Rebuffed, the Narkomindel then turned to the more realistic task of keeping Germany from slipping into an anti-Soviet con-

[1] For Soviet views see: V. B. Ushakov, *Vneshniaia politika Germanii v period Veimarskoi respubliki* (Moscow: IMO, 1958), 83–100; V. G. Trukhanovskii (ed.), *Istoriia mezhdunarodnikh otnoshenii i vneshnei politiki SSSR, 1917–1939 gg.* (Moscow: IMO, 1961), I, 279–305. Continuing Soviet interest in the subject is reflected in the collection of documents: A. F. Dobrov (ed.), *Lokarnskaia konferentsiia 1925 g.: Dokumenti* (Moscow: Gospolitizdat, 1959).

[2] Rantzau to the Foreign Ministry, December 1, 1924, 5265/E317849–52. The idea was first broached by Chicherin in 1923, at the height of the Ruhr crisis (E. H. Carr, *Socialism in One Country*, III, Part 1, 37–8). It was again discussed by him in April with an unidentified German citizen (unsigned memorandum, April 19, 1923, 1882/K482495–507).

stellation. This was Moscow's minimal diplomatic goal. It was to be reached by securing Germany's neutrality for future contingencies, an objective that explains Soviet maneuvers in 1925 to disrupt the negotiations for a Rhine pact and for Germany's adherence to the League of Nations.[1] During these negotiations the Narkomindel was frustrated in its design to impose a veto on any agreement between Berlin and London.

The most it achieved was to induce Stresemann to insist at Locarno on an interpretation of Article 16 of the League Charter that, in his words, would permit Germany to decide the 'extent to which [she] would join in taking action against a disturber of the peace'.[2] But this gesture failed to mollify Soviet diplomats, who continued to hold out for a new accord; finally, in April 1926, they elicited from the Wilhelmstrasse the modified neutrality pact of the Berlin treaty, which again cast Germany as the linchpin of Soviet Russia's security in Europe.

It would be wrong, however, to picture Soviet leaders in 1926 as sanguine about the longer-term prospects of German-Soviet cooperation. They were certain that in a time of crisis Britain would try to use her economic strength to bend Germany to her political will, or would seek to force Germany through a League resolution or at bayonet point to permit the transit of western forces across her soil. In addition, as an *Izvestiia* editorial said, they held to the dogmatic assumption that 'ultimately the German bourgeoisie, capitalist Germany, will take its stand where its fundamental class interests dictate'.[3] At best, Germany was considered to be in a transition phase: the pressures on her to opt for the west were onerous, but the link with Russia still offered her compelling commercial, political, and military advantages. The purpose of Soviet diplomacy was simply to prolong this transitional period by demonstrating to Berlin the benefits of intimate relations. Germany's neutrality could well prove decisive to Russia's survival in a hostile world that might coalesce against her under Britain's leadership.

Germany's approach to the Berlin treaty diverged markedly from Russia's, chiefly because of her more favorable international situation. In 1926 German diplomacy was no longer preoccupied

[1] E. H. Carr, *Socialism in One Country*, III, Part 1, 248–82.
[2] Cited in Gerald Freund, *Unholy Alliance*, 234.
[3] *Izvestiia*, April 13, 1927.

with the question of fundamental security, as Soviet diplomacy still was. After the formerly urgent threat of French intervention had been dissipated at Locarno, Berlin was interested in the pursuit of farther-ranging goals – the achievement of which, in German eyes, depended on continued Soviet support. Stated briefly, Stresemann negotiated the Berlin treaty in the belief that a renewed treaty relationship with Russia was essential to Germany's economy, would strengthen his hand in further negotiations with the western powers, would permit Germany to continue her evasion of the most irksome military restrictions of the Versailles treaty, and, finally, would facilitate a speedy revision of Germany's eastern border. In the contemporary language of the Foreign Ministry, a continued close working relationship with the USSR was to ensure the success of Germany's *Wirtschaftspolitik*, *Gesamtpolitik*, *Militärpolitik*, and *Ostpolitik*.

The notion that Germany's economic health hinged on intimate relations with the USSR was argued by the German business community throughout the negotiations leading to the Berlin treaty. It was rooted in the conviction that Germany's industry could not recover from the post-war slump until it recaptured its pre-1914 position in Russia's trade; such an expansion was considered dependent on close political ties. A Foreign Ministry official described German business circles in 1925–6 as 'hypnotized' by the impressive figures for pre-war Russo-German trade, which showed that Germany had supplied close to one half of Russia's total imports.[1] Suffering from overproduction, German heavy industry found these statistics appealing, the more so when Soviet officials held out the prospect of their duplication when the political precondition had been met – a counter-treaty to Locarno.

Such economic considerations effectively reinforced more crucial political motives that led to the Berlin treaty. By 1925–6 it had become an axiom in the thinking of the Foreign Ministry that Locarno was a harvest of Rapallo and that the extraction of further concessions from the western powers demanded the further use of the USSR as a political lever. Few persons in the Wilhelmstrasse would have quarreled with Rantzau's proposition that 'the

[1] Dirksen to the German Ambassador in France, Hoesch, January 12, 1926, 6698/H110936–43; cf. Alfred Anderle, 'Die deutsch-sowjetischen Verträge von 1925/26', *Zeitschrift für Geschichtswissenschaft*, V (1959), 471–502.

Soviet Union has been for us the counter that since Rapallo has raised the value of our foreign policy and in the last years has not only supported that policy but has made it possible'.[1]

Thus for Berlin's *Gesamtpolitik*, the 1926 agreement was intended as a standing threat to the western powers that it would be transformed into an alliance if Germany were not accommodated in such matters as the evacuation of the Rhineland, reparations, armaments, and political equality. Because the Foreign Ministry regarded Paris as the chief pillar of the Versailles settlement and the main obstacle to its revision it also becomes clear that the Berlin treaty was to be used as an anti-French instrument.

2. THE POLITICS OF SECRECY

THE interplay between German-Soviet diplomacy and the clandestine collaboration of the Red Army and the Reichswehr is important and yet highly elusive. One obstacle to an appraisal of the problem is the secrecy in which military relations were shrouded. We know, for instance, that Foreign Ministry officials with responsibilities in the area of eastern relations were privy to the contacts; they weighed their promise and their perils. Yet they only infrequently treated them in their memoranda as part of the intricate network of German-Soviet relations, partly because of their ever-present fear of foreign disclosure. Occasionally, in order to dramatize a point, Rantzau cited the illicit contacts as a 'strong, if not the strongest political tie' in the understanding with Moscow.[2] Yet few similarly analytical statements are to be found in the Wilhelmstrasse's files.

A further reason that contributed to the diplomat's chariness in linking diplomacy and military collaboration was the difficulty of doing so. Wilhelmstrasse officials recognized that the illicit contacts were developing in response to considerations that made them relatively immune from the friction generated by wavering diplomatic and trade alignments. For the Wilhelmstrasse and the Narkomindel diplomatic bonds were means to other ends, their utility

[1] Memorandum by Rantzau entitled: 'Das 10-Jährige Bestehen der Sowjetunion, Ein Rück- und Ausblick', November 26, 1927, K281/1097502–509.

[2] Rantzau to Schubert, July 14, 1926, 2860/D558026–30; for a similar expression see draft letter, Rantzau to Stresemann, April 12, 1928, L337/L100723–30.

largely measured by the impression they made on other states; for the Reichswehr and the Red Army military collaboration was an end in itself, its success dependent on secrecy. For this reason military ties were invested with a degree of autonomy, though not independence, from the other levels of German-Soviet relations.

Thus the *raison d'être* of military cooperation was largely defined by the indispensable military benefits, not obtainable elsewhere, that it promised both sides. These benefits, it must be stressed, were neither strategic nor tactical, but purely technical. The Germans got from the clandestine association 'space and secrecy',[1] which they needed to test weapons and equipment denied them by the Versailles treaty and to train military personnel in their use. The Russians, on the other hand, used it to exploit German military and technical prowess in the development of their deficient and backward military establishment. Joint meetings of the general staffs were never scheduled nor were common war plans worked out. To be sure, a strategic factor implicit in the situation was the mutual assumption that increments in power resulting from the contacts would pose an immediate threat only to a common adversary, Poland. This identity of interests persisted throughout the period of the Weimar Republic, making military ties more stable than other areas of German-Soviet cooperation.

Negotiations for the Berlin treaty happened to coincide with a shift in the emphasis of military relations. An earlier phase, that had started in 1921, was slowly being brought to a close. Beginning in 1921, a number of German firms (among them Junkers, Krupp, and Stolzenberg) were encouraged—and partly financed—by the Reichswehr to provide military-technical assistance for Russia in the reconstruction of her shattered armaments industry. By 1924 German assistance had led to the creation of a joint German-Soviet company for the manufacture of poison gas, a factory for aircraft production organized as a German concession, and a number of Soviet munitions plants under the supervision of German technicians. But because this line of activity was beset by insurmountable financial, technical, and personnel problems, it never flourished; and by early 1926 it was well on the way to being liquidated, a process completed about a year later. The termination of this phase of the collaboration also had an ironic sequel. The shipment

[1] The phrase appears in John Erickson, *The Soviet High Command* (New York: St. Martin's Press, 1962), 252.

to Germany in the autumn of 1926 of about 300,000 pieces of ammunition—her share of the jointly produced munitions—led to sensational disclosures of the illicit arms traffic in the *Manchester Guardian* and to stormy scenes in the Reichstag.[1]

But what these reports failed to disclose was a second phase of the collaboration, which had already moved well beyond the planning stage. This phase, discussed between the two military establishments as early as 1922,[2] had begun in earnest in 1924. It involved the exchange of officers at maneuvers,[3] the attendance of senior Red Army officers (some 120 from 1924 to 1932) at courses of the Truppenamt (the concealed general staff) and direct cooperation between the Red Army and the Reichswehr in joint training and testing stations located in the Soviet Union.

Of three German bases eventually put into operation the first and most important was a flying school at Lipetsk, about 250 miles southwest of Moscow, which was started in 1924. It conducted its initial training course for fighter pilots in 1925. Observer training was added to its program in 1928, the year that also saw Lipetsk emerge as an important center for the technical and operational testing of prototypes of new German combat aircraft.

From 1925 to 1933 the results of the instructional programs were the training of about 120 German fighter pilots and 80 observers. The testing projects, which at one stage required the services of as many as 200 German technicians, enabled the Reichswehr and German aircraft firms to freeze proven types of fighter planes

[1] For details of this phase see the following on which this summary is based: E. H. Carr, *Socialism in One Country*, III, Part 1, 46–69, Part 2, 1010–7; Francis L. Carsten, *Reichswehr und Politik, 1918–1933* (Köln: Kiepenheuer und Witsch, 1964), 253–9; Erickson, op. cit., 144–63; Herbert Helbig, *Die Träger der Rapallo-Politik* (Göttingen: Vandenhoeck und Ruprecht, 1958), 149 ff.; Hans W. Gatzke, 'Russo-German Military Collaboration During the Weimar Republic', *American Historical Review*, LXIII (April 1958), 565–78. Soviet silence concerning military collaboration has been so total that a survey of western accounts of German-Soviet relations cites Gatzke's essay without title (V. B. Ushakov, 'Otnosheniia mezhdu Sovetskim Soiuzom i Veimarskoi Germaniei v izobrazhenii zapadnogermanskoi burzhuaznoi istoriografii', *Istoriia SSSR* [1959], 182–90).

[2] Erickson, op. cit., 153.

[3] For a memoir account by a former Reichswehr officer who served Soviet military delegations as guide and interpreter see, Karl Spalcke, 'Begegnungen zwischen Reichswehr und Roter Armee', *Aussenpolitik* (August 1958), 506–13.

and short- and long-range reconnaissance aircraft for eventual mass production. The Red Army, for its part, shared fully in the benefits of both programs. Soviet ground and air personnel participated on a footing of equality with their German colleagues in the technical courses, and the Red Army was given full access to the technical, tactical, and theoretical information obtained from the development and testing programs.[1]

Soviet officials, it seems, were even more intimately involved in the activities of the other two training and testing bases, about which, however, fewer details are known. A tank school and testing center near Kazan – first used as a training ground for tanks, artillery and communications after 1926 – entered its most important phase in 1929 as a testing site for prototypes of heavy and light tanks (developed by Krupp and Rheinmetall on contract to the Reichswehr) and the adaptation of foreign-made tanks for German purposes.[2] Also scheduled to begin operations in 1926, the gas center near Saratov did not get under way until 1928 partly because of the alarm caused by the disclosures of the *Manchester Guardian*. The base, which functioned with a small group of German technicians and a Soviet staff, was used for experiments in the production of poison gas and for the testing of gas delivery devices and protective equipment such as gas masks.[3]

That the clandestine military ties played a crucial role in the build-up of the German and Soviet military establishments can no longer be doubted. Their importance, however, must be measured less in terms of the sums of money and numbers of men involved,

[1] For an excellent memoir account of the development and work at Lipetsk see, Helm Speidel, 'Reichswehr und Rote Armee', *Vierteljahrshefte für Zeitgeschichte*, I (January 1953), 9–45. See also Karl-Heinz Völker, 'Die Entwicklung der militärischen Luftfahrt in Deutschland, 1920–1933', *Beiträge zur Militär- und Kriegsgeschichte*, ed. H. Meier-Welcker (Stuttgart: Deutsche Verlags-Anstalt, 1962), III, 124–230.

[2] Erickson, op. cit., 269–70, 278; Carsten, op. cit., 257–8. George H. Stein has been able to provide new details about the operation at Kazan from files of the *Oberkommando der Wehrmacht* which contain some records of the *Heereswaffenamt* ('Reichswehr and Red Army: The Secret Collaboration, 1921–1933' [unpublished Master's essay, Columbia University, 1960], 47–56). This work suggests that further diligent search in the same records would yield other important details.

[3] Erickson, op. cit., 256–60; Stein, op. cit.; Report by Blomberg, 9480/H276183–236; Memorandum by Dirksen regarding conversation with Blomberg, December 29, 1927, 4564/E163921–3.

than against the needs of a disarmed Reichswehr[1] and a technically deficient Red Army. For the Reichswehr the bases on Soviet soil permitted the development of prohibited types of weapons and, more important, enabled a cadre of military personnel to 'maintain a continuous tradition precisely in a period of rapid tactical and technical development in other countries . . .'.[2] Senior Reichswehr officers described the contacts as 'vital for our army',[3] and termed as 'beyond question' the significance of the bases for Germany's rearmament,[4] a conclusion supported by the studies of Carr, Carsten, Gatzke, Schmidt-Richberg, Speidel, and Völkers.[5]

The pioneering work of a British scholar permits a similar judgement to be made about the value of the military contacts for the modernization of the Red Army. In *The Soviet High Command*, John Erickson notes that both the creation of the Soviet Air Force after 1924 and the absorption of the Red Army command in the subject of motorized warfare after 1928 'coincided with the intensification of work in the joint Soviet-German training and experimental centres'.[6] Likewise, the seconding of senior Soviet officers to German staff courses greatly aided in the training of a new Soviet command; it permitted military officials to 'acquire close acquaintance with the technique of modern training as well as first-hand observation of the methods of organization employed in a force dedicated to the idea of the cadre and the exploitation of ultra-modern military techniques'.[7] Finally, he argues, German technical help—particularly after 1929—'played a substantial part in remedying the defects of the native Soviet [war] industry'.[8] For

[1] Cf. Otto Gessler, *Reichswehrpolitik in der Weimarer Zeit* (Stuttgart: Deutsche Verlags-Anstalt, 1958), 200.

[2] Speidel, op. cit., 17.

[3] Cited in Gatzke, op. cit., 586.

[4] Report by General Blomberg: 'Reise des Chefs des Truppenamts nach Russland (August/September 1928)', November 17, 1928, 9480/H276183–236. 'A full exploitation of [the bases] is of vital (lebenswichtig) interest from the standpoint of our rearmament' (ibid).

[5] Carr, *Socialism in One Country*, III, Part 2, 1017; Carsten, op. cit., 253–9; Wiegand Schmidt-Richberg, 'Die Generalstäbe in Deutschland, 1871–1945', *Beiträge zur Militär- und Kriegsgeschichte*, III, 66–7; Speidel, op. cit.; Völkers, op. cit., 225–30. Blomberg commented that at Lipetsk the 'vital interests of the Reichswehr and the defense of our country were at stake' (Memorandum by Dirksen, December 29, 1927, 4464/E163921–3).

[6] John Erickson, *The Soviet High Command*, 270.

[7] Ibid., 281.

[8] Ibid., 349.

these reasons, as well as the issue of Poland, 'collaboration with the German Army was not merely incidental to Soviet military policy'.[1]

The conclusion that the Red Army and the Reichswehr gained from their illicit ties indispensable military advantages that they could not have obtained elsewhere at the time, leads to a further question, one about the linkage between diplomacy and military collaboration. Was the threat of Soviet blackmail as acute as Schubert, Rantzau, and Stresemann occasionally feared? Were Soviet leaders in a position to wring economic or political concessions from Germany by threatening to divulge details of the clandestine relationship?

On the surface the threat to Germany of blackmail did indeed seem to inhere in the military bond. Of the conspirators Germany had most to fear from an unmasking of the joint operations: before 1925 there was the risk that France might again occupy the Ruhr, subsequently that Germany's policy of conciliation in the west (Locarno, League of Nations) would be compromised. For the Soviet regime, on the other hand, disclosure would result in little more than an embarassment of the German Communist Party (KPD).

Yet against the Reichswehr's greater concern with secrecy one must weigh the Red Army's lively interest in keeping the bonds intact for purely military reasons. Since a Soviet attempt at blackmail would almost certainly have resulted in their severance, the likelihood of such action was slight so long as Soviet leaders were unable to get support for the modernization of the Red Army from other foreign sources or effect that modernization on their own – a situation that persisted to the end of the Weimar Republic.[2] Cases of Soviet blackmail are simply unknown.

Nevertheless the fear of Wilhelmstrasse officials that the secret contacts made them vulnerable to pressure from Moscow – that they 'found themselves in the hands of political blackmailers'[3] – must be counted a factor that subtly colored their thinking about

[1] John Erickson, *The Soviet High Command,* 277.

[2] The Soviet government could conceivably have hired technical help for the creation of a specialized war industry from other western countries. But it did not have a sufficient *quid pro quo* to elicit from countries other than Germany the military benefits of a tactical, technical, and theoretical kind that it derived from the officer exchanges, training courses, and operations of the bases.

[3] Rantzau to Stresemann, July 5, 1926, 4564/E163601–8.

relations with the USSR. It could, on the one hand, make them more yielding to Soviet wishes; Otto Hasse, Chief of the German Army Command, suggested to Schubert that the task of diplomacy was to ensure that 'relations with Russia are always so friendly that in practice the danger of our being compromised would not come in question'.[1]

But more often German diplomats would chafe at their lot and explore schemes for keeping the hazardous operation in bounds. In early 1926, when a disclosure of the clandestine dealings might easily have imperilled Stresemann's strategy of 'European balance', the whole issue became acute as the result of a Soviet initiative. About a month before the initialing of the Berlin treaty, a Soviet military mission headed by Unshlikht, the Deputy Commissar of War, arrived in the German capital with suggestions for an astonishing increase in military collaboration.

After discussions in the Reichswehrministerium,[2] the Soviet officials laid their proposals before an inner circle of German government leaders including Chancellor Marx, Stresemann, Schubert, General von Seeckt, and General Wetzel. The Soviet government, Unshlikht explained, needed German orders and financial and technical aid for a huge expansion of her war potential in heavy artillery, poison gases, optical instruments with military uses, and other war materials. The question at stake, Krestinskii elaborated, was whether there would be an increase of the joint activities on the 'basis of the pending negotiations for the political treaty that was ready for conclusion'.[3]

Visibly startled by these far-reaching proposals, the Chancellor and Foreign Minister responded with evasive promises that a reply could be expected through diplomatic channels. Subsequent discussions in the Wilhelmstrasse led Schubert and Stresemann to conclude that 'this project cannot be reconciled with the general lines of our policy',[4] a decision only conveyed to Soviet diplomats by Berlin's icy silence about the matter during the whole of the following year.[5]

[1] Cited by Schubert in conference with Gessler and others, July 14, 1926, 4564/E163632–42.

[2] Schubert to Rantzau, April 3, 1926, 4564/E162703–8.

[3] Memorandum by Kempner, April 1, 1926, 2860/D556967–71.

[4] 4564/E162711, quoted in Gatzke, op. cit., 582.

[5] Because Unshlikht's proposals had been made 'unofficially', Schubert

The grounds for rejecting the Soviet plan are not hard to find. Stresemann was not opposed to contacts with the Red Army as such; as a patriot and realist he believed that rearmament was as essential to Germany's continental resurgence as astute diplomacy. Since the Reichswehr argued that German bases in the Soviet Union were vital to that goal he gave them his support.[1] Moreover, he saw the illicit bonds as an earnest of Germany's fidelity, as a means of easing relations with Soviet leaders during stormy times like the Locarno negotiations. Thus in December 1925 Dirksen informed Hasse that the Wilhelmstrasse would not object to the Reichswehr continuing the secret operations within 'proper limits' because of Germany's unfulfilled military needs and the inclination of Soviet policy makers to regard them as the 'most persuasive evidence of our wish to continue our relationship with them'.[2]

Yet while these considerations argued against disrupting the contacts with the Red Army, they did not, to his mind, warrant their demonstrative expansion. Stresemann was determined that the multi-faceted bonds with Moscow should support his western policy but also that they should not supplant or jeopardize it. Consequently Unshlikht's proposals were rejected because they might discredit his policy of balance. As Schubert phrased it, the western powers would excuse Germany's previous dealings with the Soviet military because of her formerly desperate situation, 'but an extension of our activities at this moment, between Locarno and Geneva, would be condemned a good deal more harshly'.[3] In the following years Stresemann continued to support the clandestine dealings—within 'proper limits'—as valuable in their own right

considered a German reply unnecessary until a 'further official feeler' had been received from the Soviet Embassy (Schubert to Rantzau, April 3, 1926, 4564/E162703–8). Four weeks later, in response to an inquiry from Krestinskii, Chancellor Marx replied that the matter would soon be considered (Memorandum by Marx [?], April 28, 1926, 617/L194698). A year later the Soviet government was still without a reply (Memorandum by Rantzau regarding conversation with Unshlikht and others, July 24, 1927, 337/L100554–60).

[1] Memorandum by Dirksen regarding conversation between Stresemann and General Heye, February 9, 1927, 4564/E163486.

[2] Memorandum by Dirksen regarding conversation with General Hasse, December 18, 1925, 4564/E162663–4.

[3] Schubert to Rantzau, April 3, 1926, 4564/E162703–8.

and as a stabilizer of the Rapallo partnership. As for the Berlin treaty he hoped that it would serve to maintain the former level of military collaboration.

3. AN AMBIGUOUS TIE

ON a fourth important level, that of *Ostpolitik*, German diplomats viewed the Berlin accord as an anti-Polish instrument, essential to the alteration of their eastern border. It has commonly been held that the 'Polish question' constituted as firm a tie in the relations between Berlin and Moscow in the 1920s as it had earlier in those between Berlin and St. Petersburg. On the surface it seems plausible that of the many interests which brought Berlin and Moscow together in what is commonly referred to as the 'spirit of Rapallo', military collaboration and a common appetite for Polish territory formed the two elements of stability in an otherwise inherently unstable relationship.

There was, to be sure, some continuity between the Polish question in its pre-war and post-war forms, but there was probably more discontinuity. After 1918 the essential 'newness' of the question was that the war had transformed a question of Poles into a question of Poland. The effects were far-reaching both on general European diplomacy and on German-Soviet relations.

From Poland's dismemberment in the 18th century to her re-emergence as a state in World War I the 'Polish question' represented the hard core of Russo-German collaboration. For about a century St. Petersburg and Berlin were tacitly agreed that they would have to cooperate unceasingly so as to maintain the territorial integrity of their states against the ambitions of their Polish minorities to recreate their own state. This shared interest in the Polish question, stated in such terms of elemental survival, was by definition non-negotiable and enduring.

But the rebirth of Poland as a territorial state after 1918 raised an entirely new order of problems. What had previously been more of a domestic question with inescapable foreign policy implications now emerged as a foreign policy question shot through with imponderables. From a simple problem with a single solution it had changed into one dependent upon variables.

Unlike its pre-war counterpart, the 'Polish question', as is the case of a matter of inter-state relations, was now susceptible of resolution—in theory at least—in a number of ways and through a variety of political combinations. Germany and the USSR were now free to act with or against each other's interests in pursuit of a revisionist policy in central Europe. Even if Poland's neighbors should agree to collaborate against her, the variables of tactics and timing remained to be agreed upon and constituted potential sources of sharp disagreement.

In the years after 1919, the essential 'newness' of the Polish question was not immediately apparent. Indeed the function assigned Poland by the allies in 1919 to 'dam up the Russian flood and to provide a check to Germany',[1] pointed in on eclear direction. Allied with a France sternly anti-Soviet and anti-German in her goal of continental supremacy, enjoying the qualified support of a victorious England, and goaded on by territorial ambitions of her own, the new Polish state posed a standing threat both to Germany and to the USSR. As earlier, it seemed that the Polish 'cement' was again an element of stability in their relationship.

Their weakness in the face of Poland's ambition dictated defensive goals at first and restricted their cooperation against Poland to modest gestures. Two markers indicate the direction of this policy in the early 1920s: one, a posture of rigid neutrality by the German government during the Russo-Polish war of 1920, lessened the danger of France's hastening to Poland's aid; the other, threats of overt Russian action against Poland during the French occupation of the Ruhr in 1923, eased Germany's desperate situation.

With the stabilization of the European situation in the mid-1920s, Poland ceased to threaten her neighbors directly and the hitherto academic question of territorial alterations at her expense entered the field of practical politics.[2] As is well known this con-

[1] Great Britain, Foreign Office, *Documents on British Foreign Policy, 1919–1939*, ed. by E. L. Woodward and Rohan Butler, First Series, II, no. 56.

[2] This question seems to have been raised in German-Soviet conversations for the first time in December 1924. A Russian official spoke of the possibility that 'joint Russo-German pressure could be exerted on Poland' (Rantzau to the Foreign Ministry concerning conversation with Viktor Kopp, December 5, 1924, 4562/E154862–5). The Germans, it seems, first used the phrase 'that the solution of the Polish question for Germany and Russia lies in forcing Poland back into her ethnographical frontiers' (Rantzau to the Foreign Ministry concerning conversation with Chicherin, December 22, 1924, 4562/E154904–6). For a largely narrative

stituted one of the most durable of Weimar Germany's foreign policy goals, Stresemann characterizing it in April 1926 as 'not only the most important task of our policy but perhaps the most important task of European politics generally'.[1]

The German Foreign Minister believed that the achievements of Locarno had opened to Germany new perspectives for border revision in the east. At Locarno Germany had solemnly proclaimed her intention of settling disputes with her eastern neighbors 'without the use of force', but had not renounced her goal of border revision.[2] Moreover, the simultaneous weakening of the Franco-Polish alliance made such a goal seem possible. Thus during the Locarno conference tensions between France and Germany had relaxed so far that French Foreign Minister Briand remarked indiscreetly to Stresemann that 'the Poles would become very uninteresting if Germany and France were to reach an understanding'.[3]

Thus encouraged and further stimulated by events in Poland, a plan for the return to Germany of Danzig, the Corridor, and Upper Silesia slowly took shape in Stresemann's mind. After a serious crop failure in 1924 the position of the Polish economy had worsened steadily, and in the winter of 1925–6 it teetered dangerously on the edge of bankruptcy. The situation was characterized

account of these conversations see: Zygmunt Gasiorowski, 'The Russian Overture to Germany of December 1924', *The Journal of Modern History*, XXX (June 1958), 99–117.

[1] Stresemann to Sthamer, April 19, 1926, cited in Christian Höltje, *Die Weimarer Republik und das Ostlocarno-Problem, 1919–1934* (Würzburg: Holzner, 1958), 254–6.

[2] There is a large body of literature dealing with Stresemann's Locarno policy. Of greatest interest for the Polish question are: Karl Dietrich Erdmann, 'Das Problem der Ost- oder Westorientierung in der Locarno-Politik Stresemanns', *Geschichte in Wissenschaft und Unterricht*, VI (1955), 133–62; Zygmunt Gasiorowski, 'Stresemann and Poland Before Locarno', *Journal of Central European Affairs*, XVIII (April 1958), 25–47; Josef Korbel, *Poland Between East and West: Soviet and German Diplomacy Toward Poland, 1919–1933* (Princeton: University Press, 1963); Christian Höltje, op. cit., 83–116; Annelise Thimme, 'Die Locarnopolitik im Lichte des Stresemann-Nachlasses', *Zeitschrift für Politik*, III (August 1956), 42–63. For a suggestive interpretive essay by a Polish *émigré* historian, see: Titus Komarnicki, 'Polish-German Relations Between the Two World Wars', *Poland and Germany*, Part I (autumn, 1957), 24–34; Part II (spring, 1958), 24–31.

[3] Stresemann to a Conference of the Presidents of the German Länder, Memorandum, October 21, 1925, cited in Christian Höltje, *Die Weimarer Republik*, 86.

by a rapidly sinking Zloty, a murderous tariff war with Germany,[1] and an insatiable hunger for foreign credit as a means of saving the economy.

This latter need provided the occasion for the consideration of the border dispute on several levels. In March 1926, the Governor of the Bank of England asked Sthamer, the German Ambassador in London, about the viability of a formula by which Poland would give Germany border concessions in exchange for Germany's massive participation in the refinancing of the Polish economy. Sthamer transmitted to Berlin what was regarded as a semi-official British feeler and requested instructions.[2]

On April 19, 1926, several days before the signing of the Berlin treaty, Stresemann, in a remarkable letter to Sthamer, described the necessary preconditions to a settlement of the issue of the German-Polish border.[3] He regarded British interest in the border dispute as a condition of its solution, but he urged caution. The British suggestion, he wrote, would lead to an interim settlement at best: 'A peaceful solution to the question of the Polish border is possible only when the economic and financial situation of Poland reaches calamitous proportions and when the body politic of Poland is reduced to a state of complete paralysis.' Equally important, Germany's relations with the western powers were still too uncertain to support an international conference at which Germany might state her claims.

Since incomplete solutions were to be avoided, German policy must try to 'postpone a final and permanent reflation of Poland until she is ready for a settlement of the border question on our terms and until our political power has grown sufficiently'. Only then, he added, would Germany be able to gain a receptive audience for her view that 'the refinancing of the Polish economy must be tied in with the settlement of the border question on our terms'. Stresemann reiterated that the return to Germany of the Corridor, Danzig, Upper Silesia, and certain parts of Central Silesia should remain the focus of German efforts. 'Only the un-

[1] See Charles Kruszewski, 'The German-Polish Tariff War (1925–1934) and its Aftermath', *Journal of Central European Affairs*, III (October 1943), 294–315.

[2] Mentioned in Stresemann to Sthamer, April 19, 1926, reproduced in Appendix 5, Höltje, op. cit., 254–6.

[3] Ibid.

conditional restoration of sovereignty in the areas in question can satisfy us.'[1]

Here was Stresemann's unembellished plan for the recovery of Germany's 'lost territories'. It was admittedly a brutal scheme, but it did not call for war. Poland was to be squeezed into submission through the fulfillment of three conditions. The letter to Sthamer spoke of only two: a prior understanding with the western powers, which the relaxed atmosphere at Locarno suggested was feasible, and a complete collapse of the Polish economy, that was reportedly imminent.

As a third condition Stresemann expected Poland to grow more amenable to Germany's revisionist demands in the face of constant pressure from Russia. To ensure the maintenance of that pressure was one of the cardinal aims of German diplomacy in the negotiations for the Berlin treaty. After its conclusion Stresemann expressed the hope that the agreement would serve as a 'guarantee of the pursuit of a common line with Russia in questions of the Near East [Poland]'.

During the negotiations for the Locarno pact the Foreign Commissariat used the Polish question both as bait and as goad to keep Germany from approaching the west. Twice soundings were made for a Russo-German agreement directed against Poland; but both attempts were unsuccessful because Germany had too much to lose in an adventurous course.[2] Such abortive invitations to coalesce against Poland were alternated with threats of a Russo-Polish *détente*. In June 1925 Litvinov warned Stresemann that if Poland concluded that her border was no longer unconditionally guaranteed by the Versailles powers, she might turn to Russia. Such a development would be regretted by the Soviet government, he added, 'but one should not be offended with Russia if in response to the [political] development which was driving Germany into an anti-Russian position, Russia found herself constrained to review the new situation and to ask herself what the consequences might be'.[3]

[1] Ibid.

[2] Memorandum by Stresemann concerning conversation with Litvinov, August 8, 1925, 6698/H107167–71; Memorandum by Stresemann concerning conversation with Chicherin, September 30, 1925, 7129/H147979–91.

[3] Memorandum by Stresemann, August 8, 1925, 6698/H107167–71.

In September 1925, Chicherin underscored Soviet threats by breaking his journey to Berlin in Warsaw, where the Poles received him solicitously. They declined the non-aggression pact that he offered them,[1] but the effect of Chicherin's visit was nevertheless to serve notice on Germany that if the Soviet government were pressed too hard it would use the tactics of *volte-face*, reorient its policy *vis-à-vis* Poland and destroy Stresemann's dream of border revision.[2]

In December 1925, Chicherin added to his scare campaign by visiting Paris. Rantzau was almost beside himself with anxiety. Inclined to dramatize issues, he wired Berlin that an eastern Locarno – understood as a multilateral guarantee of Germany's eastern frontier – was on the verge of being concluded.[3] As the most disturbing sign of a Franco-Russian-Polish rapprochement he cited the announcement of a Franco-Soviet conference for February 1926, which was scheduled to discuss new French credits for Moscow and the perennial issue of Czarist debts. The question of a border guarantee for Poland was sure to be on the agenda, he concluded.[4]

Foreign Ministry officials were hardly immune to such pressure. They were not inclined to discount the possibility that Soviet efforts to fashion a Moscow-Warsaw-Paris alignment were serious and promising of success. Isolated and preoccupied with the issue of fundamental security, Soviet leaders were considered fully capable of satisfying their security needs against Germany's interests if they could not do so with Germany's help. The issue was particularly acute because a Russo-Polish and a Russo-French *détente* offered the three states involved real advantages. As a Foreign Ministry memorandum explained, such a development would give Poland security against Germany, free Russia of the nightmare of a British presence in Poland, and elicit French credits and ease France's onerous commitments to Poland.

[1] Fischer, *The Soviets in World Affairs*, II, 720–1.

[2] *Izvestiia* characterized the visit as an 'important achievement of the Soviet Republic. All true friends of peace must recognize improved relations between the Soviet Union and Poland as a means to vitiate the war danger embodied in the Guarantee Pact' (*Izvestiia*, October 1, 1925).

[3] Rantzau to the Foreign Ministry, February 14, 1926, 2860/D556671–2.

[4] Rantzau to the Foreign Ministry, February 3, 1926, 2860/D556691–2. Early in 1926 Moscow renewed its earlier offer of a non-aggression pact to Warsaw (Korbel, op. cit., 189–91).

Warsaw's gain would be Berlin's loss. The hope of altering the eastern border at an international conference would be torpedoed:

> If Poland were secured against Russia, then the reservation of the wealthy powers concerning a refinancing of Poland would vanish. With the threat from the east gone and Germany militarily impotent, the threat [against Poland] from the west could also be ignored. In that event the resolution of the German-Polish border question would become impossible for the duration of the reflation.[1]

Increasingly the Anglo-Soviet dispute was intruding upon the German solution of the Polish question as defined by Stresemann. For all of these reasons the Wilhelmstrasse was bent upon clarifying the Polish issue in the negotiations for the Berlin treaty.

German policy makers were not agreed about their ability to frustrate the emerging alignment. Dirksen, the cautious bureaucrat, was pessimistic, questioning whether a termination of the Russo-Polish negotiations could be exacted for a Russo-German neutrality treaty.[2] Rantzau, more astute, was hopeful. He urged the Foreign Ministry to chart an unequivocal course by telling the Soviet government that the 'binding and fundamental abandonment of every guarantee of Poland's borders' was a basic condition to the signing of a German neutrality treaty.[3]

To elicit such an undertaking from Russia was difficult. Faced by a deepening rift with Britain, officials of the Foreign Commissariat were reluctant to promise not to ease Poland's security worries as a means of keeping her out of Britain's arms. As it turned out, Moscow was disposed to make a distinction between Poland's eastern and western borders. The neutrality pact negotiations revealed that Russia's threat of an eastern Locarno had been a bargaining counter to win a stronger agreement from Germany. In late February, with such an accord in sight, Chicherin responded to a threat by Rantzau (that a guarantee of Poland's western border would 'self-evidently be synonymous with an abrogation of the existing friendly relations between Germany and the Soviet

[1] Memorandum by Dirksen for the internal use of the Foreign Ministry: 'Aufzeichnung über den gegenwärtigen Stand deutschrussischer Beziehungen', January 25, 1926, 6698/H107392–7; cf. Korbel, op. cit., 192–7.

[2] Memorandum by Dirksen, January 25, 1926, 6698/H107392–7.

[3] Rantzau to the Foreign Ministry, February 7, 1926, 5462/E373908–9.

Union') by saying that he would be on his 'guard ever to assume such a guarantee'.[1]

The question of Poland's eastern border, however, was more complicated, and here German and Soviet interests tended to diverge. While Germany demanded the 'abandonment of every border guarantee respecting Poland' so as to keep her unhinged for a territorial settlement, Russia saw a border guarantee to Poland as the one concession that might keep her out of Britain's sphere.[2] For that reason, after assuring Rantzau about one frontier, Chicherin plunged him into deep gloom about the other by stating that Russia would probably have to recognize the Riga frontiers. The sacrifice of a large White Russian and Ruthenian population to Poland's mercies was necessary, he pointed out, because of the need to 'create settled conditions along the western border and above all prevent England from using Poland as a battering-ram against the Soviet Union'.[3] The reconciliation of Soviet and German interests was becoming increasingly complicated, it seemed. While Berlin was demanding enmity between Poland and the Soviet Union as the price of German-Soviet friendship, Moscow, for tactical reasons, wanted to work with Germany as well as live peaceably with Poland.

Because his bargaining position would never be stronger, Rantzau decided to bring the negotiations to a head. In mid-March Chicherin repeated his pledge that the Soviet government would not agree to an eastern Locarno;[4] she would only accept a short, three- to five-year, non-aggression pact as a means to secure Russia's frontier. But the stabilization of the Polish-Soviet connection was precisely what Berlin feared. With great earnestness Rantzau therefore replied that a Soviet non-aggression pact with Poland would also be deemed incompatible with the proposed neutrality treaty. The German government recognized the Soviet Union's right to ease the situation along her borders, but insisted

[1] Rantzau to the Foreign Ministry, March 4, 1926, 2860/D556856–8.

[2] Although Soviet restiveness about Britain's penetration of Poland was exaggerated, the extent of it must await the publication of the *Documents of British Foreign Policy* for this period. Important for our purposes is that Soviet fears were genuine and the Wilhelmstrasse acted on the assumption that an exacerbation of Anglo-Soviet tensions would heighten British interest in Poland.

[3] Rantzau to the Foreign Ministry, March 4, 1926, 2860/D556856–8.

[4] Rantzau to the Foreign Ministry, March 15, 1926, 2860/D556896–8.

that this not endanger Germany's interests. Even a short-term non-aggression pact, he concluded, would constitute an indirect threat to Germany's territorial interests.

Chicherin fidgeted. It was a tense moment. Finally he met Rantzau half-way. The negotiations with Warsaw, he replied, could be considered terminated, although his government would continue to seek such a pact on a bilateral basis, without the participation of the Baltic states. It would be necessary to find a formula that would meet Russia's need for 'settled conditions *vis-à-vis* Poland alone, without in any manner compromising her friendly relations with Germany.'[1] Beyond this Chicherin would not go.

Thus the positions of both states had been partly clarified. An eastern Locarno was no longer to be feared from Moscow's side, and the Polish-Soviet talks, by Chicherin's own admission, had broken down. On one point only – the failure of the Narkomindel to promise not to reach an accord with Poland in the future – was the Wilhelmstrasse still anxious. With renewed urgency German diplomats tried to fill this last gap, using guidelines that Stresemann spelled out in a highly significant letter to Rantzau: 'The conclusion of a German-Soviet treaty cannot be considered until we are given assurances that Russia will not meet Poland's security needs along her eastern frontier through either a guarantee pact, non-aggression pact or even conciliation treaty.' As a written agreement would constitute a secret appendix to the treaty of Berlin, Stresemann wanted only verbal assurances.[2] He hoped for an unwritten agreement regarding Poland as an integral part of the Berlin understanding.

On March 30, State Secretary Schubert outlined Germany's broader demands to the Soviet Ambassador. He reiterated that an implicit or explicit Soviet guarantee of the Polish borders would conflict with the goals of the proposed treaty. Therefore before signing Germany would require a formal assurance that 'not only now, but also in the future such agreements would not be concluded'. Such a commitment would self-evidently place narrow limits on Russia's freedom of action. But faced with the iron alternatives of a neutrality treaty with Berlin or a *possible* non-aggression agreement with Poland, Krestinskii assented. 'For his own part,'

[1] Ibid.

[2] Stresemann to Rantzau, March 27, 1926, 2860/D556928–31.

he stated, 'he wanted to declare positively that it was his firm conviction that such agreements would not be concluded between Russia and Poland. Moreover, the proposals just made by Unshlikht for an increase in military cooperation was further evidence that Russia did not intend to conclude an agreement with Poland.'[1]

Schubert was delighted with the reply, which represented an advance over previous Soviet commitments, but thought it inadequate because it was couched in terms that did not formally bind the Soviet government. Because an 'opinion' by Krestinskii did not carry the authority of a formal pledge by Chicherin, Rantzau was instructed to seek one.[2]

In the meantime Berlin's interest in the question of Poland's borders had been broadened to include another former German territory in eastern Europe, Memel. This widening of focus was precipitated by Russia's negotiations with Lithuania for a non-aggression and neutrality treaty, which had been in progress since mid-March 1926. Lithuania was reported to be demanding a Soviet guarantee of her entire territory, including Memel. German officials took the position that Soviet recognition of the inviolability of areas that had once belonged to Germany would, by setting a dangerous precedent, help solidify the territorial *status quo* in central Europe. In a move reminiscent of their earlier reply to the threat of an eastern Locarno, German officials warned that an agreement pertaining to Memel would weaken the German-Soviet tie.[3] They also requested a more general promise that Russia would 'not assume a guarantee for the territory of other states insofar as such a guarantee would apply to territories that had earlier belonged to Germany'.[4]

A Soviet vow not to recognize the integrity of former German possessions when applied to Memel adequately served the purposes of German diplomacy; but when applied to Poland it represented an unintentional retreat from previous German demands that Soviet leaders desist from *any* agreement with her. Thus the fleeting intrusion of the Memel question in the negotiations on the Polish

[1] Memorandum by Schubert concerning conversation with Krestinskii, March 30, 1926, 4562/E156735–9.

[2] Schubert to Rantzau, March 30, 1926, 2860/D556950–2.

[3] Rantzau to the Foreign Ministry concerning conversation with Litvinov, April 23, 1926, 2860/D557353–4.

[4] Stresemann to Rantzau, April 29, 1926, 2860/D557459.

problem only served to confuse them, ultimately frustrating German attempts to incorporate in the Berlin understanding an iron-clad Soviet pledge not to bargain with Poland.

The Narkomindel responded affirmatively to the new German demands; on May 1, 1926, Litvinov informed Rantzau that an understanding between Germany and Lithuania was recognized as a condition to any Soviet guarantee of Lithuania's territory. Litvinov's reply on the Polish question was no less positive, but did not fully meet Germany's wishes. The USSR, the Deputy Foreign Commissar said, did not intend 'to guarantee Poland's possession of any of the territories . . . which had earlier belonged to Germany'.[1] Here was the Memel formula as applied to Poland.

German diplomats were moderately pleased with their success. Rantzau, concerned at the time with frustrating an emergent Russo-Polish-French combination, considered Litvinov's pledge as solid evidence that the drift toward a compact with Poland by influential Soviet circles had been countered.[2] Stresemann, more directly interested in achieving border changes with Soviet support, was somewhat less cheerful.

He interpreted Litvinov's commitment as a hopeful sign that the Berlin treaty might 'bring to maturity the fruits which we have anticipated';[3] but he was perturbed that Germany had not elicited a Soviet promise that she would not guarantee Poland's *eastern* border or conclude a non-aggression treaty with her during the life of the Berlin treaty.[4] Because he considered the perpetuation of Poland's uncertainty about Soviet intentions as crucial to his goal of revision, Stresemann urged Rantzau to again broach the subject with Soviet leaders: 'For me an essential feature (*Aktivum*) of the Berlin treaty has always been the prevention of a French-Polish-Russian combination inimical to us; also, in general, the furthest possible pursuit of a common political line with Russia in questions of the near east [the Polish question].'[5]

To sum up, since the signature of the Locarno agreements in the autumn of 1925, Stresemann had conceived of a plan for altering the German-Polish border that, viewed in its political

[1] Rantzau to the Foreign Ministry, May 1, 1926, 2860/D557508–9.

[2] Rantzau to the Foreign Ministry, April 23, 1926, 2860/D557353–4.

[3] Stresemann to Rantzau, April 29, 1926, 2860/D557659.

[4] Stresemann to Rantzau, May 11, 1926, 2860/D557659–60.

[5] Ibid.

context, was not sheer fantasy. It was a problematical scheme, to be sure, but the three circumstances deemed essential to its realization seemed to lie in the realm of the politically feasible. Stresemann's dealings with the western powers encouraged him to believe that Britain's and France's loss of interest in Poland might follow in the wake of Europe's gradual pacification.

Moreover, the hope that Poland could be made amenable to German claims on her territory in exchange for a refinancing of her economy was far from chimeric and was encouraged by sources close to the British government. Finally, the agreement on Lithuania and Poland accompanying the Berlin treaty offered hope that Poland would become more ready to entertain German wishes when persistently faced with uncertainty about Soviet intentions.

4. REVISION IN DANGER

HOWEVER sober Stresemann's plan for the redrawing of Germany's eastern frontier at an international conference may have been in the setting of April 1926 subsequent events prompted its emendation. In this, developments in Poland led the way. Soon after the signing of the Berlin treaty Marshal Pilsudski seized power in Warsaw, ended the turmoil of Poland's domestic scene and set her economy back on the road to gradual recovery.

In addition to postponing indefinitely Germany's hopes for the recovery of her lost territories, this event injected a new element of uncertainty into German-Soviet relations. From the outset Chicherin suspected that Pilsudski's hatred of Russia, his predilection for an agricultural economy trading Polish farm produce for German manufactured goods, and his pro-British and anti-French attitude would lead him to seek a rapprochement with Germany, and, worse, an alignment with England.[1] Together with the difficult state of Anglo-Soviet relations (which declined to within an inch of a rupture in the summer of 1926) this new and confused situation heightened Russia's interest in the security of her western border, and attracted her to a strategy of buffer states.

The range of alternatives open to Soviet policy was limited. The most direct way for Moscow to limit British influence in Poland would have been to offer the Poles a guarantee of their eastern

[1] Rantzau to Stresemann, May 22, 1926, 2860/D557718–19; cf. Korbel, op. cit., 202–6.

frontier. This option, however, was complicated by Poland's ambition to create a Baltic bloc, her dream of a resurrected federal state also embracing Lithuania and the Ukraine, and most important perhaps, by German stubbornness regarding any Soviet accord with Poland.

Another means of reducing Poland's influence was to isolate her in east central Europe, an alternative the more desirable because it comported with German goals. The joint interest of Germany and the USSR in preventing the emergence between them of a north–south bloc of states under Warsaw's leadership, subordinated to Britain or France, was obvious. Less clear though were the means of frustrating such a development without intruding upon what Berlin and Moscow considered to be their vital interests.

As a matter of basic security Poland's economic revival and growing influence in eastern Europe in 1926 was of relatively greater concern to the Soviet Union than Germany. For this reason the diplomatic initiative in the area passed into Russian hands while the Wilhelmstrasse was disposed to temporize. The first indication of this came in the spring of 1926, when Soviet diplomats offered Finland, Estonia, Latvia, and Lithuania separate neutrality treaties patterned on the Turkish-Soviet treaty signed some months earlier. This initiative was intended to thwart the establishment of Polish hegemony among the succession states by dealing bilaterally with each of them, to the exclusion of Poland.

But Soviet policy makers were singularly ill-equipped to work such a strategy. Their presumed territorial ambitions *vis-à-vis* Estonia and Latvia prompted those states to insist on dealing with Moscow on a collective basis with Poland, and, if possible, Lithuania.[1] By the summer of 1926 this disposition had doomed Soviet efforts to failure.

The Soviet Union, however, was provided with a second lever for checking Polish ambitions: the festering dispute between Poland and Lithuania over Vilna. Moscow recognized that a bilateral Lithuanian-Soviet accord, by aggravating the conflict

[1] A report from the German Minister to Finland described the Soviet attitude towards Estonia and Latvia: 'The majority of responsible politicians in Russia view both states as specifically Russian spheres of interest, if not as future Russian territories; in any case they are regarded as a future economic domain of Russia. This view was expressed to me quite openly by Krestinskii shortly before my departure' (German Minister in Helsinki to the Foreign Ministry, June 30, 1925, 4562/E155545–52).

between Poland and Lithuania, would help to frustrate efforts of Poland to win the support of a phalanx of Baltic states. Lithuania, moreover, was anxious to serve as a barrier to Warsaw's ambitions if the Soviet Union would stiffen her position by means of a treaty. The first negotiations for such an agreement, it will be recalled, shattered over German objections to a Soviet guarantee of Memel. They were subsequently resumed and with the support of the German Foreign Ministry culminated in a Lithuanian-Soviet treaty of non-aggression in September 1926. The specter of a Baltic bloc under Polish leadership had thus been banned by means of an agreement that Stresemann welcomed on the grounds, as he said, that 'a Polish annexation of Lithuania had become improbable', and it had been possible to draft the treaty without mentioning Memel.[1]

While Germany and the Soviet Union had thus discovered common ground in the Lithuanian question by simply not mentioning Memel, the job of finding a unified approach to the more general Polish question—of which the Lithuanian problem was really only a part—was less successful. The source of the complication, as earlier, was the conviction of Soviet leaders—an *idée fixe*—that Britain was bent on moving through Poland and the Baltic states in order to crush the Soviet Union.

In the summer of 1926 Soviet policy evolved under the banner, 'secure the western frontier'. In pursuit of this goal the tactic of dealing separately with each of the Baltic states had failed; even the Lithuanian non-aggression treaty was only of marginal importance. Therefore, with some reluctance—in view of the response expected from Berlin—Soviet diplomats again considered coming to a bilateral agreement with Poland. The result was an initiative: on August 24, Voikov, the Soviet Minister in Warsaw, submitted the draft of a neutrality and non-aggression treaty to the Polish Foreign Office.

This overture took Berlin by surprise and led to charges of Soviet dissimulation. The German State Secretary hurriedly summoned the Soviet Chargé and raged against his government for violating the spirit of the April agreement that forbade such initiatives. The absence of prior consultations, he said, had gravely impaired the usefulness of the consultation clause of the treaty.

[1] Notes, drafted by Dirksen, for a conversation between Stresemann and Chicherin, November 30, 1926, 6698/H111112–14.

And regardless of Soviet good faith towards Berlin the damage had been done—the Poles could accept or reject the draft treaty. Poland, he added, was now in the enviable position of a blackmailer who could threaten to join with Moscow unless the British pressed Germany into making concessions to her.[1] But in order that the Soviet official should not interpret this criticism as a desire for military solutions, Schubert went on to spell out Germany's policy towards Poland. In a statement that constitutes the clearest record of German aims at this time, he explained:

> . . . we would not regret a Russian treaty with Poland because it would preclude any future Russian aggressive intentions. As the Russians must know we do not consider it in our interests to permit our demands of Poland to lead to war. . . . Much rather we would regret the conclusion of such a Russo-Polish treaty because it would doubtlessly constitute a strengthening (*Rückenstärkung*) of Poland's rear. Even the mere fact that the Russians have formally disclosed their intentions to sign a pact with Poland has already strengthened Poland's position. Quite frankly we are no longer clear on what political line Russia is following.[2]

Without entering into the substance of these remarks, the Soviet Chargé sought to calm Schubert by characterizing the Soviet initiative as a strategem to put Poland on the spot, to damage her reputation.[3] A week later, having received new instructions from Moscow, Brodovskii pointed to Poland's continued demands for a collective treaty between the Soviet Union and a group of states under her leadership. Poland had discredited herself, he claimed; the Soviet objective had been achieved—a Polish-Soviet treaty would not be concluded.[4] The discussion was ended.

But the very same situation that had given rise to the incident remained. Assuming paranoiacally that Britain would appear as a

[1] Memorandum by Schubert, August 28, 1926, 4562/E157818–22. Typical of the German attitude before the offer to Poland is an unsigned memorandum of the Foreign Ministry which speaks with satisfaction of the 'exclusion of Poland' as a particular feature of Soviet negotiations with the Baltic states (Unsigned memorandum: 'Über den Stand der "Ost-Locarno" Verhandlungen, Ganz Geheim!' August 4, 1926, 5462/E374076–82).

[2] Unsigned memorandum, probably by Schubert, August 28, 1926, 4562/E157818–22.

[3] Ibid.

[4] Memorandum by Schubert, September 6, 1926.

power factor on the Polish scene, Soviet diplomats continued to weigh the various means of checking such a development, including a separate agreement with Warsaw. The USSR, as Chicherin had earlier explained, wanted 'settled conditions'[1] along her western border. But German policy called for precisely the opposite, namely the maintenance of *unsettled* conditions along that frontier. Not preoccupied with a security problem like Russia's, German diplomacy was bent on preserving the Polish question for treatment at an international conference by insisting that the Soviet Union desist from any accord with Poland, including a non-aggression treaty.

After 1924 it was a symptom of the diverging purposes of German and Soviet policy that officials in Berlin were restive lest Soviet leaders, restricted to a militarily impotent Germany in their international contacts, would ease their pressing international situation at the expense of Germany's territorial claims on Poland. Thus the lines of German and Soviet policy threatened to cross on the Polish question, putting to a hard test one of the basic assumptions of the Berlin treaty. They threatened to cross in one other respect as well.

5. REVISION REAPPRAISED

IN 1926, while German leaders suspected that Moscow and Warsaw were about to settle their differences, Soviet policy makers were apprehensive that Berlin would try to strike a separate bargain with Warsaw. It was rumored at the time that Germany was seeking a territorial settlement with Poland rather than against her, which ultimately might harm Russia. For some years past the European press had recurrently written about the possibility of effecting a reconciliation of Germany's and Poland's conflicting territorial claims. A means suggested was an ingenious compensation agreement that would grant Poland an exit to the sea via Lithuania in exchange for the transfer of the Corridor and Upper Silesia to Germany.

The return to power of Pilsudski with his alleged pro-British, pro-German, and anti-Soviet bias, revived public discussion of the 'compensation formula'. In the autumn of 1926 reports were circulated that the British Foreign Office had proposed the scheme

[1] *Supra*, 34.

as the tidiest solution to its problem of winning both Germany's and Poland's support against Russia. Given British levers of power—possible concessions in reparations to Berlin, and possible support in refinancing the Polish economy to Warsaw—the Narkomindel saw such an arrangement as being far from chimerical. For that reason Krestinskii apprised the Wilhelmstrasse that any proposal to abandon Lithuania to Poland's mercies would induce Russia to break out of her encirclement by looking to other powers for her security.

Stresemann denied knowledge of any such proposal—which had never been made to the German government—and promised to keep the Soviets informed if he were ever approached about it.[1] When dark rumors of British machinations continued to appear in the European press Chicherin was again informed that they were not true: 'Unfortunately, for the moment, the prospect of an immediate recovery of the lost eastern territories does not exist.' The German government would continue to pursue the goal of revision by all peaceful means but would not gamble away 'existing friendly relations between Germany and the Soviet Union'.[2]

The unwelcome injection of the 'compensation formula' into the discussion on border revision induced the Wilhelmstrasse to rethink its entire Polish policy. Such a reappraisal was long overdue, for by the winter of 1926–7 it had become clear that Stresemann's earlier plan for the remaking of the eastern border was stillborn and needed to be discarded or at least basically revised. The chain of events that were to have terminated in a high-level international conference at which Germany's claim to Polish territory was recognized with western and Soviet backing, had not materialized. Instead Pilsudski's steady hand had helped to stabilize Poland's economy and politics. The influence of France on Poland seemed to have diminished somewhat, but that of Britain had not, at least in the judgement of German and Soviet diplomats.

That the Anglo-Soviet dispute in Asia and the meddling of the Comintern in the coal miners' strike was drawing Britain to support Poland as a barrier to Soviet influence, and perhaps as a bridgehead for an economic or military offensive, was believed by Berlin and Moscow. For Germany the situation was doubly cheerless

[1] Memorandum by Stresemann, November 4, 1926, 2860/D558130–1.

[2] Notes, drafted by Dirksen, for a conversation of Stresemann with Chicherin, November 30, 1926, 6698/H111112–14.

because the assumption that Britain was eager to buttress Poland's position had led Soviet statesmen to consider an understanding with Warsaw as a necessary measure of self-defense.[1] Stresemann's optimistic plan of April, it seemed, lay in the dust.

By November it was high time to amend policy in accordance with the altered political circumstances. Because the situation ruled out an early solution to the border question, a viable policy would have to be geared to the longer haul. Consequently a sober Foreign Ministry memorandum recommended that the 'Locarno line' be continued,[2] admitting that British, French, and American support for German territorial claims was still improbable; and the Soviet Union was still too weak to engage Poland in a war that would result in a major redrafting of frontiers in central Europe. The memorandum concluded that the immobility of the general situation dictated a further policy of currying favor with the western powers, 'the first and most important condition to a satisfactory solution of the eastern border question in the future'.[3] This was and remained the main line of Germany's Polish policy.

Simultaneously, however, Wilhelmstrasse officials were loath to admit the finality of their defeat and continued to scrutinize the convulsive political situation in the east for a way to an early achievement of their territorial goals. Every favorable opening in European diplomacy was to be fully exploited. For a brief moment late in 1926 members of the Eastern Department suggested that an astute exploitation of the deepening crisis between Poland and Lithuania over Vilna might lead to border changes. Where Polish weakness was earlier to have led to revision, Pilsudski's greed *vis-à-vis* Lithuania was now to serve as an alternate route. Poland was to be encouraged in a policy of adventurism that, ending in fiasco, would discredit her in London and Paris and win more ready support for Germany's territorial demands.

[1] For a detailed account of the Polish side of this question see: Zygmunt J. Gasiorowski, 'Stresemann and Poland After Locarno', *Journal of Central European Affairs*, XVIII (October 1958), 292, 317.

[2] Gasiorowski has identified the author of this memorandum as Zechlin, head of the Polish desk in the Eastern Department of the Wilhelmstrasse, ibid., 303–4.

[3] Memorandum for the internal use of the Foreign Ministry by Zechlin entitled, 'Bemerkungen über die Lösung der östlichen Grenzfragen', November 19, 1926, summarized in a commentary on this memorandum by Dirksen, November 29, 1926, 5265/E318405–8.

This bellicose scheme was advocated in a Foreign Ministry memorandum which first rejected the compensation formula, discussed above. It correctly observed that the mere exchange of the Corridor for Lithuania would only partly satisfy Germany's territorial goals. Of greater moment, it would mean 'a permanent turning away from Russia by Germany. . . which we would never be in a position to advocate'.

A more viable policy would be for Germany to adopt a passive stance in central Europe so as to embolden Pilsudski to seize Lithuania and Memel. Such action might mortally wound Poland, the memorandum concluded, for by absorbing Lithuania, she would sharpen the tensions among her nationalities, harden her divisions with the USSR ('a temporary guarantee by Russia of Poland's eastern border would thus become academic, to our advantage') and isolate herself. Finally, a Polish coup against Lithuania might arm Germany and the USSR in putting forward claims for territorial compensation.[1]

German revision schemes in the mid-1920s sovereignly called for a conspiracy in Germany's favor of all contingent factors in central Europe. Actual developments, however, tended to bedevil them. Stresemann's plan of April 1926 was assigned to limbo by Pilsudski's seizure of power in May; German hopes of November 1926—that a policy of reserve would encourage Poland to swallow up Lithuania in a development that would ultimately see Germany in possession of the Corridor, Upper Silesia, Danzig, and Memel—likewise were foiled by an unexpected coup in Lithuania (December 1926). German officials at first thought that the new Lithuanian regime exhibited faint pro-Polish tendencies, which might lead to a Lithuanian reconciliation with Poland, a loosening of ties with Moscow, and a spreading of Polish influence throughout east central Europe.

Stresemann admitted that Germany's casual attitude towards the fate of Lithuania had contributed to this threat: too often in the preceding year Lithuania had been rebuffed in her overtures for closer relations with Germany. These slights had confirmed Lithuanian leaders in their interpretation that Berlin would abandon them to Poland for concessions in the question of the Corridor. To mend this situation it was decided to jettison Germany's earlier policy of reserve and cooperate with the USSR

[1] Ibid.

in the protection of Lithuania's sovereignty. This reversal, of course, meant that the facile hope would have to be abandoned that an extinction of Lithuania would serve Germany's interests. Stresemann summed up the German dilemma: 'We are deeply concerned about the ambiguity of political developments in eastern Europe, for we fear that this situation might suddenly make the whole problem of our eastern borders acute.'[1] On this note of frustration German-Soviet cooperation in eastern Europe ended in 1926.

6. ERRONEOUS ASSUMPTIONS

IN the eight months following the conclusion of the Berlin treaty the German-Soviet association was relatively free of incidents, and on the level of direct relations it seemed that a happier era had begun. The stabilization of German politics removed what had been the chief element of instability in the early 1920s; from 1924 until 1928 or 1929 the German Communist Party (KPD) was relatively quiescent, and KPD-CPSU ties were hardly a topic of conversation between Berlin and Moscow. Communist voting strength waned in 1924 and 1925[2] and the KPD was gradually transformed from the vanguard of European Revolution to an instrument for the defense of the Soviet Union.[3]

An amnesty agreement between Berlin and Moscow in August 1926 underlined the effect on mutual relations of Germany's growing domestic stability. This agreement led to the freeing of three Soviet citizens, including Skobolevskii, Moscow's agent in Germany during the abortive revolution of 1923, in exchange for thirteen Germans imprisoned in Russia for a variety of alleged offenses ranging from bribery of Soviet officials to complicity in a

[1] Stresemann to German Embassy in London, January 12, 1927, 2860/D558302–4.

[2] The KPD received 12·6 percent of the popular vote in the Reichstag election of May 1924 and 9 percent in the Reichstag election of December 1924 (Koppel Pinson, *Modern Germany: Its History and Civilization* [New York: Macmillan, 1954], 574). The KPD vote in the Presidential election of March 1925 was 7 percent (Ossip K. Flechtheim, *Die Kommunistische Partei Deutschlands in der Weimarer Republik* [Offenbach on the Main: Bollwerk-Verlag, 1948], 123–25).

[3] Otto Ernst Schüddekopf, *Linke Leute von Rechts: Nationalbolschewismus in Deutschland von 1918 bis 1933* (Stuttgart: Kohlhammer Verlag, 1960), 176–229.

plot to assassinate Stalin and Trotsky.[1] In the words of the joint announcement the exchange was to clear the air and 'support the negotiated treaty [Berlin treaty] by means of a special act of friendship'.[2]

A 300-million-mark German credit granted to the USSR in February helped further to accent the closeness of ties. By November Stresemann remarked enthusiastically to Chicherin: 'Political questions of overwhelming importance are not on the agenda of discussion between the two governments. The expectations which both sides have placed in the Berlin treaty have been fulfilled; economic relations as well have unfolded thanks to the 300-million-mark credit.'[3]

At most, however, these were peripheral benefits which the Wilhelmstrasse had expected from the treaty. For, as we have seen, Stresemann signed it in the belief that a public accord with the USSR would help intensify Germany's trade, strengthen his hand in dealings with the western powers, serve Germany's military needs, and facilitate an early redrawing of the German-Polish border. In the expectation of such support Germany had given a pledge of strict neutrality in any dispute between the USSR and a third state or states.

Both the expectation of Soviet support for Germany's policies and the obligation of neutrality assumed in the Berlin treaty rested on problematical assumptions regarding the evolution of Russia's economy and foreign relations. In the German view the political advantages of the Berlin treaty were in part to have been secured by the growth of the Soviet economy; Germany's association with an increasingly prosperous and stable Soviet Union evolving on the basis of the NEP was to have enhanced her own political stature. And the risks of such association, arising from the chance that she would become involved in foreign complications that would also entangle Germany or force her to side against Moscow, were to have been minimized by a parallel development in the area of diplomacy. A general *détente* in European relations—except, of

[1] Memorandum by Dirksen: 'Aufzeichnung über die Gründe für Durchführung der Bereinigung der deutsch-russischen Straffälle', July 10, 1926, 4564/E163615–17.

[2] Cited in Hey to the Foreign Ministry, August 22, 1926, 2860/D558071–3.

[3] Notes for a conversation of Stresemann and Chicherin drafted by Dirksen, November 30, 1926, 6698/H111112–14.

course, in those between Warsaw and Moscow—was to have made unnecessary for Germany a choice between Moscow and London.

But, contrary to Stresemann's expectations, Russia's economy did not flourish and her relations with the countries of western Europe did not improve; by the summer of 1926 the situation for the Soviet leadership was becoming economically lean and politically uncertain. After the serious economic crisis of 1923 the revival of the Soviet economy was short-lived, and by the summer of 1926 many symptoms of earlier difficulties were again visible: manufactured goods were in short supply, and a 'goods famine' developed in the countryside, with the government in need of material incentives to extract the needed grain for exports from a suspicious peasantry. Combined with a galloping inflation of the currency, this situation led to chronic trade deficits which the regime tried to alleviate by forcibly restricting imports. That these undeniably critical circumstances would have a baneful effect on the policy line represented by the Berlin treaty was predictable.

Yet what could command even wider attention was the equally unpromising development of Russia's international situation. Tensions with Poland and France continued unrelieved, and by mid-1926 the clash of Soviet and British policy in the Far East and the interference of the Comintern in the British coal miners' strike brought Anglo-Soviet relations, which had been declining steadily since late 1924, close to a complete rupture.

From the summer of 1926 Wilhelmstrasse officials were forced to recognize the widening gap between their cheerful hopes of April and Russia's bleak situation. They began to reexamine their ties with the east in a long debate that involved many of the key members of the Eastern Department and the German Embassy in Moscow. The debate began soon after the conclusion of the Berlin treaty. It ranged freely over the whole complex of relations with the USSR, and may be characterized as a resumption of the discussion about Germany's foreign orientation conducted during the Locarno negotiations.

The Soviet Union's deepening economic and social crisis was the occasion for the debate. Scarcely one month after the signature of the Berlin agreement, Eric Wallroth, Director of the Eastern Department—a Westerner—distributed in the Wilhelmstrasse and Moscow Embassy a lengthy memorandum suggestively titled,

'Nature and Political Significance of the Russian Economic Crisis'.[1] For Wallroth this report was the resumption of the battle against close ties with the Soviet Union which he had recently waged during the negotiations for the Locarno and Berlin treaties.[2] As such it consisted of an analysis, prognosis, and warning.

According to the analysis the dislocations in the Soviet economy had causes that were deeply imbedded within the system and for that reason could not be viewed as temporary. The prognosis, following logically, was that an inevitable full-scale financial and economic collapse would cause Russia to revert to an autarchic economy. The regime, however, would not collapse because the Party leadership would cling to power through a policy of ruthless repression – even at the high price of a stagnating economy. From this inevitable development, as Wallroth regarded it, arose serious risks for Germany's policy:

> Even if the Russians were themselves to put up with such an economic torso for an extended period of time, the Soviet Union would disappear as a factor in the economic combinations of her neighbors. And more important, despite her large area and population, Russia would then constitute a permanent shadow-state for the surrounding world, especially for us. Russia would then come to play only a very minor role in the foreign policies of Germany and other states, with the possible exception of her weak immediate neighbors.[3]

Coming so soon after the conclusion of the Berlin treaty, Wallroth's 'trial balance', as he termed it, was not well received by most of his colleagues. But as a well-argued brief that attacked official Foreign Ministry thought, it was sure to elicit a number of replies. Wallroth's characterization of the 'bluff effect' of bonds with Russia as meaningless *vis-à-vis* the western powers because of Russia's economic decline, for example, must have been recognized by Rantzau as aimed at him. But aside from the devastating observation that the Director's argument did not represent a trial balance

[1] Memorandum by Wallroth entitled: 'Wesen und politische Bedeutung der russischen Wirtschaftskrise', May 26, 1926, 5462/E380362–77.

[2] In the autumn of 1925 Wallroth had argued that the revolutionary commitments of the Soviet regime precluded traditionalist treaty relations, and Russia's economic and military weakness made support for Germany's negotiations in the west uncertain (Memorandum by Wallroth concerning conversation with Rantzau, November 15, 1925, 6698/H111023–7).

[3] Memorandum by Wallroth, May 26, 1926, 5462/E380362–77.

but a veritable final settlement, Rantzau left polemics to others and restricted himself to increased behind-the-scenes efforts to have Wallroth transferred to some less responsible post.

7. THE 'SCHLESINGER LINE'

A MORE explicit reply was elicited from Moritz Schlesinger, the German Foreign Ministry's expert on trade and financial relations with the USSR. In the period from 1925 to 1933 Schlesinger was an influential member of the Wilhelmstrasse, probably contributing more seminal ideas to Germany's eastern policy than anyone else. His influence, which at times extended to almost every aspect of German-Soviet relations, had a number of sources. It derived partly from the complete confidence that Rantzau placed in his intellect and judgement,[1] partly from his curious role as intermediary between the Foreign Ministry and the SPD, and partly from his considerable responsibilities for trade relations with Russia.

The unique structure of the Soviet economy coupled with special problems arising from the political uses of the Soviet trade monopoly encouraged the transfer of much authority to Schlesinger; his frequent travels between Berlin and Moscow permitted him to view the situation from a broad perspective and to win the confidence of persons in the Moscow Embassy and the Foreign Ministry. It is only one indication of the esteem in which Schlesinger was held by his colleagues that both Gustav Hilger, the German economic specialist in the Moscow Embassy, and Herbert von Dirksen, Vice-Director of the Eastern Department and later Ambassador to the USSR, describe him as a close collaborator and a trusted friend.[2]

[1] In December 1924, Rantzau recommended Schlesinger to the new State Secretary, Karl von Schubert, in these unqualified words: 'He has a complete grasp of the situation and *understands* the Russians and the "mentality" of the leading personalities here, who correspondingly fear him. . . .

. . . As for Schlesinger, I . . . emphasize expressly that I would ask you to grant him the same confidence that you have granted me; he has never disappointed it . . . since the first days of our acquaintance. I esteem him not only as a man of extraordinary intellect but am also personally on terms of friendship with him' (Rantzau to Schubert, December 16, 1924, 4562/E154899–902).

[2] Herbert von Dirksen, *Moscow, Tokyo, London: Twenty Years of*

The numerous well-knit and closely reasoned memoranda that came from Schlesinger's pen reveal keen intelligence, rectitude, first-rate analytical gifts, and, most important perhaps, a profound sense of political responsibility. In most cases they were circulated to the Ambassador in Russia and in the Wilhelmstrasse to the Director of the Eastern Department, the State Secretary, and, less frequently, the Foreign Minister. At critical moments they were often instrumental in provoking internal discussions about fundamental issues of foreign policy. Schlesinger, in short, must be credited with having contributed much to clarifying the alternatives open to Germany and with having helped her statesmen choose from among them on the basis of explicit political goals.

Before, however, treating the policy recommendations that Schlesinger made in reply to Wallroth's memorandum of May it is necessary to discuss the development of his influential ideas during the preceding year. Occupied almost constantly with German-Soviet trade relations since 1920, it had occurred to him that the Narkomindel's penchant to use Germany to pace-set the USSR's international relations posed special problems for the Wilhelmstrasse. The greatest danger was that by deepening her relations with other states, the Soviet Union would become less dependent upon Germany; carried far enough such a policy might be at the prohibitive price of Germany's isolation.

In the autumn of 1925 Schlesinger set himself the problem of divining a policy that would secure the German-Soviet tie for the longer run by eliminating from it this element of basic instability. In the negotiations that led to the signing of a series of important economic and trade agreements in October 1925, he thought at first that this goal could be reached by entangling the Soviet and German economies through treaty arrangements so that Soviet diplomats would be unable to enter another political constellation.[1] In the event, however, political considerations determined the agreements, to the annoyance of Schlesinger, who felt that 'there

---

German Foreign Policy (Norman: University of Oklahoma Press, 1952), 92; Gustav Hilger and Alfred Meyer, *The Incompatible Allies: A Memoir History of German-Soviet Relations* (Macmillan: New York, 1953), 24–5.

[1] Draft letter, Schlesinger to Dirksen, June 6, 1925, 4829/E242085–91; draft letter, Schlesinger to Schubert, June 13, 1925, 4829/E242094–103.

was no particular cause . . . to be satisfied with the results for economic reasons'.[1]

Since the two economies had not been interpenetrated by the treaties, the trade expert then urged that the same objective be sought through the extra-treaty means of German credits. In the winter of 1925–6 this policy, which Schlesinger deemed politically necessary, became economically feasible when the twin pressures of growing unemployment and overproduction won support from the business community and most political parties for a policy of extending credits to the Soviet Union. A modest short-term financial credit of 100 million marks was granted the Soviet State Bank in October 1925 by a group of private German banks.[2] In February 1926, a more significant long-term credit of 300 million marks was approved by the German cabinet.[3] It marked a new departure in international trade; although private German funds were to be used, the credit was backed by a *Reich* and *Länder* guarantee of 60 percent of its value in the event of Russian default.

German motives in offering this credit were complex. Naturally the government hoped that trade would increase and alleviate unemployment in Germany.[4] These were the arguments that featured in the cabinet session which voted the credit and in the approving German press commentaries thereafter. But the Foreign Ministry view articulated by Schlesinger stressed politics: 'The more we involve ourselves in Russia economically, the more we will strengthen the foreign policy position of the Soviet Union and thereby our own as well. That is to say, seen politically, our value as an ally (*Bündniswert*) will be raised for the balancing out of our general policy.'[5] In short, the 300-million credit was to supplement the political treaty still under negotiation.

[1] Draft letter, Schlesinger to Maltzan, Ambassador to the United States, October 6, 1925, 4829/E242067–72.

[2] Draft letter, Schlesinger to Dirksen, September 5, 1925, 4829/E242174–9; draft letter, Schlesinger to Maltzan, October 6, 1925, 4829/E242067–72.

[3] Extract from the minutes of a cabinet meeting, February 1, 1926, L617/L194592.

[4] Memorandum submitted to the cabinet by the Economics Ministry: 'Förderung des Aussenhandels mit Russland', February 1, 1926, L617/L194587–9; unsigned memorandum by the Economics Ministry: '35% Ausfallgarantie des Reichs bei Ausfuhrgeschäften nach Russland', February 18, 1926, 5265/E317456–68.

[5] Schlesinger to Maltzan, February 2, 1926, 4829/E242211–17.

In the spring of 1926 Schlesinger refined the original simplistic political idea behind the credit, namely that a strengthening of Russia's economy would bolster Germany's position. The first stimulus in this direction came from the United States. In the autumn of 1925 Ago von Maltzan, the German Ambassador in Washington—an old Russian hand—reported that Germany's credit policy in the Soviet Union was arousing suspicion in American financial circles; it was charged that American Dawes plan loans to Germany were making their appearance on the Russian market as industrial credits, bolstering Germany's competitive position against United States manufactured goods.[1]

Schlesinger realized that this interpretation could lessen America's willingness to support the German economy, a risk greater in its ultimate consequences than any possible advantages to be gained in the Soviet market. Slowly the idea took shape in his mind that a way out of the dilemma might lie in an involvement of *American capital* in the Soviet market under *German auspices*. He informed Maltzan of his views.[2]

Within a month the Ambassador in Washington replied that the Americans were interested. In fact the American President was reported to have raised the question with Maltzan in these words: 'Germany now has peace and security in the west (Locarno), and consequently has her hands free for further activity in the east.' Moreover, he had continued, with her specialized knowledge and long involvement in eastern politics, Germany had a mission to fulfill of helping to reestablish normal social and economic conditions in the Soviet Union. 'America would not object if Germany were to use American money cautiously in the rebuilding and expansion of the Russian economy (*wirtschaftlichen Auf- und Ausbau in Russland interessiere*).'[3]

[1] Draft letter, Schlesinger to Maltzan, October 6, 1925, 4829/E242067–72.

[2] He wrote Maltzan: 'The question arises whether the time has not come for us to begin negotiations about Russian economic developments with interested American financial circles. The purpose of such negotiations would be to win them to the idea of financial participation in German industrial credits to Russia' (ibid.); he wrote to the President of the German Reichsbank, about to embark on a trip to the United States, in this same vein (Draft letter, Schlesinger to Hjalmar Schacht, October 7, 1925, 4829/E242197–201).

[3] Maltzan to unnamed correspondent (Chancellor Luther?), December 9, 1925, L617/L194564–8.

In July 1926, Schlesinger clarified his thinking on the problems attending German-Soviet relations in a lengthy and highly significant memorandum addressed to Dirksen, Wallroth, Rantzau, and Schubert.[1] At this date the Foreign Ministry was reaching a *cul de sac* in its policy represented by the Berlin treaty and the credit of 300 million marks. This situation together with Wallroth's apprehensive report, on the one side, and promising developments on the American scene—which suggested a role for Germany as a mediator of Russia's economic relations—prompted a systematic analysis. But in contrast to Wallroth, Schlesinger viewed the matter from the standpoint of Russia's critical international position. How, he asked, could Germany lessen the potential threat to her position from an exacerbation of the Anglo-Soviet dispute?[2]

Schlesinger assumed that Germany desperately needed intimate bonds with the Soviet Union because of her international situation and had committed herself to the further existence of the Soviet regime in the Berlin treaty. Whatever weakened the Soviet position was therefore contrary to German interests. The most immediate danger, he felt, was that CPSU support of dissident working-class elements in Britain and revolutionary movements in China might provoke Britain to boycott the USSR economically or militarily. A more remote possibility was that Britain might act preemptively to smash the Soviet system if her leaders concluded that such action was necessary to establish peace or resolve their chronic unemployment. This appraisal led Schlesinger to conclude that Germany must keep the existence of the Soviet regime from being threatened at a time when its international ties were restricted almost exclusively to Germany.

The question of how this might be achieved brought him to two policy recommendations. Germany must try:

1. To influence the foreign policy activities of the Soviet Union in such a way as to hinder her from initiating any foreign policy conflicts.
2. To expand the economic interests of third powers in Soviet Russia and to entangle these so intimately with German interests that the

---

[1] Memorandum by Schlesinger, July 2, 1926, 6698/H109439–46.

[2] In a covering letter to Schubert he explained his purpose: it was to examine 'what Germany's position would be in the event of a foreign threat to the Soviet Union after the conclusion of the Berlin treaty and the 300 million credit' (Schlesinger to Schubert, July 2, 1926, 4562/E157743–44).

danger of an attack by a third power on Soviet Russia would be reduced substantially.[1]

The first task, to modify the policy of the Soviet regime so that it would not provoke hostile action, was to be realized through diplomatic channels. Schlesinger suggested a warning to Soviet leaders that Germany might have to loosen ties with them for reasons of self-preservation if they jeopardized their own future. Little attention was paid to this particular counsel until Anglo-Soviet relations reached their nadir in 1927.

The second recommendation, that Germany intertwine her financial interests in the Soviet economy with those of other states, was meant to free Germany of the nightmare that an armed struggle was approaching which would render her a transit zone for western armies despite her Locarno exemptions:

> . . . we dare not remain alone in Soviet Russia much longer. To the degree that we succeed in involving other interests in Russia the danger will be reduced that an intervention from abroad could shatter our general position. Our aim must be to postpone the period in which England or another power might find a reason for attacking Soviet Russia until such a time when the economic and political relations of the Soviet Union are sufficiently developed so that it is no longer possible for an attacking power to be assured of the passive concurrence of third powers. It should not be assumed that other powers will tolerate the autonomous development of German-Russian relations until the two countries represent an invulnerable force. The danger to our eastern policy will therefore be overcome only at a moment when the question will no longer exclusively be one of endangering German interests in Soviet Russia.[2]

But by what method were Russia's economic relations to be expanded without hurting Germany's interests? The technique, in all probability suggested to Schlesinger by Maltzan's conversations in the United States, was relatively simple: the 300-million-mark credit was to be systematically expanded 'through joint economic cooperation with America, France, and possibly Holland'.[3] On another occasion Schlesinger expressed it this way: Germany must seek 'to direct the inflow of capital through herself, in order that the economic strengthening of Soviet Russia does not lead to

[1] Memorandum by Schlesinger, July 2, 1926, 6698/H109439–46.
[2] Ibid. [3] Ibid.

a political development which is independent of us'.[1] Here was Schlesinger's reply to the knotty question of whether there was a course between the Scylla of Russia's and the Charybdis of Germany's isolation.

Schlesinger's memorandum of July 1926 thus marked a climax in the development of his thought on Germany's eastern policy. Starting with the problem of what Germany could do to secure her relations with Russia on a long-term basis, he had first, in the autumn of 1925, called for the establishment of a German monopoly in the economy of the Soviet Union by means of an astute credits policy. Relations with the USSR were thus to be freed from the fluctuating alignments of European diplomacy.

By July 1926, however, his proposals had come full circle. Now the Soviet Union was no longer to be insulated from intercourse with other countries by making those countries unnecessary to her economy. A strengthening of Russia's ties with other states was now inevitable—because of German inability to satiate Moscow's growing hunger for foreign credits—as well as desirable—because of the danger of a clash between the USSR and Britain being carried out at Germany's expense. The risks that this development would draw the Soviet Union into combinations hostile to Germany existed; but they were to be minimized by Germany's use of her close ties with Moscow, specialized knowledge in east European affairs, and advance position in the Soviet economy, to place herself at the center of the Soviet Union's expanding web of relations. Germany as Soviet Russia's economic middleman—here was the Grand Design for German policy.

8. BOLSTER, BLUFF, OR ABANDON

SCHLESINGER's relatively optimistic memorandum was meant to rebut Wallroth's counsel of despair as well as Rantzau's 'bluff theory' of German-Soviet relations. His denial of Wallroth's belief that the economic decline of the Soviet economy was inevitable was clear. More sophisticated was his refutation of the subtle 'bluff theory', which Rantzau had developed since becoming Germany's Ambassador to the USSR in 1922. By the mid-1920s there were two antithetical poles to Rantzau's thinking about the Soviet Union. The first was the Versailles treaty which Rantzau, as the

[1] Draft memorandum by Schlesinger, undated, 4829/E242326–32.

then Foreign Minister, had bitterly experienced at first hand. It had convinced him that collaboration with the USSR was absolutely necessary for a defenseless Germany. The second pole was the attempt in 1923 by the CPSU-KPD to explode Germany from within, which persuaded him that ultimately cooperation with the Soviet Union was impossible. Here was a conundrum – close ties with the Soviet Union defined as both necessary and as impossible – which Rantzau believed could only be resolved by arousing the impression among Germany's enemies of a 'greater intimacy with Russia . . . than actually existed'.[1] This was the 'bluff' of which he often spoke.

While Rantzau and Wallroth were agreed that fruitful relations with the USSR could not be maintained in the long run, they differed markedly in their policy conclusions. Wallroth believed that close ties with Russia were impossible and unnecessary; Rantzau asserted that they were impossible but necessary. At this point Schlesinger intervened with the counsel that such relations were not only necessary, they were feasible, and claimed that a policy based on other assumptions was fraught with the gravest risks.

Schlesinger's whole argument was meant to prove that a policy of bluff in relations with Soviet Russia (viewed solely as a means of easing relations with the western powers) broke down on its own assumptions. Those who favored such a policy believed that an inclination by Soviet policy makers to seek a political alignment inimical to Germany could be forestalled by a rapid orientation westward. He questioned whether there would be enough time in a moment of crisis to carry through such a dramatic shift. More importantly, he warned that if Germany used her connections with the USSR solely as a bluff the Russians might be disposed to do the same. What assurance, he asked in the July memorandum, did the exponents of a 'bluff relationship' have that the Soviet government might not consider it expedient 'to sell Germany's hide after they had gotten the maximum out of Germany politically and economically?'[2]

In the Foreign Ministry and Moscow Embassy Schlesinger's views received a mixed though generally favorable reception. Their overall design to ease international tensions in Europe through

[1] Draft letter, Rantzau to President Paul von Hindenburg, July 8, 1926, 9101/H224038–46.

[2] Memorandum by Schlesinger, July 2, 1926, 6698/H109439–46.

German mediation without abandoning Germany's revision goals, elicited a dual response. Those like Rantzau who expected few easy concessions from the western powers—and hence favored the resolute exploitation of the divisions among European states—feared that a general lessening of tension would only help to perpetuate the territorial and political *status quo* in Europe. Rantzau did not oppose Schlesinger's *original* plan that a monopoly for Germany be established in the economic life of the Soviet Union through a credit policy; he merely believed it was doomed to failure. Nor did he oppose economic and financial collaboration with the United States. But working with parties other than the United States was another matter, and here he seems to have lodged a strong protest.[1] We know, for example, that Rantzau did not give Schlesinger's plan for economic cooperation with third states even his grudging support until the Foreign Ministry had placed its full weight behind it.[2]

Dirksen, on the other hand, played a leading role in winning assent for the Schlesinger line in Berlin. As for Schubert and Stresemann we know that the intent of the plan was intrinsically in consonance with their views and received their general assent. Thus it was Stresemann himself who authorized Schlesinger to conduct further conversations with interested parties in the United States and France.[3]

However varied the reactions of individual members of the Foreign Ministry were to the continuing foreign policy debate on the question of *dismantlement*, *bluff*, or *intensification* of relations with the Soviet Union, it is clear that by mid-summer 1926 Schlesinger's counsel had been accepted and temporarily became the main line of Germany's policy towards the Soviet Union. On August 7, 1926, this was made official in a secret policy directive signed by State Secretary Schubert, and addressed to a number of German embassies.[4]

[1] Schlesinger wrote to Dirksen: 'I have had very detailed discussions about these questions with the Ambassador, whom I have not yet completely won for these conceptions' (Draft letter, July 3, 1926, 4829/E242359–60).

[2] Herbert Helbig, *Die Träger der Rapallo-Politik* (Göttingen: Vandenhoeck und Ruprecht, 1958), 185.

[3] Schlesinger to Wallroth, July 2, 1926, 4829/E242355–6.

[4] Memorandum by Schubert, entitled 'Geheimerlass IV Ru 4931', August 7, 1926, 6698/H109447–52. This directive is a useful summary of

This directive – drafted by Schlesinger sometime in June – instructed Germany's foreign representatives 'to pay special attention to the development of the economic relations of the Soviet Union and on the basis of the viewpoints outlined, to report immediately any opportunities that may arise for economic cooperation'. The 'viewpoints outlined' were a systematic enumeration of the considerations, outlined above, that favored collaboration between Germany and other countries in the Soviet economy.

Implementing the 'Schlesinger line', as described in Schubert's policy directive, was a knotty problem because it meant dealing with two sets of variables and required work on two fronts. It was necessary to win third countries to the idea, as well as to gain Soviet assent for such collaboration. Neither of these tasks was easy.

Unhappily, the documents of the Foreign Ministry that fell into western hands at the end of World War II do not permit a satisfactory treatment of either of these lines of activity. That must probably await the opening to western scholars of the East German archives in Potsdam, which are reported to contain records of the German Embassy in Moscow and the Economic Department of the Foreign Ministry.[1] We have, for example, little information concerning German negotiations and unofficial conversations with interested financial circles in Holland, Belgium, Great Britain, or

the Schlesinger line; draft memorandum by Schlesinger, identical in content to one cited above, undated, probably written sometime in June 1926, 4829/E242326–32.

[1] After the collapse of Nazism these documents were carried off to the Soviet Union. Since 1957 they have been returned to East Germany in lots. A general listing of the materials returned by 1960 is given in German Democratic Republic, *Archivmitteilungen*, I (1960), 13–14. The listed records relevant to this study are: Department IV, Economic Policy (*c.* 3,700 volumes, 1920–36); Economic Department (*c.* 1,000 volumes); German Embassy, Moscow (*c.* 800 volumes, 1912–41); Nachlass of Herbert von Dirksen; Nachlass of Gustav Hilger. These documents are reported to be located in Department I (Deutsches Reich 1867/71–1945) of the Potsdam Archives. The circumstances under which the Dirksen Papers fell into Soviet hands are described in Herbert von Dirksen, *Moscow, Tokyo, London*, op. cit., 262. In the spring of 1961 my request to the East German authorities to use the above files was rejected. Studies based on the documents of these archives have appeared in East Germany: Alfred Anderle, 'Die Deutsch-sowjetischen Verträge von 1925/26', *Zeitschrift für Geschichtswissenschaft*, V (February 1957), 470–502; Albert Norden, *Fälscher: Zur Geschichte der deutsch-sowjetischen Beziehungen* (Berlin: Dietz Verlag, 1960); Günter Rosenfeld, *Sowjet-russland und Deutschland 1917–1922* (Berlin: Akademie-Verlag, 1960).

France.[1] Regarding activities in western Europe we know only that Schubert's policy directive was accompanied by personal letters from Schlesinger to the ambassadors suggesting ways of fostering the proposed cooperation.[2]

But when we come to the United States our story can be documented more fully. And while cooperation with the United States bulked larger in the Wilhelmstrasse's view than cooperation with other countries—and hence is somewhat atypical—what we find in this area may serve as a sampling of German methods and an indication of the general aims of German policy.

Given the antipathy in the United States to Soviet matters it was decided to prepare the way for German-American cooperation in the Soviet economy through a broadly conceived propaganda campaign; it was to be directed in the first instance to American business circles. Foreign Ministry policy makers realized that such a campaign would have to meet head-on American preoccupations concerning the wisdom of going it with Germany.

The German selling campaign took the form of a lengthy article entitled 'The Reconstruction of Russia', which appeared in August 1926 in the *Journal of Commerce.*[3] This article was prepared in the Foreign Ministry—probably by Schlesinger himself—and its semi-official character was underlined by having it appear as the work of Werner von Rheinbaben, a close associate of Gustav Stresemann in the People's Party, and sometime cabinet minister.[4]

[1] On July 2, 1926, Schlesinger mentioned that 'the discussions conducted with Ambassador Dufour about Anglo-German cooperation have not yet given us anything positive to go by' (Memorandum by Schlesinger, July 2, 1926, 6698/H109439–46). About negotiations with French circles we have little direct evidence beyond that contained in Schlesinger's memorandum of July 2: 'The feelers in question, as well as various discussions in Paris conducted with the knowledge of Ambassador von Hoesch, suggest possibilities that could lead to concrete negotiations within a reasonable space of time' (Memorandum by Schlesinger, July 2, 1926, 6698/H224038–46).

[2] Mentioned by Herbert Helbig, *Träger der Rapallo-Politik,* op. cit., 185, footnote 93, without, however, citing source.

[3] This treatment is based on a Foreign Ministry draft of the article entitled, 'Der Wiederaufbau Sowjetrusslands', undated, 6698/H109404–409.

[4] Originally it was planned to let the article appear under the name of a prominent German economist, but those approached declined on the grounds of '*privatwirtschaftliche Gründe*' (Wallroth to German Embassy, Washington, instructing that article be sent to the *Journal of Commerce,* July 5, 1926, 6698/H109402).

By speaking in one breath of universalist principles—the need to reintegrate Soviet Russia into the economic and cultural community of 'Europe and America'—and of economic self-interest, the article constituted a clever appeal to the stereotype of the American character.

Credits from abroad, its argument began, were the key to Russia's reintegration into the *Kulturwelt*; Germany alone, however, did not have adequate means to provide them. Participation by the United States was imaginable on two levels. Germany and the United States could work side by side because there was room for all and Germany did not fear rivalry: 'Every increment in strength of the Soviet economy represents new buying power and new market possibilities for German goods as well.'

But beyond this Germany and the United States might accelerate the USSR's 'reintegration' into the world economy by collaborating on the basis of a 'fusion of German experience in and information and knowledge about Soviet Russia: German labor with American money'. Dormant American capital would thus be put to work, and the German government would be better able—through the sale of manufactured goods in the Soviet Union—to fulfill its Dawes plan obligations. The peroration was in the nature of an appeal to negotiate: 'Germany is prepared to work side by side and hand in hand with the United States in the realization of this great task.'[1]

Because of the continuing opposition of American industry to the idea of loaning money to Germany which merely 'reappeared on the Soviet market as competing industry', the scheme of marrying German know-how and American money in the promotion of German exports to the Soviet Union was soon dropped. In its place a mixed plan was suggested to increase the sale of German *and* American products on the Soviet market. Discussions in the Foreign Ministry led to a plan by which Germany was to mediate the sale of surplus American cotton to Russia along with the sale of German industrial products. Such an operation was to be financed with American money and guaranteed by the German government like the 300-million-mark credit of February 1926.[2]

[1] Unsigned article entitled, 'Der Wiederaufbau Sowjetrusslands', undated, 6698/H109404–9.

[2] Schlesinger to Maltzan, November 9, 1926, 4829/E242387–93.

Schlesinger suggested to Maltzan that a joint German-American company be organized to implement the scheme. The company would receive a five-year 100-million-dollar loan from an American financial consortium. Thirty percent of this money would be used to finance the sale of American cotton and the remaining seventy percent would help to finance the sale of products of German industry. As its contribution the German government would assume a guarantee of the whole sum.

Schlesinger stressed the advantages to both sides of such a development. It would ease the glut on the American cotton market and bring a return on capital lying idle; for Germany it would increase the sale of German industrial goods, alleviate unemployment and, best of all, constitute a first small gain in a broader program of having other governments commit themselves economically to the further existence of the Soviet Union—through Germany's mediation.[1]

But how would the Soviet government react to the 'Schlesinger line'? Wilhelmstrasse officials knew this to be a crucial question.[2] Immediate objections by Moscow would not necessarily have fatal consequences for it, although such a beginning would be inauspicious. Given the limited financial alternatives open to the Soviet Union it was considered unlikely that credits from Berlin would be rejected because of their source. But what if there were other alternatives? The Germans did not have long to wait for a first response. In the summer of 1926 rumors of German plans first reached Moscow and the Soviet government was immediately placed on its guard. It saw them as a conspiracy to create an international consortium in opposition to the Soviet trade monopoly, its chief trade weapon. Consequently the reaction was unequivocal. In press releases and in an article in a leading Soviet trade journal the government gave notice that 'there was no need for foreign capital to seek German mediation'; moreover the Soviet

[1] Schlesinger to Maltzan, November 9, 1926, 4829/E242387-93. A close study of American sources would be needed to determine the ultimate fate of this plan. Of importance for this study is that it serves as one example of the ingenious possibilities being explored by the Foreign Ministry.

[2] Dirksen was aware of the difficulties to be expected: 'Naturally we can expect the greatest opposition from the Russian side', he wrote Paul Scheffer in the summer of 1926 (Dirksen to Paul Scheffer, July 29, 1926, 6698/H109431–8).

Union would never permit her economic development to become dependent on any one country, including Germany.[1]

Soviet policy provided an equally clear reply. In her economic and trade relations Russia continued to deal with foreign states on a bilateral basis. Moscow realized that it could thwart the creation of a common economic front in the west, under whatever name, through a simple device. It need only offer better trade terms to states which had failed to give the Soviet Union credits—such as the United States and Britain—than to those which had—such as Germany.[2] By the end of 1926 this tactic of playing off one state against another had not succeeded in opening new foreign credit reserves, as the Soviets had hoped, but it had prevented Germany from emerging as the middleman in the USSR's foreign economic relations.

As 1926 drew to a close Schlesinger was frankly pessimistic. His plan had seemingly been stillborn. Russia's general economic and political situation was more precarious than it had been six months earlier, and he feared, as he wrote to Friedrich Gaus, Chief of the Legal Department, that Germany might herself no longer be in a position to keep her bonds with the Soviet Union from becoming increasingly 'looser and more effete (*lockerer und müder*)'.[3]

9. THE DILEMMA OF ISOLATION

WHILE Wilhelmstrasse officials puzzled over ways of maintaining the Berlin treaty as an active ingredient in their diplomacy, the Soviets were engaged in an analogous task. The problem, as seen from Moscow, was that there existed sedulous temptations for Germany to violate her pledge of neutrality—the interests of her bourgeoisie and her entanglements in the Dawes plan, Locarno agreements, and League of Nations. With some foreboding, the Narkomindel therefore continuously scanned the international scene for tell-tale signs of a shift in Germany's posture. Each

[1] Mentioned in memorandum by Schubert, August 7, 1926, 6698/H109447–52.

[2] Soviet efforts to use the 300-million-mark credit as a lure to get credits from other states is discussed in Stresemann to the German Ministers of Finance and Labor, December 30, 1926, 2860/D558278–83.

[3] Schlesinger to Gaus, December 28, 1926, 4829/E242450–5.

session of the League and meeting of a German leader with a representative of another state was marked by Soviet demands for a renewed German pledge of faithfulness to the 'spirit of Rapallo'.

In the autumn of 1926 at the time of the talks between Briand and Stresemann at Thoiry, for example, Chicherin expressed alarm that France would only offer Germany an early evacuation of the Rhineland in return for concessions in questions relating to the east. Stresemann admitted that French demands of that character could be anticipated, but he denied that Germany would accept them.[1] Soviet nervousness would also erupt in shrill press stories accusing Germany of acts of political disloyalty.[2] These charges, somewhat stale by now, were reiterated partly to keep alive the waning spirit of the KPD, and partly to elicit official German statements about the durability of relations with the Soviet Union. In perilous times when Russia's foreign connections were restricted almost to Germany, such repeated vows might improve Moscow's political position.

Beyond these questionable tactics to solidify their situation, however, Soviet diplomats returned in the summer of 1926 to the idea of achieving a major diplomatic realignment through the creation of a continental bloc. Chicherin had first explored the possibility of such an alignment as Russia's maximal diplomatic goal during the Ruhr crisis of 1923 and had repeated it in December 1924. Now it was Litvinov who revived it. In a conversation with Schubert in August 1926, the Deputy Foreign Commissar suggested that the French response to the Berlin treaty had been less abrupt than might have been expected. Indeed, only recently Philippe Berthelot, the French Ambassador in Moscow, had broached the idea of 'France, Germany, and Russia going it together in Europe'.[3]

A more promising combination for the USSR and a more perilous one for Germany was hard to envision. For that reason it was illusory. Nevertheless the idea of a continental bloc merits our

[1] Memorandum by Stresemann concerning conversations with Chicherin, December 2, 3, 1926, 2860/D558166–201. Printed French sources do not permit a verification of the accuracy of Litvinov's statement.

[2] Characteristic of the tenor of Soviet charges was an editorial equating Stresemann's Locarno policy with Chamberlain's openly anti-Soviet policy (*Visti*, November 29, 1926).

[3] Memorandum by Schubert, August 5, 1926, 4562/E157790–801.

attention because its airing by the Narkomindel at a number of critical points in the period 1924–31 suggests that it represented a continuing although minor theme in German-Soviet relations.[1] For the USSR the potential advantages of a continental grouping were obvious: it would have rendered unnecessary for her a choice between Germany and France as her *point d'appui* in the capitalist world; it would have relieved her of the threat of an attack by Poland that would have been supported by France; and it might also have persuaded France to drop her tutelage over Poland, an essential condition to winning Germany for it.

But clearly the most important consideration for Soviet leaders was that it would have helped to isolate Britain. If Soviet diplomacy was serious in proposing this nostrum, as seems likely, it must also have been optimistic about its leeway to remake the established diplomatic patterns in Europe. A continental grouping demanded that certain rigorous preconditions be met: it required a reconciliation of France with Germany as well as the USSR, an exacerbation of tensions between France and Britain, and a willingness on the part of Germany to be driven into an anti-British position.

For these very reasons a Franco-Soviet-German combination was never seriously considered by the Wilhelmstrasse. In December 1924, it had been turned down curtly by Rantzau; in response to Litvinov's proposal Schubert now as unhesitatingly replied that 'this was a very fine idea, but an essential precondition was first of all a reconciliation between France and Russia'.[2] For the time being the discussion of *Kontinentalpolitik* was closed. But the fundamental problem for the Wilhelmstrasse and the Narkomindel—of which it was an essential part—remained: to integrate their mutual ties into their respective foreign policies, or at least to keep those ties from thwarting the general line. The root of the difficulty was that the USSR needed German and perhaps French support in her struggle against Britain; Germany, on the other hand, needed British and Soviet support against France for her program of revision. This was a basic incompatibility.

[1] Here I am somewhat in disagreement with E. H. Carr, who writes: 'This conception, which fitted in with Chicherin's personal Anglophobe bias, was not widely shared in Moscow and had little practical influence on foreign policy' (*Socialism in One Country, 1924–1926*, II, Part 1, 38).

[2] Memorandum by Schubert, August 5, 1926, 4562/E157790–801.

Part Two

THE ANGLO-SOVIET BREAK AND GERMAN-SOVIET RELATIONS 1927

THE year 1927 was more hazardous for Soviet foreign policy than any since the end of the civil war. While Russia's economy was weakened still further, a succession of sharp foreign setbacks left her almost isolated in Europe. As in 1926, Russia's difficulties derived mainly from her dispute with Britain, which became critical early in 1927. A measure of Britain's impatience was a curt Foreign Office note of February; the note demanded that Moscow desist from revolutionary activity in China or suffer the consequences of an abrogation of trade relations and 'even the severance of ordinary diplomatic relations'.[1]

Some weeks later the Italian government, in an openly anti-Soviet move, recognized Rumania's right to Bessarabia. But so long as Soviet activities in China were promising of victory, confidence in Moscow remained at a high level. In April, however, the tide in China shifted as Chiang Kai-shek crushed his former ally, the Communist wing of the Kuomintang—a defeat more stinging for Moscow than any since the abortive revolution in Germany in 1923.[2] Others soon followed. On May 12, the offices of Arcos, a branch of the Soviet trade delegation in London, were raided by the British police, and two weeks later Sir Austen Chamberlain suspended diplomatic relations with the USSR.

Chamberlain's action brought on the first great international crisis of the post-Locarno period. Although Germany was not

[1] Quoted in Fischer, op. cit., II, 682; the Soviet reply is given in Degras, op. cit., II, 159–64.

[2] For Soviet military-strategic considerations in China, see: Erickson, *The Soviet High Command*, 217–39.

directly involved, it nevertheless came also to disturb German-Soviet relations. By raising the possibility of a wide-ranging diplomatic, economic, and perhaps even military confrontation between London and Moscow, the dispute put to a hard test Germany's diplomatic system, which rested on the Locarno and Berlin treaties. Were the policies associated with those agreements compatible only in fair weather? Did Germany have the power to remain neutral if the dispute should deepen? Was it still realistic to believe that Germany could maintain equally intimate ties with London and Moscow? These, for the Foreign Ministry, were the fundamental questions posed by the crisis.

Since a balancing role had previously been defined by Stresemann as the *sine qua non* of Germany's international revival, the imbroglio could not help but evoke another great debate in the Wilhelmstrasse. The issue on which it turned was, as a leading participant described it, 'whether Germany's ties with Russia are worth enough to our present and future political interests so that it pays to assume the political expenses and risks involved in maintaining them?'[1]

Germany's posture in the dispute—cautious neutrality with an edge in favor of London—tended to confirm Soviet suspicions that the lines of the Dawes plan and the Locarno agreements had entangled Germany in the purposes of the western powers. Even though the dispute petered out without forcing Germany to opt for either of the sides, it made the Soviet leadership increasingly skeptical about the value of shifting diplomatic alignments—such as the one with Germany—as buttresses to the security of a militarily weak USSR. This attitude probably influenced both the militant resolutions of the Sixth Comintern Congress (1928), that were to mobilize non-Soviet Communists to the defense of Russia, and the decision (in the same year) that the muscle for Russia's security would from henceforth be sought primarily in industrialization.

1. REASSURANCES

BEFORE the reversal of Russia's position in China in April 1927, Soviet leaders had been concerned but not overly alarmed about their increasing isolation. Although they had played on the theme

[1] Memorandum by Dirksen, September 19, 1927, K281/K097454–60.

of Britain's enmity since mid-1924, they had not described an Anglo-Soviet showdown as imminent.[1] Even after Chamberlain's stern reprimand in February, Stalin had spoken of war as only a future possibility.[2] As late as March 29, Rykov had characterized the threat of a military clash in the coming year as slight 'if the present distribution of powers could only be maintained'.[3]

Moscow's measured optimism had several roots. One was the expectation that the Chinese revolution would be successful, another the conviction, as Chicherin confided to Rantzau, that '*nous sommes géographiquement inattaquables*'.[4] The Soviets also assumed, as Krestinskii observed, that England was crippled for serious action so long as the dominions were chary in giving her their aid and British public opinion was inclined toward pacifism.[5] Finally, and of greatest moment, it was anticipated that the links with Germany would bear the strain of an international crisis.

Earlier in 1927, Soviet leaders had been much less sanguine about the stability of Germany's policy, expressing concern that it was about to veer towards the west. Although such suspicions were expressed in temperate forms by the Narkomindel, they would, when transmitted through party loudspeakers, often become strident enough to occasion a sharp rejoinder from Berlin. In such instances the Narkomindel would again have to mend the damage.

In January 1927, in a polemical address to a party gathering of the Moscow district, Bukharin asserted: 'Now [Germany] is joining the concert of fully-fledged imperialistic states and is turning her back on the east.' He accused her of having had a hand in the recent Lithuanian coup that had brought a fascist-type government to power. His one hope was that the German bourgeoisie's interest in the Soviet market would prompt the Foreign Ministry to adopt

[1] In a speech to the press in Berlin on December 6, 1926, Chicherin had stated: 'The policy of encirclement which is being followed with regard to us is a hard fact, and we are fighting back, not without success' (Degras [ed.], II, 144–7.)

[2] Cited in Otto Hoetzsch, 'Russlands aussenpolitische Lage und Aussenpolitik', *Osteuropa*, II (February 1927), 396–7.

[3] Ibid., 397.

[4] Rantzau to Schubert, March 6, 1927, 2860/D558454–65.

[5] Köpke to the German delegation at the League of Nations reporting conversation between Paul Scheffer and Krestinskii, March 8, 1927, 2860/D558471.

policies toward Russia friendlier than those of other western states.[1] These harsh words were not suited to win German favor, and they elicited the expected sharp protest from Rantzau and the Foreign Ministry. Both Litvinov and Shtein, with whom Rantzau spoke, replied in embarrassment that the Narkomindel was not able to take up the matter with Bukharin. They suggested a German denial of Bukharin's charges, but asked that not too much be made of the matter.[2]

That the issue would be blown up in Germany was precisely what Rantzau feared. He did not deny the vexing nature of Bukharin's speech, but was uneasy that advocates of a pro-British policy in and outside the German Foreign Ministry would use it in support of their claim that such conduct precluded businesslike relations with the USSR. Because this was a recurring problem for Rantzau, he again tried to guide criticism into safe channels in a long despatch to the Foreign Ministry. 'It has,' he wrote, 'been possible for us during the last four years, to make progress here politically as well as economically.'[3] While the paths of Germany and the Soviet Union might ultimately diverge, Rantzau was convinced that for the time being they still ran parallel.

A further incident early in March led the Narkomindel to question publicly whether Russo-German cooperation would be realized even temporarily. In a sensational report, the Paris paper *Excelsior* quoted an alleged statement by von Schubert:

> The German public does not like to be reminded of unpleasant concessions which Germany has had to make. This is the case in the familiar question of transit rights for France in case of an attack on Poland or Czechoslovakia. This reminder was especially embarrassing for Germany in view of the fact that her relations with Poland are quite precarious.[4]

If true, this disclosure would perforce cause the Narkomindel to lose its trust in German policy. Chicherin had been repeatedly reassured about the involved negotiations at Locarno so as to free

[1] *Pravda*, January 13, 1927; Rantzau to the Foreign Ministry, January 13, 1927, 2860/D558306–11; characterized in *Osteuropa* as symptomatic of the increasing nervousness of Soviet foreign policy (O. Hoetzsch, *Osteuropa*, II [February 1927], 396–7).

[2] Rantzau to the Foreign Ministry, January 18, 1927, 2860/D558315–7.

[3] Rantzau to the Foreign Ministry, January 20, 1927, 2860/D558323–6.

[4] Quoted in *Berliner Zeitung*, March 8, 1927.

him from the nightmare that by joining the League Germany would be forced to permit foreign troops the right of transit through her territory. That this was not the case was also the substance of Germany's promise of neutrality in the Berlin treaty. The *Excelsior* report therefore led to a hurried exchange of diplomatic communications and a spate of articles in the Soviet press speaking of German dissimulation.

The incident was further inflamed and prolonged through the Wilhelmstrasse's inept handling of it. The immediate German response, for instance, heightened Soviet wariness by depicting the interview not as a perversion of Schubert's words, but as a breach of confidence by the correspondent.[1] The offending passage, as it turned out, was a quotation from one of Briand's interviews that Schubert had characterized as erroneous.[2] The incident dragged on for two weeks, only ending after Stresemann had explained it to the Reichstag[3] and the Narkomindel had received a top secret Foreign Ministry memorandum containing excerpts from the negotiations concerning Article 16 at Locarno.[4] Since the dispute with England involved the risk of war the Russians could take no chances concerning Germany's intentions.

The Soviet response to the *Excelsior* interview offers some useful insights into the Soviet approach to relations with Germany in the months before the break with England. On the one hand Berlin was asked to clarify its position regarding Article 16 and the Locarno conference. Litvinov remonstrated that Russia was less interested in discovering the substance of the reported interview than in knowing 'if at Locarno Germany had actually declared herself ready if necessary to grant French troops transit rights'.[5] Editorially the *Ekonomicheskaia Zhizn'* suggested that perhaps

[1] Rantzau to Stresemann, March 19, 1927, 2860/D558543–7; *Izvestiia*, March 10, 12, 1927.

[2] Memorandum by Schubert, concerning interview with correspondent from *Excelsior* on March 6, 1927, dictated on March 15, 1927, 4562/E158354–7.

[3] Stresemann to Rantzau, March 22, 1927, 2860/D558556; copy of statement made by Stresemann in Reichstag, March 22, 1927, 4562/E158445–6.

[4] This memorandum was transmitted to the Soviet government after the rupture between England and Russia (Memorandum by Wallroth concerning conversation with Chicherin and Rantzau, June 14, 1927, 5265/E319015–16).

[5] Rantzau to the Foreign Ministry, March 15, 1927, 2860/D558508–9.

Schubert's *Excelsior* disclosure was timed to thwart the Wilhelmstrasse's eastern policy because it 'does not suit the followers of wholesale cooperation with anti-Soviet groups in England'.[1] The ill-starred interview was combined in Soviet thinking with the March session of the League, at which Chamberlain, it was alleged, had sought both Germany's passive acquiescence (the troop transit question) and her inclusion in an anti-Soviet bloc. *Pravda* suggested in an article entitled, 'Germany and the spirit of Locarno', that by signing the Locarno accords Germany had opened the sluicegates to a development that was drawing her ever more deeply into Britain's anti-Soviet intrigues.[2]

At the same time Germany was reminded of the possible consequences of a change in alignment. *Pravda* pointed out that collaboration against the USSR would prevent Germany from recovering her freedom of political action and force her to abandon 'her plans for the revision of her eastern borders'.[3] An effort was also made to mobilize German commercial interests against what were regarded as anti-Soviet influences. *Pravda* commented that Germany's obligations to the Dawes plan could not be met without the Soviet market. And since politics and trade were linked Germany 'cannot run the risk of breaking the treaties relating to mutual neutrality and non-aggression'.[4]

The argument that Germany's interest in the Polish question was incompatible with a one-sided western orientation was further explored by *Izvestiia* on April 13.[5] In an article entitled 'Germany and the Border States' a bold new departure on the Polish issue was aired. Germany and the Soviet Union, the article read, had a 'common goal of fundamentally guaranteeing the real independence of the border states'. These states were circumspect in their relations with Germany because they were dependent on France and becoming increasingly dependent on Britain. Indeed, Britain's recent support of Warsaw was interpreted as a reward to Poland at 'Germany's expense for Polish services in the encirclement of the Soviet Union'. Thus the Polish problem was becoming more insoluble.

The article implied that Britain's appearance in central Europe

[1] *Ekonomicheskaia Zhizn'*, March 15, 1927.

[2] *Pravda*, March 15, 1927.

[3] Ibid., March 21, 1927.

[4] Ibid., March 15, 1927.

[5] *Izvestiia*, April 13, 1927.

was at one and the same time an overt threat to Soviet security and a covert challenge to German interests in that the goal of border change was being thwarted. That this was the effect of the unresolved quarrel between Britain and the USSR on Germany's interests agreed with German views. What broke fresh ground, however, was the proposed way out of this dilemma. Germany should try to free Poland 'from foreign influence on her policy' by temporarily abandoning her revisionist goals. Britain's alleged efforts to reconcile Germany's and Poland's conflicting territorial claims for anti-Soviet purposes were to be foiled by temporarily reconciling these differences using a Soviet formula to heighten Poland's security. In short, Germany's previous objections to a Russo-Polish non-aggression pact were to be overcome by involving her in a similar agreement with Poland—in this way Britain would be denied the use of Poland as a base from which to counter Soviet activities in China. But this radical proposal meant a temporary abandonment of Germany's territorial claims, a course that no German government in the 1920s could choose. For this reason the Soviet initiative was never answered by the Foreign Ministry, a fact that may also explain why it was not ventilated again by the Soviet press nor supported by a diplomatic sounding from the Narkomindel.

On the eve of Russia's setbacks in China and the rupture with Britain relations between Berlin and Moscow had been smoothed over. The March session of the League had not led to the feared anti-Soviet front,[1] and Stresemann's statement in the Reichstag explaining the *Excelsior* interview had buoyed up the Soviet regime by giving public notice that efforts to isolate the USSR would not enjoy German support. As late as March 21, 1927, *Pravda* had expressed a feeling of discomfort about German intentions: 'Germany must remain neutral in the Anglo-Soviet Russian conflict, for only this policy corresponds with her own interests.'[2] A month later Rykov, Chairman of the Council of People's Commissars, was more optimistic. He admitted that recent rumors of changes in German foreign policy had upset his government, but he

[1] 'Germany, on which English diplomacy counted the most, has rejected the invitation to join the anti-Soviet bloc, because an open anti-Soviet orientation at this time in no way accords with the interests of the German bourgeoisie' (*Pravda*, March 21, 1927).

[2] Ibid.

affirmed: 'in our future relations with Germany we shall proceed on the assumption that in the event of any intrigue against the USSR Germany will not allow herself to be used for any armed attack upon us'.[1] Events proved this assumption to be correct.

2. A THREAT OF *ALLEINBLEIBEN*

IN 1926–7 German diplomats saw the directions in which relations with the USSR might develop in terms of a continuum with limits of extreme instability and a center of relative stability. In the contemporary language of the Wilhelmstrasse the one limit, a point of high danger to Germany's diplomatic system, would have been termed *Ausschaltung* (exclusion). It described the potential situation in which Russia was integrated into European diplomacy through an accord with Poland and France. The result would be a Germany isolated on the continent. The other limit, called *Alleinbleiben* (remain alone), defined the converse situation in which Germany was associated with an increasingly insular USSR and hence was in danger of being drawn into the sphere of Russia's isolation. The clock of history would again be turned back to the situation that had existed at Rapallo.

The most lively threat of *Ausschaltung* would coincide with intervals in which the diplomatic component of Soviet policy was receiving top priority. And the risks of *Alleinbleiben* would tend to be greatest at times when the revolutionary aspect was in the foreground. Thus Germany's efforts to integrate her relations with the Soviet Union into her general foreign policy may be characterized as an attempt to stabilize them at a mean position between these extremes. It would be a point where the international situation of the USSR was not firm enough to let her dispense with Berlin's support and yet not desperate enough to render her an international pariah.

The Berlin treaty, it may be recalled, was an attempt by Germany to stabilize relations with Russia at precisely such a point. It was concluded, in part at least, to hinder the creation of a Russo-Polish-French grouping that was then being rumored by Moscow for tactical reasons. This was an example of meeting the threat of *Ausschaltung*. Moreover, in the next six months the Foreign

[1] Rykov to the Fourth Soviet Congress, April 17, 1927, Degras (ed.), op. cit., II, 190.

Ministry debate leading to the 'Schlesinger line' centered on the question of how to inhibit the development of German-Soviet relations toward either of the extreme limits of the continuum. Schlesinger's idea, to repeat, was that Germany could hasten the emergence of Russia from diplomatic and economic isolation without risking her own isolation by placing herself, as mediator, at the very heart of Russia's expanding web of relations, trade relations in particular.

These expectations were bitterly disappointed. The long shadow cast by Soviet activity in China accented Moscow's insularity and narrowed the threat to Germany to *Alleinbleiben*. While this development simplified the problem of analysis by sharply limiting the policy alternatives, it did not, of course, ease Germany's position. And again as in 1926 another debate was stimulated within the Wilhelmstrasse—this one about even more fundamental issues. The debate may be described as revolving around the question of how to temper the Anglo-Soviet dispute so that it would not terminate in a break; such a result, it was thought, could place Germany before the barren options of having to side with the west, at the price of abandoning her revisionist objectives, or of having to tie her future to that of Russia, at the equally prohibitive price of imperiling her economic position and postponing her military and political recovery.

There was little inclination to loosen relations with the Soviet Union still more unless radical Soviet policies made this necessary. That links with Moscow were essential to the realization of Berlin's chief political goals—the restoration to Germany of sovereignty over the Rhineland and the Saar and the recovery of territories from Poland—continued as an axiom of Germany's policy. Indeed, the progressive non-fulfillment of the revisionist hopes that Germany had placed in Locarno made friendly relations with the Soviet Union seem as crucial as ever.

Rantzau, as the chief proponent of this view, warned against placing too much emphasis on the revolutionary outbursts of Soviet leaders. A balanced interpretation, he said, would recognize that it had been possible 'in the course of the last four years to make progress here politically as well as economically', despite the strongly dogmatic views of the Bolshevik leaders.[1] Germany's

[1] Rantzau to the Foreign Ministry, January 20, 1927, 2860/D558323–6.

general and eastern interests would also continue to depend in large measure on Soviet support.

Concerning general policy, he reminded Stresemann early in January 'that we cannot dispense with the support (*Rückhalt*) which we have sought and which in part we have found in the east or we would be exposed to an otherwise unavoidable political and economic oppression from the west'.[1] In March he wrote to Schubert that it would be catastrophic for 'German-Soviet relations and hence for our eastern policy . . .' if Germany were forced to side with England.[2] Rantzau made many similar statements during this period, and while they constitute a more categorical formulation of the need for close ties with Russia than those of his colleagues, the difference is only one of emphasis.[3]

In the first months of 1927 Wilhelmstrasse officials recognized the need to allay Soviet suspicions about a shift in German policy. Contributing to these suspicions was Berlin's treatment of the sensational *Manchester Guardian*-SPD revelations concerning military collaboration (December 1926); they disclosed details about that phase—already almost ended—involving the manufacture of munitions, poison gases, and military aircraft. By late February, when it was clear that a major change in French and British policy had not been provoked,[4] a course of action was chosen. Two government officials, Reichswehr Minister Gessler and Schubert, appeared before the Reichstag's Foreign Affairs Committee to admit only what had already been divulged. They explained, without giving details, that in 1923 the German government had been driven to take up the illicit contacts by the circumstances of the Ruhr crisis; in the meantime those ties had been unravelled and further agreements with Moscow that violated the Versailles treaty

[1] Rantzau to Stresemann, January 10, 1927, 2860/D558297–9.

[2] Rantzau to Schubert, March 6, 1927, 2860/D558454–65.

[3] Schubert's attitude was given to the Foreign Affairs Committee of the Reichstag on February 23, 1927: 'For the moment Germany will have to adopt a wait-and-see attitude and guard herself against being drawn into the conflict between Russia and the western powers. One should try not to lose contact with both sides and in particular attempt further to build economic bridges to Russia so that the connection with Russia will later be there' (Sächsisches Landeshauptarchiv Dresden, Embassy Berlin, Committee for Foreign Affairs, 1919–33, no. 367, cited in Alfred Anderle, *Die deutsche Rapallo-Politik*, 202–3).

[4] Noted by Dirksen as early as December 24, 1926, 4564/E163465 ff.

did not exist.[1] Not a word was said about the training and testing bases in the Soviet Union.

German leaders could no more avoid making these admissions than Soviet officials could help taking umbrage at them. The Soviet Chargé in Berlin protested to Schubert that the German government, by first admitting to the clandestine dealings and then reporting their termination, was creating the impression that the direction of its foreign policy was being altered.[2] The ill-feeling thus engendered seemed, however, to be only temporary. The established lines of military collaboration remained secure even though the December disclosures had prompted Schubert to question whether the anticipated military gains from the bases at Lipetsk and Kazan would be great enough to offset the 'political risks' involved in maintaining them.[3]

Early in February Stresemann gave General Heye his formal consent to a continuation of the training and testing stations on the condition that active Reichswehr members would not use them in 1927.[4] The Soviet government, for its part, showed an equally lively interest in keeping the military bonds intact. Both Lunev, the Soviet military attaché in Berlin, and Berzin, Unshlikht's deputy in Moscow, stated that their government attached the 'greatest importance' to the work at the bases, the seconding of Soviet officers to German staff courses, and the exchange of information at maneuvers.[5]

[1] Memorandum by Lütgens (?) regarding: conference of Marx, Gessler, Schubert, Heye, and others with Reichstag party leaders and session of Foreign Affairs Committee, undated, probably February 23, 1927, L617/L194852–5; Schubert to Rantzau, February 23, 1927, 4564/E163516–20.

[2] Memorandum by Schubert regarding conversation with Bratman-Brodovskii, February 18, 1927, 4562/E163487–9.

[3] Memorandum, probably by Dirksen, 4564/E163480 ff., cited in Gatzke, op. cit., 586–7.

[4] Memorandum by Dirksen regarding conversations with Major Fischer: February 9, 1927, 4564/E163486; February 19, 1927, 4564/E163494–5. Stresemann's agreement with Heye was approved at a cabinet meeting on February 26 and confirmed by a conference of leading Reichswehr and Wilhelmstrasse officials on May 18 (copy of agreement, February 26, 1927, 2860/D558404; memorandum by Köpke, May 18, 1927, 6698/H111738–41).

[5] Memorandum by Dirksen: Fischer reports talk with Lunev, February 19, 1927, 4564/E163494–5; Lieth-Thomsen reports talk with Berzin, March 3, 1927, 4564/E163861–2.

But as a condition to further collaboration Soviet officials demanded formal changes in the organization of the operations; these were to minimize the chances of further disclosures or at least ensure that such developments would not again have the effect of a bombshell. They asked that the bases be 'legalized', organized as concessions, or state-supported limited-liability companies. This was to be accomplished through diplomatic channels.[1] In addition they requested that the Foreign Ministry associate itself with the proposed tank base at Kazan by formally declaring that it agreed to its establishment.[2] These Soviet requests were probably all directed to one goal, the formal involvement of the German government (not only the Reichswehrministerium) in the clandestine relations. Under such altered circumstances, they may have reasoned, Wilhelmstrasse officials would in future be unable to dissociate themselves from the military contacts as Moscow suspected they had tried after the December revelations. As a means of winning German assent to these requests the Red Army held back on cooperation for some weeks in March;[3] agreement was finally reached although developments in the Anglo-Soviet crisis caused the Foreign Ministry to postpone the requested official statement acquiescing in the setting-up of the tank station.

While military dealings were thus formally being put on a new basis, Schubert's ill-starred *Excelsior* interview further burdened relations. Moreover, in the area of commercial contacts the reluctance of German financiers (early in 1927) to expand the trade credit of the previous spring was likewise interpreted by Moscow as a sign of waverings in German foreign policy.[4] Finally Soviet leaders were especially concerned over indications that some political parties and interest groups which had previously supported Berlin's eastern policy were reconsidering their commitments.

There was considerable substance to these latter suspicions. It seemed that in Germany new battle lines were forming against

[1] Memorandum by Dirksen regarding conversations with: Lieth-Thomsen, March 4, 1927, 4564/E163861–2; Major Fischer, March 10, 1927, 4564/E163867–8.

[2] Conference of Stresemann, Gessler, Heye, Blomberg, Schubert, Köpke, May 18, 1927, 4564/E163880–4.

[3] Fischer to Seeckt, March 12, 1927, cited in Carsten, *Reichswehr und Politik*, 302.

[4] Memorandum by Dirksen concerning conversation with Krestinskii, March 24, 1927, 4562/E380385–92.

close relations with the USSR, a development unsettling to both the Eastern Department and the Narkomindel. The situation involved the loss of interest in ties with Moscow of German commercial circles and elements in the Center Party. Contrary to earlier expectations, the Berlin treaty, supported by generous industrial credits, had failed to open the Soviet market to a large volume of German goods; by early 1927 German commercial circles were freely venting their frustrations. Trade had not boomed and they were bitter. The Wilhelmstrasse believed that Soviet officials had transferred orders from Germany to Britain, a tactic designed to break up the anti-Soviet front of British interests. In May the Moscow Embassy reported knowledge of a secret directive ordering Soviet purchasing agencies 'henceforth to transfer the center of gravity for orders for producer goods, etc., more from Germany to other countries'.[1]

A shift in Russia's trade policy or an improvement in the absorptive capacity of her market could conceivably reverse the tide of industrial opinion that had earlier stood firmly behind the Berlin treaty. But waverings in the foreign policy outlook of the Center was a more critical matter because the coalition government of that day contained a number of Center Party members: Chancellor Marx and three out of eleven cabinet members. Josef Wirth, another of its leaders, had earlier maintained the party as a staunch supporter of the Rapallo policy; in the first months of 1927 a change in its orientation was noted. In a memorandum with the title 'The Altered Attitude of the Center Party in Questions Relating to German Eastern Policy', Dirksen reported that the Center was veering from its former course and might soon demand a 'departure from Soviet Russia and a policy of open reconciliation with Poland . . .'.[2] A member of the British Commons, he noted, had recently asked the Chancellor and members of his party about their attitude in the event of a worsening of Anglo-Russian relations.[3] Moreover, a conference of leading Center members had voiced concern that 'Germany would miss the opportunity to join

[1] Memorandum by Hey: 'Gegen Deutschland gerichtete Geheimdirektiven über Erteilung von Auslandsaufträgen. Englische Kreditangebote', May 19, 1927, Embassy Moscow: Department D, Special Folder (not filmed).

[2] Memorandum by Dirksen, March 21, 1927, 6698/H114427–9.

[3] Memorandum by Dirksen, February 12, 1927, 5265/E319167.

the western powers' through her adherence to the Rapallo policy. Wirth's supporters were alleged to have suffered a defeat. Totally new in the situation was the readiness of one wing of the party to seek an understanding with Poland – a trend ascribed to Vatican influence[1] – that was being more frequently expressed in the columns of the Center organ, *Germania*.[2] Dirksen recommended that this trend be countered by means of an approach by Stresemann or Schubert to the leaders of the Center. German interests, Dirksen concluded, required a halt to the 'undesirable splitting of the formerly united political parties in questions relating to Germany's eastern policy . . .'.[3] The Foreign Ministry files do not further document the fate of Dirksen's suggestion, an indication in itself that the Center's reserve towards the USSR was kept from assuming the form of an explicit demand for an orientation to the west. These were, however, straws in the wind warning the Wilhelmstrasse that a further exacerbation of the tensions between London and Moscow would inflate demands in Germany for a western option.

3. RISKS AND REWARDS

COULD Germany, bound both to London and Moscow by treaty ties, obviate the need for a choice between them by mediating the Anglo-Soviet dispute? On this question turned a deadly serious debate in the Foreign Ministry during the first months of 1927. Almost every important person in the Wilhelmstrasse took part in

[1] Memorandum by Dirksen, March 21, 1927, 6698/H114427–9.

[2] Commenting on the Anglo-Soviet dispute, *Germania* of March 28, 1927, warned against a continuation of a see-saw policy between east and west: 'We have realized that our ascent can only be accomplished by way of honest reconciliation with our erstwhile enemies. Since Locarno our place is on the side of the western powers. . . . Let us guard ourselves against the childish impression that we could exert pressure on England or France by flirting occasionally with Moscow. Such pseudo-machiavellian tactics would merely have the effect of heightening the present mistrust of us in Paris and London without bringing us any advantages in Moscow.' It was suggested that relations with Russia should be restricted to intensive trade relations. Concerning Poland it said: 'An effective European eastern policy can only be achieved when a good neighborly relationship exists between Poland and Germany. The more intimate it can be made, the better. If Europe is to recover, Poland and Germany belong together, not in opposition.'

[3] Memorandum by Dirksen, March 21, 1927, 6698/H114427–9.

it: Stresemann, Schubert, Rantzau, Schlesinger, Wallroth, his chief deputies in the Eastern Department, Dirksen and Trautmann, and others. Hindsight tempts us to dismiss their entire discussion as a futile exercise in contingency planning for the improbable occurence of an Anglo-Soviet war. But that would mean passing blindly over one fundamental element to an understanding of the politics of this period – the charged atmosphere in which decisions were being made.

For the Wilhelmstrasse the question of the outcome of the Anglo-Soviet wrangle was still open. The response to a break of Italy, France, Poland or the other border states was not certain. And the Soviet view that the situation was fraught with the danger of war was crucial: at the moment of crisis the Soviet reading of British intentions could determine the course of the dispute. German interests and political responsibility therefore dictated the need for a prognosis of the dispute and a judgement of Germany's freedom to modify its course.

As early as August 1926, Rantzau had urged Stresemann to study the possible consequences for Germany of a rupture between London and Moscow, and to discuss the matter with Chicherin.[1] The Foreign Minister, however, had let slip the opportunity to raise the question when Chicherin had visited Berlin in December,[2] and in early 1927 it was still not the subject of systematic study. The Foreign Ministry was generally uncomfortable about the drift in Soviet policy but had few suggestions on how to stop it.

This was the picture on January 12, 1927, when Schlesinger distributed to Schubert, Rantzau, Wallroth, and Dirksen a report entitled 'The Present Condition of the Soviet Union as it Relates to Germany's Foreign Policy'. It concluded with this controversial recommendation: 'Germany's important and dangerous task [in the Anglo-Soviet dispute] consists in being able to bring about a speedy compromise through her pressure'.[3] Thus the stage was

[1] Rantzau to Schubert, March 6, 1927, 2860/D558454–65.

[2] Memoranda by Stresemann concerning conversations with Chicherin, December 2, 3, 1926, 2860/D558166–201.

[3] Memorandum by Schlesinger entitled: 'Die gegenwärtige Lage der Sowjetunion in ihrer Bedeutung für die deutsche Aussenpolitik', January 12, 1927, 6698/H105686–700. In an accompanying letter to Schubert, Schlesinger described it as a report 'which I have submitted to the ambassador as the conclusion of an exhaustive analysis of the present

set for a protracted debate that was still inconclusive at the time of the Anglo-Soviet break.

Schlesinger's report was a tacit admission that his earlier plan to restrain Soviet policy through an astute credit policy was impracticable. It was now necessary to explore other ways of arresting Russia's drift into isolation. This task was all the more urgent, he thought, because the Soviet economic crisis was of such a character that it would not prompt Moscow to seek a *modus vivendi* with London, as some observers had predicted it might. It was inconceivable, he wrote, that the CPSU would circumscribe its revolutionary goals in China in order to ease a domestic problem—mainly involving the interests of Russia's large but docile peasantry—that did not threaten its rule.[1] A further circumstance making likely an intransigent policy was the competition for Lenin's mantle among members of the Politburo, which forbade them advocating policies that could stigmatize them as 'liquidators of the Revolution'.

Schlesinger was hardly less pessimistic about *Germany's* capacity to take the sting out of Soviet pertinacity. Since Locarno, he wrote, her efforts to 'draw along the Soviet government into an evolutionary course' had all been shattered. Germany had unsuccessfully sought to 'erect a bridge for the Soviet Union to the international economy and thence to international policy'. The deepening of political relations by means of another bilateral treaty or a multilateral grouping including third powers was also barred by Moscow's radical objectives.

The prognosis was therefore melancholy. Schlesinger predicted that the Soviet Union's achievements in China and in the British coal miner's strike would provoke London to organize economic or military sanctions against her. Proposals in this direction, he observed, would probably gain a wide measure of European support. And Germany, confronted with pressures from abroad, the disenchantment of her commercial circles with the USSR, and widespread domestic anti-Communist sentiment, would have a hard time remaining neutral. The imperative for Germany was to

---

general situation of the Soviet Union' (Schlesinger to Schubert, January 15, 1927, 4562/E158142–4).

[1] Schlesinger felt that economically only a general crop failure coupled with structural irrationalities in the Soviet economy might topple the regime (Schlesinger, ibid.).

keep this 'approaching struggle from being carried out because it is improbable that we would not ourselves become involved'.[1]

He suggested that German mediation take the form of approaches to both Russia and Britain, so as to maintain the balance between Locarno and Berlin. A threat of a shift in Germany's orientation was to dissuade Moscow from sharpening the dispute. The German government

> would in the long run not be able to resist domestic pressures against the Soviet Union which could be expected. The reasons for this were that German economic circles were disenchanted with the Soviet market, and there was opposition to the spread of the Communist system. Finally, Germany's general European situation had to be considered.[2]

In London, on the other hand, Berlin's appeal would stress the hazards of an anti-Communist crusade: Europe's brittle social fabric would prevent the mobilization of public opinion against the USSR, and a break might result in a social upheaval, a 'colossal explosion of revolutionary energies'.[3]

This report was well-timed, reaching Berlin at a moment when Anglo-Soviet relations were reaching their nadir. By initiating a series of consultations it helped to fill a policy vacuum.[4] The result was a consensus in the Wilhelmstrasse to take the initiative in the 'approaching Anglo-Russian conflict'.[5] On February 19, 1927,[6] three days before it was given greater urgency by Chamberlain's threat to sever ties with Moscow, Schubert sent Rantzau a proposal for his evaluation.

Schubert's summing-up of how Germany might 'minimize the threatening dangers or at least improve [her] political position for the various eventualities' may be given in terms of a series of propositions. Germany, he felt, would have great difficulty in remaining neutral if the Anglo-Soviet crisis should lead to a conflict, even of an economic nature. The impasse had been caused by Soviet policy in southern China and in the British coal miners' strike and could scarcely be termed an achievement of Moscow.

Moreover, a further sharpening of the dispute would lead

[1] Schlesinger to Schubert, January 15, 1927, 4562/E158142-4.

[2] Ibid. [3] Ibid.

[4] Dirksen to Schlesinger, January 20, 1927, 4829/E242481–6; Dirksen to Rantzau, February 10, 1927, 6698/H111696–702.

[5] Dirksen to Schlesinger, January 20, 1927, 4829/E242481–6.

[6] Schubert to Rantzau, February 19, 1927, 2860/D558379–86.

Britain to use her many political levers to meet the Soviet threat, and Russia would suffer defeat in the ensuing conflict. Finally, he noted, if revolutionary euphoria had come to inform Soviet policy, as some believed, Germany was tied to a 'state that does not wish to follow a policy based upon national interests, but rather one of world revolution. And for this reason it is not in a position to coordinate its policy with ours on a scale commensurate to our relationship.'

But contrary to Schlesinger's recommendation that Germany offer to mediate in the dispute, Schubert suggested a *démarche* which would encourage Moscow to consult with Berlin on all aspects of Anglo-Soviet relations. If the Soviets were to be further assured that Germany would 'live up to the terms of the Berlin treaty even if it should come to the worst', they might entertain a query as to the possibility of a *modus vivendi* with Britain. Although the picture was not totally bleak, Schubert harbored no illusions about the chances of a German initiative meeting with success. Yet the attendant risk of alienating Moscow had to be taken for tactical reasons. If Germany were forced to side with Britain the fact that attempts had earlier been made to temper Soviet policy would enhance the Wilhelmstrasse's position both with domestic opinion and the British government.[1] The Wilhelmstrasse, in short, was thinking of all eventualities, including a change in political fronts.[2]

But while Schlesinger's analysis and some of his recommendations received unusually wide support in Berlin, Rantzau vigorously dissented. In a lively exchange with the State Secretary that marked a resumption of the Locarno debate, he questioned Berlin's appraisal of the dispute and showed himself unalterably opposed to the suggested measures for alleviating it. Instead of rendering Soviet attitudes more conciliatory, Rantzau's opinions, which he conveyed to Litvinov, were stiffening them.[3]

The Ambassador made his objections explicit in a lengthy telegram to Stresemann and Schubert on March 6; the telegram[4]

[1] Ibid.

[2] After Chamberlain's provocative speech of February 22, Dirksen urged that a German *démarche* be postponed in order to escape the Soviet charge that 'we were acting in secret agreement with the English' (Dirksen to Schlesinger, February 25, 1927, 4829/E242522–4).

[3] Rantzau to Schubert, February 26, 1927, 2860/D558401–3.

[4] Rantzau to Schubert with a request that it be transmitted to Stresemann, March 6, 1927, 2860/D558454–65.

rebutted point by point Berlin's interpretation of Soviet policy as given in Schubert's letter. Rantzau denied that Germany would have to opt for the west in the event of an Anglo-Soviet rupture—the Berlin treaty had freed her of the fatal compulsion to do so. Nor was Russia solely to blame for driving matters to a head. Schubert's claim that the forward policy of the Soviets in the Far East had weakened their position was also countered: 'He who weakens his enemy, gains indirectly in strength himself.' As for Soviet purposes, ultimately the salient question, he rejected the view that the USSR had veered towards a strategy of revolution that barred state-to-state relations on a *realpolitisch* basis: 'She wishes calm and peace in order to prepare herself sufficiently for the decisive blow.'

This dissenting view on fundamental questions prompted Rantzau to warn that a German *démarche* would appear as pro-British to Moscow and constitute a death blow to German-Soviet cooperation. It would vitiate Germany's *Ostpolitik* and leave her to the mercies of the western powers. What purpose, he asked rhetorically, would there be in 'losing the east without winning the west?' As a surer method of diffusing the crisis he urged that Moscow be reassured of Germany's fidelity and London warned that Germany would under all circumstances stand by her obligations in the Berlin treaty.[1]

Rantzau's dissent put Berlin in a quandary. It was feared that his refusal to intervene in Moscow would frustrate Germany's strategy of making complementary representations to the two disputants; it would evoke a British charge that Berlin was siding with Moscow. This was a likely development because since mid-February 1927 one phase of the policy was indeed being implemented. In the months before the rupture, Anglo-Soviet relations were treated in conversations between London and Berlin on four occasions, once by Stresemann and Chamberlain at Geneva and three times by Schubert and Lindsay, the British Ambassador in Berlin.

These conversations persuaded the Wilhelmstrasse that the theme of its peacemaking efforts—the Soviets would lose interest in revolution if their isolation were ended through involvement

[1] Rantzau to Schubert, March 6, 1927, 2860/D558454-65 cf. memorandum by Dirksen, March 10, 1927.

with the west[1]—was restraining British policy. Chamberlain, for instance, confessed to Stresemann at the League of Nations that Germany's representations had strengthened his hand against powerful anti-Soviet opinion in the British cabinet.[2] (Stresemann had reiterated that Bolshevism could be overcome by bringing 'Russia into connection with western policy and thereby favor an evolution . . .') Heartened by these small gains the Wilhelmstrasse considered whether Rantzau should not be overruled and a similar intervention made in Moscow. Yet first some of the arguments raised by Rantzau needed elucidation. Was the mainspring of Soviet action revolution or *Realpolitik*? Would a *démarche* in Moscow compromise Germany's trade and external policies? And if the chances were slim for a successful intervention what other considerations might nevertheless argue for one? Against a background of further incidents between London and Moscow these questions were the subject of hurried consultations in the Wilhelmstrasse between Schubert, Wallroth, Dirksen, and Trautmann.

Again the result was a consensus in favor of German intervention that was supported for a variety of reasons. Wallroth, an extreme Westerner, ironically at the head of the Eastern Department, argued that for Germany the risks of making a *démarche* were minimal. German diplomacy, he wrote, should not mute her voice for fear of Russia turning against her in anger: the substance of German-Soviet cooperation had already been squandered through Soviet recklessness. Economically Germany's gains had been nil; her goals of economic recovery and rewriting of the Versailles treaty depended on British support—support that would evaporate if the Anglo-Soviet dispute persisted and Germany remained neutral. And her policy of border revision had been made illusory by a crisis spawned in Moscow that had drawn Britain and Russia to court Poland.[3]

[1] Memoranda by Schubert regarding conversations with Lindsay: February 15, 1927, 4562/E158202–3; February 22, 1927, 4562/E158220–221.

[2] Memorandum by Stresemann, March 3, 1927, 2860/D558446–53; Stresemann to the Foreign Ministry, March 8, 1927, 2860/D558481–4. In his alleged efforts to win Germany for a massive conspiracy against the Soviet Union, Chamberlain did not go beyond expressing a mild regret that German industrial credits to the Soviet Union had probably freed considerable Soviet funds for propaganda against Britain.

[3] Wallroth to Rantzau, March 4, 1927, 5265/E317688–95; Memorandum by Wallroth: 'Betrifft: Bemerkungen von Herrn von Dirksen vom

A more typical view in the Foreign Ministry was that held by Trautmann, the able Deputy Director and later Director of the Eastern Department. In a report that blended caution with firmness, he weighed the risks and advantages of German intervention. The Soviet Union, he warned, construing a note from Germany as heralding a shift in her position, might liquidate her dispute with London while blaming Germany for her defeat, or seek an alignment with France and Poland. In either event Germany would have 'lost forever the use of Russia as a counterpoise to the west'.

Nevertheless, he urged action. The perils inherent in a German initiative, he felt, could be minimized by making the case for Soviet concessions to Britain in terms of purely Soviet interests. At the same time Trautmann made the point that German diplomats should not suggest that they were disappointed with the 'results of our treaty relationship with Russia'.[1] Emboldened by Trautmann's and Wallroth's interventionist counsel, Dirksen urged mediatory action that would demand of the Narkomindel concessions that would enable Germany to 'carry through a successful action with the English'.[2]

A draft dispatch to the German Embassy in Moscow suggests that Stresemann, fortified by these and similar opinions in the Foreign Ministry, drew back on the verge of ordering an initiative.[3] Probably he recognized that retribution might be the only reward of a successful mediation – Bismarck's experience after the Berlin Congress; failure, on the other hand, might undercut Germany's status in Britain and Russia. Stresemann may also have been influenced by a sudden change in Schlesinger's counsel, largely prompted by considerations of timing: 'In view of the fact that they were now progressing very well in China, the extraordinarily suspicious Russians would say that we were taking this initiative on English instigation and that we had probably been

10 d.M. zur Antwort des Herrn Botschafters Graf Brockdorff-Rantzau', March 14, 1927, 6698/H103778–83.

[1] Memorandum by Trautmann entitled: 'Russland und England', March 14, 1927, 6698/H105784–98.

[2] Memorandum by Dirksen: 'Bemerkungen zur Antwort des Herrn Botschafters Grafen Brockdorff-Rantzau auf die Anfrage des A. A., betreffend den englisch-russischen Konflikt', March 10, 1927, 5265/E319128–38.

[3] Draft dispatch, Stresemann to Rantzau, 'Ganz geheim! Ausschliesslich für Botschafter persönlich!', March 31, 1927, 6698/H105802–7.

promised some type of reward by the English.'[1] Yet the main grounds for Stresemann's hesitancy were surely Rantzau's opposition. If the highly sensitive Ambassador were overruled on so fundamental a question he might resign, as he had twice threatened to during the Locarno negotiations. Since his presence in Moscow was regarded as the seal of Germany's fidelity to Russia his sudden departure would have led to the opposite conclusion, precisely the result that Rantzau feared from a German offer of mediation. All in all the risks seemed too great and German policy vacillated. The debate in the Wilhelmstrasse continued. In the midst of such equivocation London on May 27 peremptorily cut its relations with Moscow.

4. WAVERING NEUTRALITY

STRANGE as it may seem, Britain's sudden action came as a shock to the USSR, upsetting her relative composure about Anglo-Soviet relations. That mood had recently been enhanced by the downturn in Soviet fortunes in China, a sharp reversal that in Moscow's view should have eliminated the grounds for an unyielding British stand. And, in general, the Soviets had been inclined to consider a showdown with Britain as only a future possibility. They were unable to conceive of their opponent's purposes as less than Russia's destruction and had therefore reasoned that England would not bring matters to a head until she had won the collaboration of Finland, Poland, and Rumania, the acquiescence of France, and the connivance of Germany.

Above all Germany's will and capacity to assert her neutrality was deemed central to the issue of whether Britain would break relations. Thus Germany's efforts in the first months of 1927 to demonstrate the stability of her policy had served to heighten Moscow's sense of equanimity. But now, for the same reason, there was a tendency to suspect that Britain's action had been triggered by a prior agreement with the Wilhelmstrasse.

Not surprisingly Moscow's first response was to focus on Berlin, and what it observed was initially reassuring. Stresemann immediately declared Germany neutral and after some hesitation acceded

[1] Memorandum by Schubert regarding conversation with Schlesinger, April 2, 1927, 4562/E158648–9.

to a Soviet request that Germany represent her interests in England.[1] Equally heartening for Moscow, a domestic consensus in support of official policy emerged in Germany. The German press, including the Center organ *Germania*, held that the meagre findings of the raid on the Arcos offices were too slender a peg for the British to hang such a weighty political departure. Indeed any action was unnecessary because of the fiasco of Moscow's policy in the Far East.[2]

In the spate of articles supporting neutrality, only one jarring note appeared, first parenthetically in the *Kölnische Zeitung*,[3] and then in the semi-official *Deutsche diplomatisch-politische Korrespondenz*. It was that Germany must likewise take measures to protect herself from infection spread by Soviet propaganda agencies like the Comintern. The Narkomindel attached symptomatic value to this warning, particularly since it appeared in the semi-official voice of the Foreign Ministry soon after the break.[4]

This was the one ripple on the surface of German-Soviet relations that otherwise remained placid in the three weeks after May 27. During this time the Soviets maneuvered astutely to frustrate alleged British efforts to forge a ring about them. Again they hoped that Germany would serve a critical role in the crisis. She would, as before, be the missing link in the chain of capitalistic states, and, in addition, a timely demonstration of the 'intimacy' of the German connection might inhibit other countries from following the British lead. Since the center of danger was thought to be Geneva, where Chamberlain was expected to continue his intrigues in the League Council, Chicherin hurried off to Germany, in order, as Stresemann irritably said, 'to pose as a special adviser to the German politicians travelling to Geneva'.[5]

On June 8, the day of the assassination of Soviet Minister Voikov in Poland, Chicherin conferred with the German Foreign Minister

[1] Stresemann to various German missions, May 27, 1927, 2860/D558728–9.

[2] *Berliner Tageblatt*, May 25, 1927; *Kölnische Zeitung*, May 25, 1927; *Vorwärts*, May 25, 1927; *Germania*, May 25, 1927.

[3] *Kölnische Zeitung*, May 25, 1927.

[4] 'Sowjet-Propaganda', *Deutsche diplomatisch-politische Korrespondenz*, June 2, 1927.

[5] Excerpt from the minutes of a cabinet meeting, May 30, 1927, L617/L194974–9.

at Baden-Baden.[1] The talk indicated that Russia's chief concern at the time was less the possibility that Britain was readying for action than that British nationalists would goad Poland into an anti-Soviet adventure that France would support, so as not to risk losing her allies in eastern Europe. Chicherin asked if Germany would be able to resist western demands for troop transit rights across her territory in the event of such a crisis. Stresemann repeated that the concessions given Germany at Locarno were still valid and promised to give the Narkomindel a full record of them.[2] Chicherin was gratified at the outcome of his visit, and on his departure seemed confident that the German wing of his policy would bear the weight of the Anglo-Soviet crisis.

Soviet diplomacy remained optimistic about its international situation beyond the feared League Council session in mid-June; this was about three weeks after the rupture and ten days after Voikov's assassination, an event usually cited as the trigger to the 'war scare' of the summer. Such confidence was reflected for the last time in an *Izvestiia* leader of June 18, which lauded Germany for her deportment at Geneva in frustrating efforts to create an alliance against Russia. Anxious to rebut arguments that a policy of neutrality would damage Germany's national interest, it maintained that 'through her resistance, which undoubtedly rests on a complete understanding of her own interests, Germany has strengthened her political prestige in the international sphere'.[3] It was to be some time before the Soviet regime would again assess the international situation so hopefully or speak so confidently of German policy. It seems that reports of what had transpired at Geneva were slow in trickling into Moscow, but when they did, as will be shown, they revived Soviet fears that London might be closing a deal with Berlin.

While the Russians fixed their gaze on Berlin, the Germans

[1] Wallroth to Moscow Embassy, June 14, 1927, 2860/D558857–9; from the minutes of a cabinet meeting, June 9, 1927, L617/L195003–4.

[2] Ibid.; cf. memorandum by Wallroth concerning conversations with Chicherin and Rantzau, June 14, 1927, 5265/E319015–16.

[3] *Izvestiia,* June 18, 1927. German reluctance to accede to English blandishments at Geneva was attributed to German interest in the Soviet market: 'The question of a financial blockade of the Soviet Union played a leading role at Geneva. Exactly on this point the greatest pressure was exerted upon Germany . . . . We are convinced that those economic circles which are resisting English pressure understand the meaning of Chamberlain's blackmail.'

looked to London, wondering whether the dispute could long be localized. Were the British following limited goals that would not go beyond the formal act of diplomatic rupture, or would they try to limit Germany's neutrality? Indeed, might they offer Germany tantalizing concessions in questions of the Rhineland, reparations, or the German-Polish border in exchange for her adhesion to an anti-Soviet front? Or, if the dispute petered out in a stalemate, would Britain seek retribution against Germany for her neutrality, or might both antagonists weary of their conflict and seek to resolve it at Germany's expense? These were the kinds of questions about potential risks and rewards that coursed through Wilhelmstrasse channels after May 27. Germany was weak, perhaps expendable both to Russia and Britain, and hence had to tread cautiously.

What contributed to Germany's difficulty in evolving a viable policy was the seeming confusion of Britain's goals. Conversations with British statesmen were punctuated with signposts indicating London's intentions, but they did not seem to point in any clear direction. British diplomacy, for instance, characterized the rupture as an 'isolated act' that was unrelated to its other international ties. Yet three weeks after the break, the British king twice ventured the hope to the German Ambassador that the Soviet regime would disintegrate if France and Germany were to follow Britain's example.[1]

On a more responsible level a British Foreign Office official shortly after the break combined the theme of 'isolated act' with a most unsettling question: 'Why Germany was perpetually looking east, when the west was consolidating for peace and endeavouring to combine for an effort to secure the traditional civilization of Europe?' Germany, he added, must not let public opinion in England 'crystallize in a sense unfavourable to her. The Locarno policy still held the field. But it was not a finite act that was just done and left to itself.' The Wilhelmstrasse must 'do nothing to impede its growth'. Yet so long as the British were reluctant to spell out the meaning of the latter phrase no one in Berlin wanted clarification. Because such sentiments were balanced by assurances that London would not preach a 'crusade against the Soviet Union',[2] Stresemann thought he might succeed in carry-

[1] Sthamer to the Foreign Ministry, June 16, 1927, 6698/H105930–1; 2860/D558892–3.

[2] Memorandum by Gregory, of the British Foreign Office, concerning

ing on Germany's diplomatic business both in London and Moscow.

To the German cabinet the Foreign Minister expressed a sense of relief that England had not attempted to build up a moral or financial front against the USSR. He remarked that the European response to the imbroglio suggested that England had suffered more as a result than Russia. The outbreak of war he termed as unlikely even though the Conservative right wing would try to push Chamberlain to such a step. In this connection he reported that British agents had 'transferred their field of activity primarily to Germany'; English rightist elements might try to create 'domestic difficulties for the Soviet government' by supporting separatist groups in the Ukraine and in Georgia.[1]

As for Germany's neutrality Stresemann defended it to the cabinet in purely *realpolitisch* terms. A choice between *east* and *west*, he contended, was neither wise nor possible; the USSR was too feeble to play the role of an ally, and an alignment with Britain was impossible because of her inability to offer Germany concrete advantages:

> At most it would be a case of vague promises concerning territories which England did not control. In particular this would apply to the areas of Poland, Danzig and the Corridor, in which Germany was interested. It must also be said that until now not a single time has there been so much as a vague reference to compensations by any official British party.[2]

Thus a week after the severance of Anglo-Soviet relations Stresemann's evaluation of the political situation was reasonably hopeful. England, he felt, was isolated, and his conversation with Chicherin on June 8 suggested that Russia was avoiding any step that might render more difficult a resumption of diplomatic relations. There was, however, some ambivalence in the situation indicating a quiet before rather than after the storm.[3] Reports were

---

a conversation with Dieckhoff, Counsellor of the German Embassy, May 25, 1927, 4562/E158835–9.

[1] Extract from the minutes of a cabinet meeting, May 30, 1927, L617/L194974–9.

[2] Extract from the minutes of a cabinet meeting, May 30, 1927, L617/L194974–9.

[3] In a memorandum dated June 3, 1927, Dirksen warned that 'this

received from Rome,[1] and confirmed in London,[2] that Italy was planning an incident which would serve as a pretext for following Britain; and there was good reason to believe that frustration about the failure of British policy was as likely to strengthen the hand of those in Britain favoring an even stiffer one as it was to make that policy more amenable. Germany's capacity to influence events was limited, as before, to diplomatic means; these, it was decided, should to be used to dissuade Britain from boycotting Moscow and to encourage her to resume formal relations.

For this purpose Schubert received the British Ambassador on June 10, ostensibly in order to inform him of the conversations with Chicherin. At the outset he indicated that Germany would not be enticed into an anti-Soviet bloc – Chicherin, he confided, had been given assurances on the troop-transit question. He then requested a candid statement of England's plans. When Lindsay confirmed that a second step was not contemplated, Schubert asked about the possibilities of a rapprochement with Russia 'and how such a development might be envisaged'. Lindsay was taken aback by this unpolitic gesture and mumbled words about the need in politics to keep open a path for retreat.[3]

Since May 27 the British government had been on the defensive regarding its Soviet policy and eager to emerge from isolation, as the talks at Geneva in June were to show. Stresemann, on the other hand, went to Geneva to win support for his thesis that overt means were powerless to check Communist activity – the USSR should be guided along an evolutionary path by opening alternatives to her.[4] At a meeting of the League Six on June 14 Chamberlain initially found little support for his policy, even when it was characterized as an 'isolated act'.[5] Both Vandervelde of Belgium and Briand of France supported Stresemann's plea that

---

localization of the conflict cannot long be maintained' (Memorandum by Dirksen entitled: 'Die durch Abbruch der englisch-russischen Beziehungen geschaffene Lage', June 3, 1927, 6698/H106612–18).

[1] Neurath to the Foreign Ministry, June 11, 1927, 5265/E319014.

[2] Dieckhoff to the Foreign Ministry, June 13, 1927, 5265/E319013.

[3] Memorandum by Schubert, June 10, 1927, 4562/E158894–6.

[4] Position paper for the occasion submitted to Stresemann by Dirksen: 'Leitsätze über die deutsche Stellungnahme zum englisch-russischen Abbruch', June 12, 1927, 2860/D558849–51.

[5] Memorandum by Stresemann, June 15, 1927, 2860/D558876–82.

the maintenance of diplomatic relations with USSR was a first condition of her transformation into a state that one could 'get along' with. The session, it seemed, was vindicating Germany's neutrality.

Then, however, discussion turned to Russia's deteriorating relations with Poland, and Stresemann was maneuvered into an awkward position. As the statesmen met, word had just been received of Moscow's aggressive demands on Warsaw in the Voikov case, which to some were disturbingly reminiscent of those made on Belgrade in 1914.[1] Moreover, the rather good European press that Russia had been enjoying after the break began to turn against her in response to the execution without trial in Russia of twenty persons charged with treason.

Against this background Briand called for preventive action that might keep Moscow from giving Warsaw an ultimatum that could result in war. Here was a situation ready-made for Chamberlain to brighten Britain's Soviet policy and reduce her isolation, and he played it to the hilt. In the midst of a lengthy discussion he turned in Stresemann's direction. 'Join with me', he said grandiloquently, 'in an urgent appeal to Germany to use her relationship with Russia and in an appeal to Mr. Stresemann to use his relations with Chicherin in order that we may guard the world against the eventuality that the peace of Europe should be jeopardized because of this incident.'[2]

At this moment the German Foreign Minister was faced with the difficult situation that he had foreseen as early as 1925, namely that as a member of the League Germany might have to acquiesce in some of its unwelcome decisions rather than brave the odium of disturbing the unity of Geneva.[3] He agreed to carry out the wishes of the group.

[1] It characterized the assassination as one 'manifestation of the systematic and organized struggle against the USSR by dark forces of world reaction and the enemies of peace' (note from Litvinov to the Polish Minister in Moscow, June 11, 1927, cited in Degras, op. cit., II, 228–31). For a fuller discussion of the Voikov incident see Louis Fischer, *The Soviets in World Affairs, 1917–1929* (London: Jonathan Cape, 1930), II. A Soviet account is given in F. O. Volkov, *Anglo-Sovetskie otnosheniia*, 322–44.

[2] Memorandum by Stresemann concerning conversation with Krestinskii, April 25, 1925, 7129/H147795–801.

[3] Memorandum by Stresemann, June 15, 1927, 2860/D558876–82.

Stresemann, it should be noted, was nervous at the time about Russo-Polish relations; he was also deeply disturbed by the continuing executions in Moscow, which he termed the greatest moral defeat suffered by Russia since her foundation. This sudden upsurge of emotion, his deep personal animus towards the Soviet system,[1] and his undeniably awkward tactical position at Geneva, may explain why he accepted what was a Six-Power mandate without first consulting Schubert and Rantzau and with so little thought to the impression that would be aroused in Moscow. Beyond question, this undertaking was sharply at variance with Germany's neutrality. In circumstances where Moscow viewed international events paranoiacally, a warning in defense of Poland, given in the name of a concert of states including England, was a graver threat to the German-Soviet partnership than the previously suggested policy of mediation that had been rejected after interminable debate.

But if clear reasons are lacking for Stresemann's hazardous behavior, the Soviet response may be amply documented. Stresemann instructed the Wilhelmstrasse to warn the Soviets against sharpening their quarrel with Poland in the name of the League Six; he repeatedly used the expression, it is the unanimous opinion of the 'representatives of all the states gathered here', and the dispatch bristled with words such as 'war danger', ultimatum, 'world opinion', 'moral defeat'.[2] Nevertheless the collective authorship of the initiative was at first kept from them. Conveyed to Krestinskii by Köpke,[3] and to Chicherin by the German Chancellor on June 15, the warning was initially accepted by the Soviets as voicing the concern of a staunch political friend;[4] this trust in German policy appeared for the last time in the already mentioned *Izvestiia* editorial of June 18.

The situation changed abruptly, however, when Stresemann re-

[1] Stresemann's personal antipathy toward the Soviet system is discussed in: Hans W. Gatzke, 'Von Rapallo nach Berlin: Stresemann und die deutsche Russlandpolitik', *Vierteljahrshefte für Zeitgeschichte,* IV (1956), 13, 29.

[2] Stresemann to the Foreign Ministry, June 15, 1927, 5265/E319007–8.

[3] Köpke to Stresemann, June 15, 1927, 2860/D558885–7.

[4] Köpke to Stresemann, June 16, 1927, 2860/D558890. It was reported that the Chancellor's remarks to Chicherin, 'though friendly, were very earnest and obviously impressed him. He agreed to try to influence the government in Moscow in the desired sense.'

turned to Berlin and told Krestinskii about the source of the warning. This disclosure, the Ambassador exclaimed, showed that Germany had, 'so to say, acted on the instructions of the other participating powers'.[1] The situation was further inflamed on the following day by Stresemann's speech to the Reichstag, his first after the Anglo-Soviet rupture.[2] He denied that pressure had been used at Geneva to win Germany for an anti-Soviet coalition; this assertion Moscow interpreted as a cover-up. And with hardly a word about the importance of Rapallo and only brief mention of trade relations he labelled Communist propaganda as incompatible with the non-intervention principle of international relations. Here, as *Pravda* made clear,[3] it was not the substance of Stresemann's words but the context in which they were made that was baffling. Yet most disquieting for Moscow was his publicizing of Germany's initiative in the Voikov case, which he characterized as in 'conformity' with the tendencies of the Geneva conversations.[4]

While it is difficult to cite one factor as the key to the Soviet 'war scare' in the summer of 1927, it seems that more important than the Voikov case—usually cited in treatments of the subject—was the erosion of Soviet confidence in Germany following the disclosure to the Reichstag of Stresemann's acceptance of the Six-Power mandate. Germany had been regarded, both before and since the break with England, as the linch pin of Soviet security. If she faltered the worst might occur. Moscow was nervous. *Pravda*, for example, after berating Stresemann for his questionable deportment at Geneva and in the Reichstag commented: 'In view of the evident bankruptcy of Locarno and Thoiry and the complete impossibility of changing the present situation with England's help, a policy of enmity towards the Soviet Union would spell suicide for Germany.'[5]

Chicherin was even more explicit. Unsheathing his most telling argument he reminded Rantzau that the main goal of their common partnership, to force Poland back within her 'ethnographical boundaries', had been compromised by Stresemann's publicly

[1] Memorandum by Schubert, June 23, 1927, 4562/E158981.

[2] Quoted in full under the headline 'Stresemanns grosse Reichstagsrede', *Vossische Zeitung*, June 24, 1927.

[3] *Pravda*, June 26, 1927.

[4] *Vossische Zeitung*, June 24, 1927.

[5] *Pravda*, June 25, 1927.

taking Poland's side at a highly dangerous moment for the USSR. An anti-Polish policy, he added, had seemed to him 'an axiom for the direction of German-Russian relations'.[1] Implicit in his words was the threat that if Berlin continued to take 'sides against Russia . . . before the whole public forum', Russia might reconcile her differences with Poland. Somewhat later Chicherin revealed the full gravity of the situation when he informed Rantzau that since Geneva his politics had been 'grievously burdened within the cabinet'.[2] This statement was not designed merely to frighten Berlin, for the evidence suggests that Chicherin had staked his career on Germany's neutrality, and its apparent dilution was now accelerating his decline in the Narkomindel. And before the summer was out he was to show even greater signs of desperation.

Soviet leaders were doubly uneasy because the ambivalence that marked Stresemann's diplomacy seemed also to be affecting military collaboration with the Reichswehr. This became evident at the end of July during a visit to Berlin of Unshlikht, the Deputy Commissar of War, who again brought with him a startling proposal for an acceleration of military dealings. This urgent appeal was in one sense a follow-up to proposals for intensified joint arms production which he had made on a similar visit one year earlier, to which the Foreign Ministry had not replied. This initiative was equally barren of results. On leaving the German capital Unshlikht was downcast in the summary of his impressions to Rantzau. Although the Army Command had expressed a willingness to continue the existing lines of cooperation his new proposals had been turned down by General Heye on the grounds that the Reichswehr lacked the necessary funds. 'Militarily', he explained to Rantzau, 'we understand each other completely, but politically there exists a great difference in the interpretation of each side. General Heye had told him that he did not believe in an imminent danger of war for years to come. But the Soviet government is reckoning with a catastrophe in the near future.'[3] Indeed a Polish-Rumanian attack

[1] Private letter, Rantzau to Stresemann, concerning a series of conversations with Chicherin, August 27, 1927, 1841/H419295–300. The exact dates of the conversations with Chicherin are not given; Rantzau merely refers to a 'number', the earliest of which was on his return to Moscow.

[2] Ibid.

[3] Memorandum by Rantzau, July 24, 1927, L337/L100554–60.

on the USSR had to be considered a matter not of years but of months.[1]

During these critical summer months the German government not only rejected Soviet proposals for an increase in military collaboration but seemed to be having second thoughts about maintaining the existing level. At the time of Unshlikht's visit Gessler confided to Rantzau that the confused international situation dictated a policy of marking time with the Russians – the bases would be maintained but other lines of cooperation would not be considered.[2] At the same time Rantzau and Stresemann questioned the wisdom of allowing German officers to appear in uniform at Soviet maneuvers for the duration of the Anglo-Soviet crisis.[3] (This right had been granted them during the talk between Stresemann and Heye in February.) German indecision was demonstrated to Moscow officials more clearly by the Wilhelmstrasse's persistent failure to give the Narkomindel a formal statement – promised some months earlier – signifying its support for the establishment of the tank base at Kazan. Unshlikht complained bitterly about this during his visit to Berlin as did Soviet officials to the Reichswehr representative in Moscow.[4] German wariness in this matter, it was reported, was being interpreted in Moscow as a further step in 'Germany's withdrawal to the west'.[5] It was not until the Soviets showed themselves disinterested in the tank base that Stresemann finally in mid-August authorized Rantzau to make the long-promised statement.[6] But in the meantime the Foreign Ministry's circumspection had contributed to the war scare.

Fear of war mounted throughout the summer. In late June Rantzau reported information that the Red Army had assumed

[1] Memorandum by Schubert regarding talks with Rantzau and Heye, July 26, 1927, 4564/E163899–901.

[2] Memorandum by Rantzau, July 24, 1927, L337/L100554–60.

[3] Memorandum by Dirksen, June 4, 1927, 4564/E163891–2.

[4] Memorandum by Rantzau, L337/L100554–60.

[5] Memorandum by Dirksen regarding talk with Fischer and Lieth-Thomsen, July 28, 1927, 4564/E163902–3.

[6] Stresemann to Rantzau, August 12, 1927, 4564/E163916–17; Rantzau to Stresemann, August 15, 1927, 4564/E163920. Erickson has exaggerated the meaning and significance of the sudden show of Soviet disinterest through a failure to see the incident in its context (*The Soviet High Command*, 257–8, 281).

battle positions along the western frontier.[1] In early July the German Embassy sent further details indicating the concentration of troops at Gomel, the movement of men and equipment from the interior to the west, the construction of new military airfields, and the speeding-up of work in munitions plants.[2] The 'war scare' reached its crest in September, with a 'leading member' of the Narkomindel sketching an imminent situation in which Britain would blockade the USSR by sea and urge Poland on to a land-attack that would be joined by Rumania in the south and by Finland in the north.[3] Köpke wrote of a war psychosis flooding over Russia.[4] And when the erroneous information reached Chicherin that Germany was supporting Finland's candidature for a seat on the League Council, the Foreign Commissar dashed off a hand-written message to Rantzau; the message contained the cryptic threat that the 'consequences' for Germany of siding with Poland and then supporting Finland as the designated staging area for an attack against the USSR did not have to be pointed out.[5] Stresemann, informed of the Soviet accusations, wired his indignant rejection of them.[6] Chicherin, by now somewhat embarrassed, replied that his outburst had been 'an expression of sorrow over the evil consequences for the future of German-Soviet relations that could have developed'.[7] In Berlin the Soviet Chargé explained that Moscow had been 'extremely nervous'.[8] The incident was thus closed by a flurry of diplomatic exchanges, but it remained as a symptom of Chicherin's close identification with the policy of the Berlin treaty and of Moscow's growing conviction that close relations with Germany were becoming a fair weather phenomenon.

[1] Rantzau to Foreign Ministry, June 29, 1927, 9524/E671669–70.

[2] Dirksen to Behschnitt of Reichswehr Ministry, July 2, 1927, 9480/H276430–1.

[3] Rantzau to the Foreign Ministry, September 5, 1927, 2860/D558955–56.

[4] Memorandum by Köpke, September 8, 1927, 5265/E318948–52.

[5] Rantzau to Stresemann, September 12, 1927, 2860/D558977–8; cf. *Pravda*, August 23, 1927.

[6] Stresemann to Rantzau, September 14, 1927, 5265/E318932; 2860/D558980.

[7] Rantzau to Stresemann, September 15, 1927, 5265/E318920–3.

[8] Memorandum by Köpke, September 16, 1927, 5265/E318918–19.

5. *ALLEINBLEIBEN* TO *AUSSCHALTUNG*

IN August and September Russia's already critical international situation was worsened when French rightist circles agitated for the recall of Rakovskii, the Russian Ambassador; Moscow suspected that their purpose was to provoke a Franco-Soviet diplomatic break.[1] To forestall such a development the Soviets in mid-September offered France a non-aggression treaty, agreed to resume negotiations on the debt question, and revived the non-aggression pact discussions with Poland, which had been languishing since the previous autumn. It was a familiar tactic. Now, as during the Locarno talks and in the summer of 1926, the Soviets were again taking a cautious step in the direction of France and Poland in order to counter the menace of isolation.

For about a week the Wilhelmstrasse was apprehensive that its own recently ambivalent policy might bar the way to border revisions or even result in Germany's isolation. To Rantzau and others Trautmann's earlier forecast seemed prophetic, namely that a shattering of Russia's confidence in Germany would be followed by her rapprochement with France and Poland.[2] Germany, to be sure, feared the possible consequences of a break between Russia and France, and favored anything short of a Russo-Polish accord to inhibit such a development. But such an accord seemed now to be in the offing. It was reported that Paris would only consider an agreement with Moscow as part of a collective non-aggression pact embracing Poland and perhaps Rumania or one accompanied by a tandem Polish-Soviet security and non-aggression agreement. Russia, it was said, was ready to negotiate on these terms. Moreover the failure of the Narkomindel to give the Germans advance notice of their plans confirmed them in their worst suspicions. (Since December 1926 Moscow and Berlin had been consulting on Polish-Lithuanian relations.[3]) For years to come Moscow's talks

[1] Hoesch to German delegation, Geneva, September 17, 1927, 2860/D558996–8.

[2] Rantzau to Foreign Ministry, September 21, 1927, 2860/D559006–9.

[3] In 1926 Germany had been reserved in her attitude toward Lithuania, secretly hoping that Poland would discredit herself internationally by following an aggressive policy toward Lithuania. Following a *putsch* in Lithuania in late 1926, however, Germany's policy turned 180 degrees and she entered into consultations with the Narkomindel in order to 'preserve the common goal of Russian and German policy, namely, the

with Warsaw and Paris were to remain inconclusive, but that they might succeed was something that German diplomacy continued to reckon with.

Because Moscow's negotiations were abortive – Chicherin explained that the approach to France had been a defensive tactic and nothing else[1] – Germany's irritable response is not substantively important. But it is nevertheless of considerable interest as one measure of the changing role of the 'Polish question' in German-Soviet relations in the eighteen months after the conclusion of the Berlin treaty. In April 1926, it will be recalled, the Wilhelmstrasse asked Russia for a promise that she would refrain from concluding any treaty with Poland. This condition, deemed necessary to early border changes, was restated on the occasion of Russia's offer of a non-aggression treaty to Poland in August 1926. Subsequently, however, the course of Anglo-Soviet relations had strengthened Poland's position by winning greater support from France and Britain. The result was that Germany now had to substitute minimal for maximal goals. Plans for an early settlement with Poland had to be abandoned; instead a more limited policy was necessary that would merely keep alive the question of border change.

This circumscribed objective was reflected in Germany's response to Russia's negotiations with France and Poland. Germany's policy, as enunciated in a series of diplomatic conversations,[2] accepted a bilateral Franco-Soviet non-aggression treaty in prin-

---

independence of Lithuania; and for this purpose to support the present Lithuanian government as much as possible. . . .' An east European bloc under Polish leadership was as repugnant to Germany as it was to Russia (Köpke to Rantzau, March 3, 1927, 2860/D558418–20). This policy continued to hold sway throughout the summer and autumn of 1927. In a conversation Schubert agreed to a statement by Litvinov that 'there was a need, because of Poland, to tie Lithuania to Germany and Russia . . .' (Memorandum by Schubert, August 29, 1927, 5265/E318962–70).

[1] Rantzau to Stresemann concerning conversation with Chicherin, September 27, 1927, 2860/D559045–7.

[2] This summary is based on the following documents: Rantzau to Foreign Ministry regarding conversation with Chicherin, September 21, 1927, 2860/D559006–9; Köpke to German delegation, Geneva, September 23, 1927, 2860/D559014–15; Stresemann to Rantzau, September 24, 1927, 2860/D559028–31; Memorandum by Wallroth regarding conversation with Bratman-Brodovskii, September 26, 1927, 5265/E317519–24; Rantzau to Stresemann, September 27, 1927, 2860/D559045–7; Rantzau to Foreign Ministry, October 7, 1927, 2860/D559065–7.

ciple. But a multilateral pact embracing Russia, France, Poland, and perhaps Rumania, was termed incompatible with the Berlin treaty. Equally unacceptable was a separate Russo-Polish non-aggression pact that included a guarantee of Germany's border with Poland. Indeed on this point Wallroth informed the Soviet Chargé (at the time Russia was believed on the verge of a *volte face*) that for Germany 'an essential condition of Rapallo had been that the eastern question would be kept open for a solution favorable to Germany's interests'.[1] Yet Stresemann, Rantzau, and Wallroth also knew that they would be vulnerable to charges of war-mongering if they tried to block a simple non-aggression agreement between Poland and Russia.

This recognition of the effective limits to Germany's forward policy in the east signified a retreat by the Wilhelmstrasse from its adamant opposition to any Polish-Soviet accord announced in 1926. As such it came to represent Germany's eastern policy during the following years. But the Soviet thesis that Germany's support for her international policy was a condition to keeping alive the 'Polish question' was matched by a German counter-thesis that the Soviets would indeed have to give life to that question or risk forfeiting their partnership with Germany.

6. 'A BALL WITHOUT BOUNCE'

AFTER the Anglo-Soviet rupture, attention in the Wilhelmstrasse intermittently returned to the possibility that Germany might mediate the dispute.[2] By early August the crisis was thought to have matured to the point where the antagonists might welcome such an offer. In a conference between Schubert and Rantzau on August 5 it was decided to ask Chicherin what conditions the Soviets would consider necessary for a *modus vivendi* and whether they would accept a German offer of mediation.[3] This strategy, laid down in written instructions to Rantzau, was modified in a

[1] Memorandum by Wallroth regarding conversation with Bratman-Brodovskii, September 26, 1927, 5265/E317519–24.

[2] Cf. memorandum by Dirksen entitled: 'Die durch Abbruch der englisch-russischen Beziehungen geschaffene Lage', June 3, 1927, 6698/H106612–18.

[3] Memorandum by Schubert concerning conversation with Rantzau on August 5, 1927, and with Stresemann and Rantzau on August 6, 1927, 4562/E159068–70; 6698/H106686.

further consultation involving Stresemann. Now the German Ambassador was merely to ask for Chicherin's appraisal of Chamberlain's recent speeches.[1]

Germany's flickering desire to intervene was, however, quickly snuffed out. Chicherin informed Rantzau on his return to Moscow that he regarded an offer of mediation as a sign of weakness on the part of the state making it and was not considering 'calling upon a third power to mediate . . . in the present conditions of the Anglo-Soviet conflict'.[2] The bulky Wilhelmstrasse file 'to mediate or not to mediate' was herewith closed.

At the same time, however, consultations in Berlin began to focus on the more fundamental question of the interplay between Germany's revision goals and her relations with Russia. This was a perennial problem. In 1925 and 1926 the question had been, *how* can Russia be rendered into a useful partner for Germany. The solution had been the Berlin treaty. In the interval, that question had changed from *how* to *whether*—evidence that the situation had fundamentally changed. As Dirksen phrased it: 'Are Germany's ties with Russia worth enough to our present and future political and economic interests that it pays to assume the political expenses and risks involved in maintaining them?'[3]

Leading opinion in the Wilhelmstrasse agreed that the issue was acutely pertinent because of Russia's failure to reach her Thermidor, as the NEP had earlier suggested. 'Gradually to neutralize the revolutionary and subversive tendencies of the Soviet government and to bring it closer to the west',[4] was the way Dirksen, for example, described the goal of Germany's relations with the USSR. Wallroth, on the other hand, saw that a removal of the revolutionary core from Russia's policy would have rendered that policy more independent of Germany. But he also cited the 'failure of an evolution to appear in Soviet Russia', as the chief

[1] Memorandum by Schubert, August 6, 1927, 6698/H106686.

[2] Rantzau to the Foreign Ministry, August 12, 1927, 6698/H106689. *Pravda* of June 25, 1927, warned against a German attempt to mediate in the propaganda question: 'He [Stresemann] clearly will have seen that under the existing circumstances such mediation could in no sense have been viewed as friendly.'

[3] Memorandum by Dirksen entitled: 'Bemerkungen zur Aufzeichnung von Gesandschaftsrat Hahn über die deutsche Russland-Politik', September 19, 1927, K281/K097454–60.

[4] Memorandum by Wallroth, June 3, 1927, 6698/H106612–18.

reason why intimate relations with her would be without tangible benefits for Germany.[1] Even Rantzau, who earlier had defined Communist purposes in China and Britain in terms of national interest, confessed in autumn that the bourgeois world had turned against the USSR because she had not 'evolved' in the direction expected in 1921.[2]

Yet this consensus among Dirksen, Wallroth, Rantzau, and even Schubert, that the USSR's failure to evolve toward the right had shaken a major assumption of the Rapallo and Berlin treaties, was not paralleled by any agreement on policy. Dirksen, an *Ostler*, with a national-interest view of foreign policy, contended that at the base of German-Soviet relations was a stable community of interests that was independent of the internal nature of the Soviet system: 'If . . . Germany's and Russia's interests are parallel, then the policy of both sides will not change – at least not permanently – even if a radical change should occur in the Russian system, let alone a gradual shift (*allmähliche Mauserung*).' For that reason Germany's policy, in his view, should not risk a lurch to the west in response to Russia's temporary weakness.[3] Not since before 1922 had the *Ostlers* assumed so defensive a posture. They no longer seemed sure that the path to revision led through Moscow. They were alarmed at the erosion of domestic German support for the tie with Russia, and put on their guard by the concerted attack launched on the bases of official policy from within the Wilhelmstrasse.

In the summer and autumn of 1927, Wallroth, Director of the Eastern Department, and his close associate, Consul Hahn, the occupant of the Russian desk, pleaded for a drastic reorientation of Germany's policy. Their plea was a further chapter in the continuing dialogue between *Ostlers* and *Westlers*, although it must be stressed that the positions of the participants were not as rigid as the labelling suggests. Early in August, Hahn argued that Germany could no longer choose between east and west. The eastern option, he wrote, had succumbed as a result of Russia's weakness at home and her isolation abroad: the Red Army was technically deficient

[1] Wallroth to Rantzau, December 31, 1927, 5265/E318789–91.

[2] Memorandum by Rantzau entitled: 'Das 10-jährige Bestehen der Sowjetunion, Ein Rück- und Ausblick', November 26, 1927, K281/K097502–9.

[3] Memorandum by Dirksen, September 19, 1927, K281/K097454–60.

and unreliable, the economy near paralysis, and the Party divided against itself. The universal recognition of Russia's malaise had robbed relations with her even of their 'bluff effect'.[1]

Some months later Wallroth expanded these views in a lengthy report that concluded with the assertion: Russia is a 'ball that has ceased to bounce'. There is a dogged quality to the persistence with which Wallroth clung to his views over the years. Since becoming head of the Eastern Department in 1925 he had grown progressively more skeptical about the value of maintaining a partnership with Russia. In this statement, his final one as Director before being transferred to Oslo as German Ambassador, he went beyond his earlier pleas for a shift in Germany's policy.

The crisis of the Soviet economy was not temporary, he argued, nor was there a long-term congruity of German and Soviet interests, as Dirksen claimed. Bolshevik ideology had cut a clean line between the foreign policies of pre- and post-revolutionary Russia. Likewise he rejected as fallacious the *Ostlers*' assumption that Soviet support was either dependable or essential to Germany's foreign policy. An alliance with Russia against the Versailles system was precluded by the revolutionary core of Soviet thought. The 'bluff effect' of relations was spent because the threat of a German-Soviet alliance was no longer credible. Economically the gains for Germany had been nil; and as for the Polish question the Anglo-Soviet conflict, by stiffening Poland's position, was well on the way to extinguishing Germany's dreams of border revision.[2]

If relations with Moscow had indeed begun to threaten Germany's interests, one key unexplored question remained: what other diplomatic alternatives existed? Hahn was able to suggest a panacea—Britain's support against Versailles could be secured by means of an ingenious plan that would also wean the Soviet system from its ideological commitment. He suggested that London

[1] Memorandum by Hahn, August 8, 1927, 5462/E380438–52. In a letter to Schubert, introducing his reply to the Hahn memorandum, Dirksen wrote: 'An investigation of these statements seems important to me because they are designed to disturb our official Russian policy and to strengthen the diverging tendencies present in certain parties' (Dirksen to Schubert introducing his memorandum entitled: 'Bemerkungen zur Aufzeichnung von Gesandschaftsrat Hahn über die deutsche Russland-Politik', September 24, 1927, 6698/H112327–8).

[2] Memorandum by Wallroth entitled: 'Russlands Selbstausschaltung und deren Folgewirkung für Deutschland', November 20, 1927, 5265/E318838–53.

and Berlin jointly offer the Soviets an ample loan on the condition that they accept a Dawes-type plan and agree to reconstruct their political system.[1] When this incredible proposal, based on the postulate of the primacy of economics, was first made in August, Wallroth thought it might have some chance of success under the right conditions.[2] But by November he had concluded that ideological rigidity was an essential feature of the Soviet system, and for that reason was not susceptible of modification by means of political strings attached to an international loan.[3] Dirksen was willing to grant that Hahn's scheme might in future serve to blunt the radical point of Soviet policy. But it was ludicrous for the present because of the pinched state of German finances and, more seriously, because it might provoke a break with the USSR.[4] In short Hahn's panacea was rejected because it was based on too optimistic a reading of Germany's freedom of action.

Wallroth was more sober and suggested the careful plotting out of a gradual change in orientation so that the delicate matter of altering course could be implemented at the exact moment when Germany's bargaining position was strongest. He was sure that a slight inclination towards Britain would elicit reciprocal gestures and eventually the offer of major concessions to Germany for her complete separation from the USSR. The question of timing, he admitted, would be crucial in such a venture. But regardless of when that moment arrived Germany 'dare not miss it'. The immediate need, he wrote, was not to postpone the discussion of basic decisions concerning the direction of Germany's policy because of an 'erroneous fundamental attitude'. And so that Germany's hands not be tied for such dealings he urged that no further economic concessions be granted Russia.[5]

[1] Memorandum by Hahn, August 8, 1927, 5462/E380438–42. It should be mentioned that the idea of an international loan to Russia with the rider that the revolutionary goals of Soviet policy be abandoned was first adumbrated in May or June by so hard-headed an observer as the Nationalist Reichstag Deputy and editor of *Osteuropa*, Hoetzsch (Memorandum by Dirksen, June 3, 1927, 6698/H106612–18).

[2] Memorandum by Wallroth entitled: 'Deutsch-englisch-russisches Verhältnis', August 27, 1927, K281/K097443–6.

[3] Memorandum by Wallroth, November 20, 1927, 5265/E318838–53.

[4] Memorandum by Dirksen, September 19, 1927, K281/K097454–60.

[5] Memorandum by Wallroth, November 20, 1927, 5265/E318838–53.

Yet given the nature of Germany's revisionist ambitions throughout the period of the Weimar Republic, was this recommendation not too facile as well? The opinion represented by Dirksen, Trautmann, Schubert, Rantzau, and Stresemann, took a gloomier view of the political choices open to Germany. Since 1923, a year of truth in Germany's foreign policy, the Wilhelmstrasse had become increasingly skeptical about the possibility of maneuvering between London and Paris. This important conclusion had dictated Germany's negotiation of the Locarno agreements. The Wilhelmstrasse recognized that so long as London clung to the dictum that Paris would not be sacrificed to Berlin, and so long as France continued to support Poland, Germany would be foolish to expect British concessions for an unravelling of her eastern ties. Germany's frustration about her limited freedom was epitomized in a reply by Dirksen to the recommendations of Hahn: 'The principle that the English will approach us only so far as this is possible without encroaching on Anglo-French relations has run like a red thread throughout the development of our foreign policy in the past few years.'[1]

Other officials in Berlin shared this frustration. It was expressed by Trautmann during the Wilhelmstrasse's 'mediation debate' when he admitted that the possibility of alienating Russia would not trouble him if Germany could 'win England permanently by giving up Russia'.[2] The inference was that he would have been jubilant about such a development if it had been possible. And in the same debate, as already mentioned, Rantzau expressed a kindred view, although more extreme, when he warned that a loosening of relations with Moscow would be tantamount to 'losing the east without gaining the west'.[3] 'Gaining the west', was indeed a big order when it was defined in terms of Germany's revision goals—goals which so far as we know were assumed and not debated. Stresemann ventured such a definition to the German cabinet soon after the Anglo-Soviet break when he spelled out the minimum concessions that Germany would demand to become associated with Britain: the 'Polish territories, Danzig, and the Corridor'. He added regretfully that thus far there had not been so

[1] Memorandum by Dirksen, September 19, 1927, K281/K097454–60.

[2] Memorandum by Trautmann entitled: 'Russland und England', March 14, 1927, 6698/H105784–98.

[3] Rantzau to Schubert, March 6, 1927, 2860/D558454–65.

much as a 'vague reference to compensation by any official English party'.[1] This statement remained true throughout the crisis.

By late 1927 Stresemann's buoyant hopes of the mid-1920s, that a balance between the policies of the Locarno and Berlin treaties would mark Germany's political resurgence, lay in the dust. The worst, to be sure, had been avoided. The crisis was easing and Germany had not faced the barren alternatives of having to chose sides. The goal of revision had, moreover, been kept intact, and the absence of other paths to its achievement dictated that special ties with Moscow be retained.

Yet relations with Moscow, stripped as they now were of some of their earlier illusions, had chilled. The Wilhelmstrasse's debate had served at least to drive home the hard truth that the economic decline and international isolation of the USSR had rendered collaboration with her an uncertain weapon in Germany's anti-Versailles armory. At the same time Germany's ambivalent policy during the crisis had heightened Russia's conviction that the sinews necessary for her security would have to be sought less in diplomacy than in industrialization. For the Soviets as well, however, the absence of other diplomatic bonds meant that the partnership with Germany, however tenuous, would have to be retained. On this level, then, the relationship defined by the Berlin agreement was to continue for many years. But the elements of instability inherent in it had become explicit.

[1] Extract from minutes of a cabinet meeting, May 30, 1927, L617/L194974–9.

Part Three

VANISHING ILLUSIONS, 1927–1929

FROM the autumn of 1927 to the spring of 1929 German-Soviet relations matured and underwent fundamental change. During this period the accumulated frustrations of German commercial circles over the disappointing development of trade with the USSR were dramatically brought into the open, combining in the spring of 1928 with other factors to inflate the Shakhty case (which grew out of Soviet charges that German firms were involved in the sabotage of industry in the Donetz) into a first-class political emergency. The period ended in a partial resolution of differences and a new level of economic interaction.

At the same time the issue of revolutionary Communism, which had lain dormant for some years, reemerged in Germany. Since about 1924 both governments had viewed the call of other alignments as the gravest threat to their partnership. Soviet leaders, as we have seen, had been agitated over the possibility that Germany might be drawn into Britain's alleged anti-Soviet orbit; they had tried to meet this danger by assuring themselves of German neutrality through policies part carrot and part stick. German policy makers, on the other hand, had been uneasy that Russia might thwart their goals of revision either by combining with France and Poland or by aggravating her relations with Britain. As a means of lessening the risks and increasing the advantages of association with Russia the Wilhelmstrasse had evolved the ingenious though stillborn policy of Germany mediating Russia's foreign contacts.

Although such considerations continued to strain the bonds between Berlin and Moscow after 1927, they became more marginal as new complications arose out of domestic affairs in both countries. An interplay between the radical politics in the Soviet Union accompanying the First Five-Year Plan and the social instability in Germany caused by the depression came to disturb mutual relations, particularly after 1929. Already from the summer of 1928, however, the electoral gains and heightened militancy of the KPD prompted government officials to explore the potential conflict between Germany's internal security and her partnership with the Soviet Union.

The questioning mood that became a feature of German-Soviet relations in 1928 may be traced in part to an understandable yet fundamentally mistaken reading of Soviet intentions. German government leaders were aroused by incendiary resolutions at the Sixth Comintern Congress (1928), calling for a sharpening of the class struggle and placing Social Democrats and fascists in one category. Attracted to an interpretation that causally linked the excesses of German Communists, inflammatory outbursts by Comintern officials, and Stalin's new course, they came to view all three as part of one development—the 'Cominternization' of Soviet policy. This sloganizing, it seems, barred the path to fruitful analysis.

1. STABILIZING BONDS

As we have seen, the Wilhelmstrasse's debate in the fall of 1927 led to the recognition that Russia's economic decline and political isolation weakened her support for a speedy achievement of Germany's revision goals. Nevertheless it was also assumed that a close association with Moscow would have to be retained because of a lack of other approaches to the same goal; indeed, in 1928 as German public opinion grew restive about the meager benefits of the conferences at Locarno and Thoiry, this policy seemed all the more necessary. Similarly, although Soviet leaders had expressed irritation about Stresemann's ambivalent policies in 1927, the following year did not provide viable alternatives that would have permitted them to drop their German connection. After the crisis of 1927 the USSR's relations with Britain stagnated, those with France worsened, and in the spring of 1928 the fear revived that Poland was planning to intervene against the Soviet Union. A neutral Germany was consequently still recognized as the crucial gap in any alliance against the Soviet Union and a brake on Polish inclinations to move eastward.

In 1928 the residual congruence of Germany's and the Soviet

Union's interests in international questions was seen most clearly in two areas: in the Soviet Union's effort to break out of isolation through association with the League and in Germany's attempt to mediate her adherence to the Kellogg pact. Soviet representatives made their first appearance at Geneva in 1927 to attend sessions of the world economic conference and the preparatory commission for the disarmament conference, both held under League auspices.

The Soviet Union's first tenuous association with the League was welcomed by Wilhelmstrasse officials even though it could have presaged a more independent Soviet course. This reaction was not surprising because in past years German policy had favored developments that would ease Russia's international situation, including membership for her in the League;[1] it had never sought an exclusive relationship with the USSR for fear of *Alleinbleiben*. For Germany an added attraction of the departure in Soviet policy was that it introduced disarmament as a new subject for collaboration. On the Soviet side, Litvinov journeyed to Geneva with the intention of proclaiming proletarian virtue, clearing the roadblocks to a rapprochement with other countries, and strengthening existing ties with Germany.

At Geneva the German and Soviet delegations agreed at the outset to coordinate their policies in the disarmament discussions of the first session of the Preparatory Commission.[2] But, typical of Germany's delicate international situation, a Wilhelmstrasse memorandum supporting this policy urged that it 'not be made too evident outwardly'.[3] The reasons for such caution became evident in the first sessions at Geneva, when Briand informed German representatives that the solidarity developing between the German and Soviet delegations in disarmament policies could have baneful consequences for Germany – Russia and Italy were already suspect in French eyes and Germany must be wary not to let herself be drawn into the same universe of isolation.[4]

French ire was explicable. Litvinov's revolutionary proposal for

[1] Nadolny, German Ambassador to Turkey, to Schubert, July 24, 1926, 4562/E157679–84.

[2] Stresemann to Köpke regarding conversation with Litvinov, December 4, 1927, K281/K097515–16.

[3] Notes by Dirksen for conversation of Stresemann with Litvinov, November 24, 1927, 2860/D559190–2.

[4] Köpke to Rantzau, March 7, 1928, 2860/D559477–9.

immediate, general, and complete disarmament supported the German thesis that disarmament must take priority over security, and for this reason was warmly greeted by Johann Bernstorff, the German spokesman. In short, the opening of this new area of co-operation helped to muffle the growing dissonances in German-Soviet relations. It was more than an empty phrase for Litvinov when he assured Stresemann that for him further collaboration with Germany was the most significant result of the Soviet Union's first appearance at Geneva.[1]

Roughly the same motives that brought Litvinov to Geneva led to the Soviet Union's eventual adherence to the Briand–Kellogg pact. Soviet leaders interpreted the pointed absence of their country from the list of states originally invited to sign the agreement as a further effort at their quarantine. In public statements, however, they kept the door to participation ajar.[2] German officials likewise saw Russia's exclusion as planned, and emboldened by a session of the Reichstag's Foreign Affairs Committee – in which all parties (with the exception of the KPD) voiced support for the USSR's adherence[3] – they sounded Moscow and Washington about including the USSR among the original signatories.

Soviet diplomats recognized that association with the Kellogg plan would have the double advantage of frustrating efforts aimed at their international quarantine and link them to the United States in an inter-state action.[4] In addition, mediation by Stresemann would advertise the 'intimacy' of the German tie, only recently mended after the Shakhty incident. For that reason the Soviet press encouraged the Wilhelmstrasse's efforts by alluding to them.[5] The Wilhelmstrasse's mediation was partly successful: although the Soviet Union was not included among the original signatories of the Kellogg pact, German officials were able to obtain a face-saving formula from Washington which specified that

[1] Stresemann to Köpke, December 4, 1927. Litvinov expressed similar sentiments to Schubert and Stresemann on April 5, 1928, 2860/D559482–84, D559490–6.

[2] Degras, op. cit., II, 322–5.

[3] Schubert to Moscow Embassy, July 11, 1928, 2860/D559608–12.

[4] Schubert to Moscow Embassy, July 17, 1928, 2860/D559622–3; Memorandum by Schubert regarding conversation with Krestinskii, July 21, 1928, 6698/H112682–4; Memorandum by Dirksen regarding conversation with Bratman-Brodovskii, July 25, 1928, 6698/H112690–2.

[5] *Izvestiia*, July 27, August 8, August 11, 1928.

a distinction would not be made between original participants and those that adhered later.[1] On the basis of this formula the Soviet Union, together with a number of smaller states, participated in the original Kellogg pact by means of a supplementary protocol. To a modest degree the German government had helped to increase the Soviet Union's foreign connections, a goal that it had earlier hoped to reach through the 'Schlesinger line'.

But the area in which German leaders were prepared further to tolerate and even promote such a development found its extreme limit when it came to Poland. This had been made clear earlier during the negotiations preceding the Berlin treaty, again in August 1926, and for a third time late in 1927 when Wilhelmstrasse officials had lodged strenuous objections against proposals for a Polish-Soviet treaty of non-aggression. The arguments then adduced against any such agreement were revived late in 1928 and early in 1929 to serve against the Litvinov protocol.

The Litvinov protocol, whose object was to make the Kellogg pact immediately applicable to the relations between Poland and the Soviet Union, was part of the same defensive Soviet policy that had led to Geneva and the Kellogg pact. But it was not from Berlin's standpoint, because it involved Poland and had features of an eastern Locarno. Since the ostensible purpose of the Soviet proposal was to lessen tensions in eastern Europe German diplomats could not oppose it publicly. But in conversations with members of the Narkomindel they voiced their reservations freely.

German objections focused on the situation that would arise if the Kellogg pact remained inactive because one of its original signatories had failed to ratify it. A new security system, the German thesis was, would then have arisen in eastern Europe. On the other hand, even an implementation of the treaty that removed Germany's juridical worries, would leave untouched the political fact that 'such a protocol would cover Poland's back (*Rückendeckung*)'.[2] German restiveness about the proposed agreement increased as the border states were brought into its purview and the

[1] Memoranda by Schubert regarding conversations with American Ambassador, July 20, 1928, 6698/H112667–75; July 25, 1928, 6698/H112695–705; August 1, 1928, 6698/H112759–71.

[2] Memorandum by Schubert regarding conversation with Krestinskii, January 2, 1929, 4562/E159839–46.

idea revived of a Baltic bloc under Poland's leadership.[1] Finally, the prospect that foreign pressure might compel Germany to adhere, with disastrous consequences for her revision claims in eastern Europe, made Wilhelmstrasse officials balky.[2]

Soviet spokesmen tried to meet German objections by demonstrating that the protocol served their common interests. It was designed, Litvinov explained, to strengthen Lithuania against Poland by interposing the Soviet Union as a guarantor of the peace between the two states; if Germany were to express interest in becoming a second guarantor the matter could be arranged.[3] Schubert's and Stresemann's allegation that a system was emerging that bore a disturbing resemblance to an eastern Locarno was countered. The protocol, Litvinov said, did not contain any border guarantees and was preferable for Germany to a Polish-Soviet non-aggression accord. The more political reservation that Poland was nevertheless receiving a *Rückendeckung* was dismissed as unimportant because Germany was under no immediate threat from Warsaw.[4]

On February 9, 1929, six months before the implementation of the Kellogg pact, the Litvinov protocol was signed in Moscow. The Wilhelmstrasse, faced with the accomplished fact and recognizing that its fears had been exaggerated, accepted the new situation. But the Litvinov protocol as well as Moscow's recurring negotiations with Warsaw for a non-aggression treaty reflected some of the same diverging German and Soviet interests that were to culminate in open differences some years later.

2. A DISILLUSIONED AMBASSADOR

In 1927–8 the direct contacts of the Rapallo partners were markedly less harmonious than their association at Geneva and in the negotiations for the Kellogg pact. In 1928 the chanceries of Europe

[1] Dirksen to Foreign Ministry regarding conversation with Litvinov, January 7, 1929, 2860/D560110–12.

[2] Schubert to a number of German embassies, January 14, 1929, 4562/E159895–8.

[3] Dirksen to Foreign Ministry regarding conversation with Litvinov: January 20, 1929, 2860/D560118–20; January 22, 1929, 2860/D560125–7; January 24, 1929, 4562/E159938–9; February 1, 1929, 2860/D560163–4; February 27, 1929, 2860/D560217–18.

[4] Ibid.

watched with malicious pleasure as a dispute between them suddenly flared up in the Shakhty case. This incident involved the arrest of fifty Soviet and three German engineers and technicians who were brought to trial on charges of having sabotaged the coal mines in the Donetz area in preparation for a war of intervention. A conspiracy of international capital was alleged. The trial might easily have blown over as other incidents had before. But unexpectedly the German government and press reacted abruptly, and in the spring and early summer of 1928 the 'Soviet-German horizon was blackened'.[1] Considered in isolation, this precipitous development is inexplicable.[2] But in context, viewed as the culminating of a process, as the unleashing of pent-up frustrations, it takes on the importance of a symptom.

In what did this context and process consist? What were the sources of these frustrations? In the spring and summer of 1928 three developments converged to produce the Shakhty crisis. The first we have already discussed: it was the reluctant admission of German officials that the relationship defined by the Berlin treaty had been exploited by the Soviets but would have to be maintained. The conclusion, 'we will have to make the best of our relationship with Russia', was, however, accompanied by the resolve that mutuality would have to be reestablished. In the late autumn of 1927 German frustration about the limited worth of the partnership began to merge with a view held by Rantzau and some of his associates that radical Soviet domestic policies were being paralleled by radical Comintern policies, directed at the base of German democracy. As a last development German business interests were critical of the stagnation in trade and financial dealings with the USSR. Together these three developments produced so resentful a mood in Germany that the occasion of the Shakhty case in April 1928 led the Foreign Ministry, German security agencies, and German business circles to cry out with one voice: 'not one step further'.

[1] Fischer, op. cit., II, 773.

[2] Published accounts of the Shakhty case have not gone beyond a description of the trial, the vehement reaction of the German government and press, and an indictment of Soviet justice. (Fischer, op. cit., II, 772–4; Kochan, op. cit., 134; Hilger, op. cit., 217–22; Dirksen, op. cit., 69–70.) For a purely descriptive account of the Shakhty case based on the German Foreign Office documents see: Kurt Rosenbaum, 'The German Involvement in the Shakhty Trial', *The Russian Review*, XXI (July 1962), 238–60.

The opinion that Soviet foreign policy had become more militant since the fall of 1927, that the NEP was being supplanted by the class struggle at home and revolution abroad, was first aired by Rantzau. Representing a sharp departure in his thinking, this interpretation made a correspondingly sharp impact in the Foreign Ministry. Previously, as late as the spring of 1927, Rantzau had argued that recurring incidents should not divert attention from the fact that it had been possible for Germany to use the Soviet Union for her purposes.[1] Even at the height of Soviet activity in China—when Soviet leaders were using diplomacy to secure their potential revolutionary gains in Asia or to minimize their risks if that revolution should fail—Rantzau had denied that Moscow was following a leftist strategy.[2]

Occasionally the Ambassador's deathless hatred of the authors of Versailles blinded him to the broad sweep of Soviet policy and reduced his assessment to generalizations based on limited German experience. In early 1927 all was quiet in Germany, from which he inferred that the Soviets were pursuing a rightist course. In November 1927—ironically at a moment when Stalin was shedding the goal of foreign revolution in favor of the penultimate objective of 'Socialism in one country'—Rantzau began noting a leftward shift in Soviet foreign policy.

His first observations about this trend were made in an important memorandum commemorating the tenth anniversary of the October Revolution, which concluded with an assertion and an apprehensive question. The partnership of Rapallo had served German purposes despite numerous disappointments, he observed. But what of the future? This fundamental question troubled the Ambassador:

> Decisive for our policy towards the Soviet Union is the increasingly acute question of the political and economic development here. Will it follow moderate lines that permit us to deepen and broaden our friendly relations as a counterweight to an unconditional dependence upon the west, or will developments here prevent the future maintenance of German-Soviet relations in spite of their importance for the international reputation of Germany?[3]

---

[1] Rantzau to the Foreign Ministry, January 20, 1927, 2860/D558323–6.

[2] Rantzau to Schubert, March 6, 1927, 2860/D558454–65.

[3] Memorandum by Rantzau entitled: 'Das 10-jährige Bestehen der

As a thesis that was generally applicable to German-Soviet relations this statement was sound enough. But what, in Rantzau's estimation, had rendered the question acute in November 1927? What had happened since March to warrant such a drift into gloom? The Soviet war scare was, of course, only just ebbing, relations with France were still burdened by the Rakovskii incident, and those with Britain remained difficult. But more important for Rantzau's mood than this general Soviet malaise was an incident at the tenth anniversary celebrations of the October Revolution bearing on the ties between the KPD and Moscow.

On November 12, Voroshilov, the Soviet Commissar of War, summoned the International Congress of the Friends of the Soviet Union to greater exertions in the cause of world revolution. The October Revolution, he said, was only the 'introduction to the greatest drama that had ever been enacted in the human arena. But we know that the following acts of this drama are going to start soon.'[1]

Following this general summons, the Revolutionary War Council awarded the coveted Order of the Red Banner to a number of prominent Hungarian, French, and German Communists. Among the latter it was granted *in absentia* to the German Communist Max Hölz, at that time imprisoned in Germany as a common criminal. The rhetorical words of General Budenny in making the awards were pointed: 'The blows of the proletariat will soon make the chains fall from our brothers languishing in capitalist prisons.' The response of a German Communist in accepting the award for Hölz was that the KPD looked with confidence to the USSR and Red Army for support in its struggle to topple the established order in Germany.[2] These words were without question incendiary. But the conclusion seems unassailable that following the recent collapse of Communist plans in China they represented the militancy of the despaired and an avowal of eschatological hope, not a genuine call to action.

Rantzau was, however, wont to view the episode differently. Rarely since 1923 had he shown such irritation or voiced such pessimism as on this occasion. He called on Chicherin almost immedi-

---

Sowjetunion, Ein Rück- und Ausblick', November 26, 1927, K281/K097502–9.

[1] Hilger and Meyer, op. cit., 157. [2] Ibid.

ately and raged about the matter as a grave provocation.[1] And he unsuccessfully requested authorization from the Foreign Minister to leave his Moscow post as a demonstration.[2] On November 26 Rantzau characterized the 'Hölz case', as a 'brazen challenge'.[3]

The Hölz incident seems to have marked a turning point in Rantzau's view of the prospects for long-term cooperation with the Soviet Union. From henceforth he interpreted each new incident in mutual relations as confirmation of a leftward trend in Soviet policy. There were many more to come. The endless train of revolutionary celebrations in Moscow provided occasions for numerous incidents. Thus, in February 1928, during the tenth anniversary celebrations of the founding of the Red Army, Voroshilov was made an honorary member of the Young Pioneers in Berlin.[4] Again through word and deed he was closely identified with the KPD's alleged revolutionary purposes in Germany. Rantzau considered that the Rapallo structure could only be saved if, as Paul Scheffer commented, the 'boundaries to Revolutionary caprice as regarded Germany were definitely set'.[5]

The Ambassador now demanded an unequivocal answer to each new provocation. The Hölz incident was to be countered by his departure from Moscow. A speech by Tomsky urging Soviet workers to hurry to the aid of their foreign proletarian brothers regardless of the risks to Russia's diplomatic system was to be met by a blanket ban on travel to Germany of Russian trade union members.[6] He called for toughness all along the line.

Rantzau's motives in demanding a purifying crisis were threefold. He feared that inaction would encourage Soviet party organs to become yet more abusive and that a further proliferation of incidents might undermine support for the Rapallo policy in Germany. Decisive measures were needed, he wrote Stresemann in November, or all 'of the opponents of our eastern policy will take the conduct of the Soviet Union as expressed during the tenth anniversary celebrations—in particular the incident involving

[1] Rantzau to Foreign Ministry, November 14, 1927, 2860/D559138.

[2] Rantzau to Stresemann, November 23, 1927, 2860/D559175–9.

[3] Memorandum by Rantzau, November 26, 1927, K281/K097502–9.

[4] Rantzau to the Foreign Ministry, February 26, 1928, 2860/D559458.

[5] Scheffer, op. cit., 322.

[6] Rantzau to the Foreign Ministry, February 19, 1928, 2860/D559440–43; Schubert to Rantzau, February 23, 1928, 2860/D559447–9.

Hölz—as a pretext to press for a shift away from Russia and a western orientation'.[1] Yet what made Rantzau most restive was that Soviet leaders like Voroshilov were prominently involved in the incidents. Hence, he felt, a dualism between the utterances of Party and government leaders—which had earlier been a comforting feature of the Soviet scene—was being replaced by a monism in which Party and government spoke with a single revolutionary voice.

Previously the Ambassador had often cited military contacts as important 'ties' with Moscow, and had supported them for this reason despite the risks of foreign disclosure.[2] But now that the War Commissar had implicitly injected the issue of German politics into German-Soviet relations through his support of the KPD, Rantzau demanded that military collaboration be reappraised with a view to its possible liquidation.[3]

At first Rantzau did not gain much support among his colleagues in the Foreign Ministry for his ultimatum-type proposals, and his relations with Stresemann, which had always been a bit touchy, suffered.[4] By this time the Foreign Minister was disposed to take ties with the USSR for granted as a constant in his western plans; only infrequently did he attend to their details.[5] When the Narkomindel therefore tried to placate Berlin by explaining that the Revolutionary War Council had acted without the approval of the Soviet government and had honored Hölz not for his partisan activities in Germany but for his military contributions toward the end of the war, Stresemann was ready to view the incident as closed.[6] But Rantzau saw the apology as only a means of preventing a break and continued to press his more stringent demands.[7]

[1] Rantzau to Stresemann, November 23, 1927, 2860/D559175–9.

[2] Memorandum by Rantzau regarding talk with Groener, August 1, 1928, L337/L100545–53; Instructions from Rantzau to Hencke for talks in the Foreign Ministry, April 23, 1928, L340/L101048–52; Memorandum by Rantzau, June 9, 1928, L340/L101053–4.

[3] Rantzau to Stresemann, April 12, 1928, L337/L100723–30.

[4] Ibid.

[5] For an opposite view, based largely, it seems, on familiarity with Stresemann's very active involvement in the negotiations for the Berlin treaty, see E. H. Carr, *What is History?* (New York: Alfred A. Knopf, 1962), 16–20.

[6] Memorandum by Schubert, December 23, 1927, 4562/E159527–9; Schubert to Rantzau, January 2, 1928, 2860/D559392.

[7] Rantzau to Foreign Ministry, January 3, 1928, 2860/D559398–9.

3. AFTER HYPNOSIS, DISCONTENT

WHILE Rantzau was arguing that Soviet foreign policy had set out on a revolutionary course German industry was giving vent to its accumulated frustration over the unfavorable development of commercial relations with the USSR. It is a superficial view to dismiss German-Soviet trade as unimportant in mutual relations before 1931 because it was not substantial. The oscillation in attitude of the German business community toward trade relations from *hypnosis* early in 1926 to *disappointed hopes* in the winter of 1927–8, is a political fact of great importance and merits our close attention.

In the autumn of 1927, the German government initiated a conference to clarify the October 1925 economic and legal treaties with the USSR. German and Soviet delegations assembled in Berlin early in February 1928; the atmosphere bordered on hostility with the German press creating an inhospitable setting with commentaries blaming the continuing passivity in trade on Russia's failure to treat with Germany in a spirit of reciprocity.

Krämer, the spokesman for German industry in the negotiations, was more blunt. In a first plenary session he took the offensive by declaring that except for a 'small group in the iron-using industry, there is no longer any interest in the German industrial community for trade with Russia. . . .'[1] This distressing conclusion was more than a bargaining maneuver to inflate the price for further German cooperation. It reflected accurately the mood which pervaded German industry at the time, and serves as a measure of the change in psychology of German commercial circles since early 1926, when Dirksen had described them as 'hypnotized' by the dazzling prospects of the Soviet market. That transformation in mood is worth documenting.

The inflated expectations for trade with the Soviet Union that German businessmen had earlier placed in the 300-million-mark credit were soon upset. The objectives of that credit—to give Germany an advance position over rivals on the Soviet market, to ease her unemployment, and to serve as an entering wedge for her as middleman in extending the USSR's economic connections to third countries—were all thwarted. As early as August 1926,

[1] Minutes of the plenary sessions of the Russo-German economic negotiations, address by Krämer, February 15, 1928, 6698/H115218–22.

Dirksen had raised a subject that was to become familiar in subsequent commercial negotiations with Moscow. He complained about the political motives that seemed to guide the activities of Soviet purchasing agencies, reducing the role of Germany's credit to that of Russia's pace-setter. This policy, he observed, was leading to the diversion of valuable orders to France, England, and the United States.[1]

By the end of 1926 the Eastern Department recognized that Berlin's credit policy was not serving to increase German exports.[2] Equally abortive was the 'Schlesinger line' of mediating Russia's foreign economic ties because the Soviet economy had a limited capacity for foreign goods and because Moscow was unalterably opposed to anything resembling an international financial consortium.[3]

A final cause for bitterness in commercial circles was the striking contrast between the treatment of Soviet economic and trade agencies in Germany and that of German business enterprises in the USSR. German businessmen and *Reichsdeutsche* in the USSR

[1] Notes by Dirksen for conversation between Schubert and Litvinov, August 5, 1926, 6698/H110877–80; Memorandum by Schubert regarding conversation with Litvinov, August 5, 1926, 4562/E157790–801.

[2] Stresemann to the Minister of Finance and the Minister of Labor, December 30, 1926, 2860/D558278–83.

[3] As early as May 1927 the Eastern Department had come to the conclusion that the British and Americans were not inclined 'to work together with the Germans in their business dealings with Russia' (Unsigned memorandum regarding a conference of Köpke, Wallroth, de Haas, Schlesinger, May 16, 1927, 5462/E380381–4). In the subsequent period attention concentrated more on France, from where an initiative for the joint financing of trade to the Soviet Union had come in early 1928. The French aired the idea publicly and the Soviets responded that such efforts were part of a plan to encircle Russia economically (Schlesinger to Hilger, January 28, 1928, 4829/E242600–2). Rantzau warned of the obstacles in the path of joint Franco-German economic cooperation (Rantzau to Schubert, February 22, 1928, L356/L107560–1). In view of Soviet reservations the Wilhelmstrasse, which was favorably disposed to the French plan, decided to let negotiations with Paris develop on a non-governmental level and only step in later with a credit guarantee. Consultations commenced between German industrialists such as Otto Wolff, and French leaders such as Briand, Berthelot, and Clémentel. (Unsigned memorandum concerning the history of efforts to cooperate economically with France in the Soviet market, March 22, 1928, 6698/K109288–92). They seem to have continued intermittently into 1929, though without success, for by that time Russo-French relations were declining rapidly (Memorandum regarding a conference of Trautmann, Dirksen, Bülow, etc., March 22, 1929, 6698/H109295–8).

found that the increasing centralization of the Soviet economy was drastically limiting the range of economic activities in which they might engage. In Germany, on the other hand, Soviet agencies continued to expand their operations on terms of equality with local enterprises.[1] The lesson from this situation was that the principle of 'equal-treatment-between-foreigners-and-nationals (*Inländergleichbehandlung*)', that lay at the base of the October agreements, was badly suited to establish reciprocity in the relations between a reasonably permissive economy and a centralized command economy.

In 1927 the Soviet Union's increasing economic and political isolation tempted her leaders to make political use of their limited financial and trade resources to buy off Britain and entice the United States. After the Anglo-Soviet rupture the German Embassy in Moscow reported that a secret Soviet directive had been sent to Soviet purchasing agencies late in April, instructing them to divert their principal orders for machines and other producer goods from Germany to other industrial countries. This action was believed to be designed to win British industry for a pro-Soviet policy and to elicit further credits from Germany;[2] this interpretation was supported by independent observations of the Eastern Department.[3]

In 1927 the crisis in Anglo-Soviet relations followed by the war scare of the summer further complicated trade and financial relations. By then, German industrial leaders and Foreign Ministry officials were agreed that Moscow's use of trade relations as a political instrument had transformed them into a casual affair for which long-range plans could not be made. Together with the increasing precariousness of the Soviet Union's international position this appraisal prompted a resolution of the German cabinet (June 9) that 'the Reich guarantee for deliveries to Russia is not to be expanded beyond the limits (*Risiko*) set down in earlier resolutions'. For Wilhelmstrasse officials this measure had the unwelcome political consequence of making German industrial circles

[1] Schlesinger to Gaus, December 28, 1926, 4829/E242450–5.

[2] Memorandum by Hey: 'Gegen Deutschland gerichtete Geheimdirektiven über Erteilung von Auslandsaufträgen. Englische Kreditangebote', May 19, 1927, Embassy Moscow: Department D, Special Folder (not filmed).

[3] Dirksen to Embassy Moscow, June 24, 1927, Embassy Moscow: Department D, Special Folder (not filmed).

more reluctant to grant further credits to the USSR. Concerned that political relations not be damaged, the Foreign Ministry tried to inhibit this development by encouraging German businessmen 'not to leave the field of Russian business prematurely. . . .'[1]

Rantzau repeatedly brought the complaints of Germany's trade leaders to the attention of the Soviet government, warning that the diversion of trade to England and the United States stood 'in sharp contradiction to the spirit of Russo-German relations'. Cautiously he hinted that as a countermeasure Germany might abrogate the economic agreements.[2] Almost invariably Soviet officials bluntly denied German charges, but occasionally they were candid enough to admit that the Soviet Union, lying under a desperate political necessity, must try everything 'to prevent a worsening of relations through economic concessions to England'.[3]

As the summer lengthened into fall and the 'war scare' in the Soviet Union failed to abate, Narkomindel officials finally began to show concern over the German business community's growing reserve toward the *Russengeschäft*. In September Bratman-Brodovskii asked Wallroth whether treatment by the Soviet press of the danger of foreign encirclement was still agitating German businessmen. On receiving an affirmative answer he replied fatalistically that this would then have to be the economic price of keeping Russia's fighting spirit alive.[4]

In this setting Stresemann was asked by the *Reichsverband der deutschen Industrie* to initiate a conference with Soviet officials so as to clarify the provisions of the 1925 economic and trade agreements. In a letter to Rantzau the Foreign Minister requested that the subject be broached to the Narkomindel; at the same time he expressed a feeling of disquiet that economic matters might soon have unwelcome consequences for political relations. Contrary to the impression occasionally aroused by Stresemann's conversations with Briand and Chamberlain—that his chief interest in the Soviet connection lay in trade relations—these negotiations again demonstrated that he was primarily concerned that estrangement over trade matters not spill over into the political field.

[1] Dirksen to Embassy Moscow, June 24, 1927, Embassy Moscow: Department D, Special Folder (not filmed).

[2] Rantzau to Stresemann, November 10, 1927, 2860/D559103–5.

[3] Ibid.

[4] Memorandum by Wallroth, September 26, 1927, 5265/E317519–24.

To inhibit such a development he suggested that the proposed talks pursue the goal of establishing mutuality in trade and economic contacts; it was necessary to counter the growing disillusionment that threatened a 'withdrawal of German business from Soviet Russia. . . .'[1] Rantzau agreed that the hesitancy of German finance to extend new credits to the Soviet Union might inimically affect political ties,[2] a view confirmed in late autumn by articles in the German press combining questions about the solvency of the Soviet economy with attacks on the Soviet Union.[3]

The subsequent negotiations (which began in January 1928, were interrupted by the Shakhty trial, later resumed and concluded in December) were approached by the two sides with incongruent objectives and bargaining styles. They were important—indeed of a pioneering nature—because they were to interpret the treaties of October 1925, which had served as the 'first encompassing attempt to regulate the entire economic life between Soviet Russia and a differently organized country'.[4] For that reason the Soviet government could not risk their failure, at least openly. Publicity was therefore avoided by representing the talks as part of a continuing series to iron out minor problems that had arisen in the course of everyday business.

Above all the Soviet negotiators wanted to avoid an open debate about the bases of the October agreements: Germany's recognition of the foreign trade monopoly, and the key principles of 'most-favored-nation treatment' and 'equal-treatment-between-foreigners-and-nationals (*Inländergleichbehandlung*)'. In this way established positions were to be defended. Moreover, the Soviet Union's shaky credit and precarious international situation dictated a muffling of the theme of 'disappointed hopes', which German industry was sure to develop. It was necessary in such uncertain times to bluff, to conceal the slack in German-Soviet cooperation.

Finally, the Soviets were out to gain as far-reaching credit concessions as their weak bargaining position would permit. Given the Soviet Union's shaky economic position, the credit question was the key to her approach. Moscow's tactic was to insist that action

[1] Stresemann to Rantzau, October 22, 1927, 6698/H115089–92.

[2] Hencke to Schlesinger, October 14, 1927, 4829/E242580–3.

[3] Rantzau to Stresemann, November 10, 1927, 2860/D559103–5.

[4] Wallroth to Reichstag, first reading of bill to approve agreements of October 12, 1925: December 1, 1925, 5265/E316831–41.

on German complaints depended on the prior satisfaction of Soviet credit demands. This was made clear in pre-conference discussions a week before the plenary negotiations by a high-powered Soviet delegation headed by the President of the State Bank, Sheinman, and the Commissar of Transportation, Rudsutak.

On February 6, the Soviet negotiators sought to entice their German counterparts, Stresemann, Schubert, and the German Economics Minister, Curtius, with a statement about the scintillating prospects of the 'Soviet market'. Orders to a limit of 600 million marks would be placed in Germany in the next two years, Rudsutak announced, if Soviet demands were met: a trade credit of 600 million marks on terms better than those of the 300-million credit; a long-term financial credit of unspecified value; and the right to list Soviet bonds on the German stock exchange.[1]

These conditions evoked a surprised and largely negative reaction from Stresemann, who countered with a list of Germany's complaints regarding the failure of the 300-million credit to increase German-Soviet trade. A consideration of such questions, he insisted, would have to precede discussion of new credits. Rudsutak dismissed the German gravamina as 'technical questions' which would 'solve themselves' when credits were granted. Finally, he concluded with the threat that credit concessions were 'now even more urgent because Russia had arrived at a crossroads in her relations with various countries. Her relations with these countries would depend largely upon how Germany reacted to the Russian suggestions. The question was, could Russia or could she not depend on German help.'[2] Since the Soviet negotiators did not possess the alternatives to give this statement meaning, the German delegation correctly interpreted it as bluster, and did not respond. The 'hypnosis' of 1926 had obviously given way to a healthy skepticism.

In the subsequent negotiations (the Soviets had no choice but to agree to German priorities)[3] it became evident that the niggardly

[1] Memorandum by Wallroth regarding a conference between Stresemann, Curtius, Schubert, Posse, Schäffer, Wallroth, on the German side, and Rudsutak, Sheinman, Krestinskii and Bratman-Brodovskii on the Soviet side, February 6, 1928, 4484/E096961-9. [2] Ibid.

[3] In the meantime the Soviet government apparently was informed of the rejection of its request for a financial credit and the right to list bonds in Germany. Consideration of a trade credit would depend on the creation of suitable 'psychological conditions' in the negotiations (Notes by

'technical questions', referred to by Rudsutak, were considered to be of a fundamental character by the German negotiators. German specialists ascribed many of the difficulties in economic and trade relations with the Soviet Union to the transformation of Soviet economic and social policy which was accompanying the dismantling of the NEP. The implicit assumption on which the October treaties rested, they argued, was that the NEP represented a long-range policy that would gradually lead to a relaxation of the foreign trade monopoly.[1]

The conclusion reached in a report of the Eastern Department was that the principles underlying the October agreements were viable in business relations between states with similar economic and social systems but could no longer adequately regulate economic intercourse with the USSR.[2] Since these principles could not, however, be excised from the existing agreement without jeopardizing political ties (the most-favored-nation principle, for instance, was anchored in the Rapallo treaty) it was decided to seek parity in economic and trade relations without altering the treaty base. The Soviets were to recognize that German business interests would not further tolerate the imbalance of concession without counterconcession (*Leistung ohne Gegenleistung*).

The opening address of Wallroth, head of the German delegation, lacked nothing in dismal precision regarding 'the undeniably deeply rooted disappointment of German business concerning the form taken by Russo-German economic relations. . . .'[3] He developed the theme of 'disappointed hopes' in terms of two subjects – 'imparity' and 'purchasing policy'.[4] The basic cause of the imparity in economic relations, Wallroth began, was the arbitrary functioning of the foreign trade monopoly and the unconscionable application by Soviet agencies of the principles of 'most-favored-

Dirksen for a conversation between Curtius and Sheinman, February 14, 1928, 5265/E317783–5).

[1] Germany, *Reichstag Debates*, Session 128 (December 1, 1925), 4669–91.

[2] Memorandum by Hahn, January 12, 1928, 6698/H115102–4.

[3] Minutes of the plenary sessions of the Russo-German economic negotiations, opening address by Wallroth, February 13, 1928, 6698/H115144–62. Cf. *Ekonomicheskaia Zhizn'*, February 18, 1928.

[4] Ibid.; Memorandum by Wallroth listing German complaints under the headings '*Bestellungspolitik*' and '*Imparität*', February 6, 1928, 4484/E096936–9.

nation treatment' and 'equal-treatment-between-foreigners-and-nationals (*Inländergleichbehandlung*)'. A variety of international agreements had granted foreign enterprises and individual foreigners in Germany those rights enjoyed by German individuals and firms to carry on trade and engage in a craft or profession.

The Soviet government, however, had used its trade monopoly to exploit them to its one-sided advantage. The freedom to carry on business operations had been used by the foreign trade monopoly to cover Germany with a closely woven net of trade and economic organizations that had almost excluded German middlemen from participation in Soviet business activities in Germany. Germany's shipping to the Soviet Union was being strangled, her forwarding agencies were being edged out, and the Soviet insurance monopoly was expanding its operations to every corner of Germany. By playing off one firm against another the Soviet trade monopoly had also developed a bargaining style that was causing ill-feeling among German business interests.

In the Soviet Union, on the other hand, Wallroth continued, German commerce was being crippled by restrictive legislation and the growth of state enterprises. Freedom to trade stopped at the Soviet border, while questions of entry and residence were made extraordinarily complex. Finally, the principle of 'most-favored-nation treatment', which accorded German firms those rights enjoyed by foreign enterprises and Soviet citizens, was empty of meaning in an economy monopolized by the state. The anticipation of this problem, Wallroth added, had led German negotiators in 1925 to ask for treaties based on the principle of 'reciprocity'. They had finally agreed to Soviet terms only for political reasons and in the hope that the NEP would gradually lead to a 'lessening of the contradictions [between the two systems]'.[1]

This analysis of the differential effect of the 1925 treaties on German and Soviet interests brought Wallroth to his first conclusion. In future, he warned, the question for Soviet leaders should be less whether they were entitled in international law to continue as before than if it was prudent for them to make unrestrained use of their juridical freedom. *Summa jus* was *summa injuria*. His delegation wanted only to forestall a rupture in com-

[1] Minutes of the plenary sessions of the Russo-German economic negotiations, opening address by Wallroth, February 13, 1928, 6698/H115144–62.

mercial relations; it did not ask the Soviet government to abandon its economic principles but only to modify them so as to re-establish mutuality in economic relations.

In treating the subject of imparity Wallroth only charged that the October treaties had been perverted by an overloading of their basic principles. But when he dealt with the more concrete matter of the hiatus in trade contacts he alleged a Soviet violation of key provisions of the trade treaty. He denied the claim made by the Soviet propaganda organs that trade with Germany had flourished by establishing the miniscule extent of that trade: 15 percent of pre-war trade, little more than Germany's exports to remote and colonial India, and much less than Germany's exports to Denmark, Sweden, Czechoslovakia, Switzerland, and Poland.[1]

He then documented a Soviet violation of every provision of Article 1 of the trade treaty, which read:

> The contracting parties undertake to promote mutual trade relations in every possible way, to achieve stability in the volume of trade, and, in proportion to the economic recovery of both countries, raise mutual imports and exports to the percentual pre-war levels. In this endeavor they will be led by economic considerations.[2]

A Soviet effort to foster trade, he said, had not been made; trade contacts remained chronically unstable; Germany's pre-war percentual share of Soviet imports had not been reached; and political not economic considerations were determining Soviet purchasing policies. In 1926, Germany had accounted for only 24·2 percent of Russia's total imports, barely half of Germany's pre-war percentual share, which had hovered around 47 percent to 50 percent of a much larger total. In contrast, Britain's share had risen from a pre-war 12·6 percent to 18·2 percent in 1926, while America's share had climbed even more steeply from 5·8 percent before the war to 20·8 percent in 1926. What made the situation particularly distressing for Germany was that her large credit of 1926 had not thus far shown an 'additional effect'. Was it economically sound or politically wise to treat a proven friend in so cavalier a manner, Wallroth concluded.[3]

[1] Ibid.

[2] Cited in unsigned memorandum regarding the Russo-German treaties of October 21, 1925, March 22, 1926, 5265/E317091–102.

[3] Minutes of the plenary sessions of the Russo-German economic

Consistent with their purpose of adhering to an achieved position which served as a model for contacts with other states, the Soviet negotiators refused to consider the subject of 'imparity' in a manner that could restrict the working of the most-favored-nation principle.[1] This was a highly political question that he was not empowered to discuss, Shliefer, head of the Soviet delegation, maintained. And in any case the Soviet Union could never accept a treaty based on 'reciprocity' because it would result in a penetration of her economy by capitalist forms of business; it would set her back a hundred years in the regulation of her foreign economic contacts. Only one question was therefore pertinent: had the Soviet government violated the most-favored-nation principle? Since this had not been charged he considered the first part of the discussion ended.[2]

But Shliefer was prepared to debate trade relations (i.e. the question of Soviet purchasing policy) in greater detail. He skirted around the German accusation about the political motives behind the USSR's purchasing policy and concentrated on trade statistics. Shliefer suggested that a study of the figures for orders rather than delivery figures would show that Germany's trade with the USSR was continuing to edge upwards despite German claims to the contrary. He also rejected the interpretation that Germany's credit of 1926 had been proferred in charity and not self-interest to ease domestic unemployment. In conclusion he characterized the depressed tone of Wallroth's address as typical of a small sector of German industry whose ill-humor derived from minor incidents and passing dislocations.

This claim was promptly refuted by Krämer, the spokesman for German industry.[3] On this strained note the plenary sessions ended

negotiations, opening address by Wallroth, February 13, 1928, 6698/H115144–62.

[1] The Soviet bargaining position was anticipated by *Izvestiia* on February 9, 1928, in a programmatic article by Gorkin, entitled 'Soviet Russian-German Economic Relations'.

[2] Minutes of the plenary sessions of the Russo-German economic negotiations, opening address by Shliefer, February 14, 1928, 6698/H115177–91. In a private letter to Paul Scheffer, Schlesinger described Soviet behavior: 'In response to each of our ever so modest demands a cynical smirk and the answer: "the system" ' (Briefwechsel Schlesinger–Scheffer).

[3] Minutes of the plenary sessions of the Russo-German economic negotiations, address by Krämer, February 15, 1928, 6698/H115218–22.

and the detailed negotiations in committee began. It would go beyond the scope of this study to detail them. Suffice it to note that the mood of frustration and hostility evident in the plenary sessions did not abate in the subsequent committee debates, which were suddenly interrupted by the Shakhty trial.

German businessmen continued to view the stagnation in mutual trade as the result of Soviet ordering policies which discriminated in favor of Britain and the United States, countries that not only offered the Soviet Union less generous trade terms than Germany, but did not even maintain diplomatic relations with her. The defensive strategem of Soviet leaders in using their limited trade capacity to better their position with the most hostile of their antagonists was understandable. But recognition of this fact did not soothe ruffled feelings among German commercial leaders or weaken their resolve to use the next affront from Moscow to place an ultimatum before the Soviet government.

4. 'NOT ONE STEP FURTHER'

AGAINST this background the arrest on March 7, 1928, of five German engineers on charges of sabotage, industrial espionage, and collaboration with the former owners of the Donetz coal mines, must be considered less the cause than the occasion of the political crisis that ensued.[1] Some fifty Soviet engineers and technicians were arrested with the Germans on similar charges. This set the stage for one of the noisiest and most disastrous of the show-trials of the early period of Soviet industrialization. The Supreme Court of the USSR underlined the public nature of the affair by issuing an indictment charging the existence of an extensive anti-Soviet 'economic counter-revolutionary conspiracy' with a foreign center, and the collaboration between this center and 'individual agents of German firms'.[2] Without awaiting the verdict of the courts Rykov then declared that he regarded the guilt of the

[1] Hilger and Meyer, op. cit., 217–22; Fischer, op. cit., II, 772–4; Herbert Helbig, *Die Träger der Rapallo-Politik*, 200–1; Kurt Rosenbaum, 'The German Involvement in the Shakhty Trial', *Russian Review*, XXI (July 1962), 238–60. It is noteworthy that neither V. B. Ushakov, *Vneshniaia politika Germanii v period Veimarskoi Respubliki* (Moscow: IMO, 1958), nor F. D. Volkov, *Anglo-sovetskie otnosheniia 1924–1928 gg.* (Moscow: Gospolitizdat, 1958), make mention of the incident.

[2] *Pravda*, March 9, 1928.

accused as proven.[1] The Soviet press fell into this pattern with a strident attack on the good faith of German industry.[2] Thus the trial was given a highly political tone and transformed into a question of prestige for the German government.

Rantzau as well as German industrial and financial leaders saw the provocative nature of the incident as confirming the trend in Soviet policy that they had abstracted from previous developments. For that reason they became steeled in their individual resolves to achieve a squaring of accounts. In a report to Stresemann one day before the arrests Rantzau noted that the economic negotiations were exacerbating tensions that had been present since the incidents involving Hölz and Voroshilov.[3] Subsequently he described the Shakhty episode as a further step in the same process in which revolutionary were replacing *realpolitische* considerations as determinants of Soviet policy. He wired Stresemann indignantly: 'These eternally conceited and brazen elements in the Communist Party and the Comintern have, since they escaped so lightly in the Hölz case, now become cockier than ever. They think that they can now take any liberties at our expense that they wish. A lesson at the proper time would probably have brought them to their senses.' The incident had vastly increased the dangers to Germany's general position; Moscow's diplomatic corps, he reported, showed malicious pleasure, spreading the view that Germany's demure acceptance of the provocation would mean that she was linked to Moscow 'for better or for worse . . . and therefore had to accept everything passively, or that [she] did not possess the strength to defend [herself] against such behavior'.[4]

But there was no reason for Rantzau to fear that his colleagues in Berlin would again refrain from parrying Soviet blows as they had in October and November of 1927. Unlike the Hölz incident, the Shakhty case was of such a character as to elicit the broadest possible German response. Widely publicized by the Soviet press and involving powerful persons in German industry (some of whom, such as Felix Deutsch, President of AEG, had always favored close ties with the east), it aroused a sharp reaction in Germany. After the arrests Stresemann reported a 'feeling of

[1] Stresemann to Rantzau, March 15, 1928, 5265/E319203–5.

[2] Hilger and Meyer, op. cit., 218.

[3] Rantzau to Stresemann, March 6, 1928, 2860/D559468–70.

[4] Rantzau to Stresemann, March 16, 1928, 2860/D559755–6.

indignation' sweeping over German public opinion and business circles.[1] In the Reichstag, all parties, with the exception of the Communist, expressed strong doubts about the possibility of continuing economic cooperation with the Soviet Union.[2]

Buoyed up by this solid domestic support Stresemann moved to demonstrate Germany's anger by abruptly interrupting the economic negotiations in Berlin.[3] In addition, German industry, led by the AEG (the firm whose employees were most directly involved), announced in a first flush of indignation that all German technicians in the Soviet Union would be recalled.[4] A solid front thus emerged, apparently under government control. Soon, however, ranks were broken as circles in Germany began pressing for an abrogation of the Rapallo and Berlin treaties.[5]

Although the Foreign Ministry was eager to make a 'cleansing crisis' of the provocation, which would startle the Soviet hierarchy, strengthen the right wing in Soviet politics, and reestablish a modicum of equality in political and economic relations, talk of a rupture was deemed hazardous to German policy. Since that policy was soon to be exposed to a prolonged season of bargaining with the western powers it needed the link with Moscow as further support. In the Foreign Affairs Committee of the Reichstag Stresemann tried therefore to moderate the impatience of the political parties, stressing that the Rapallo connection was still essential to Germany's purposes and must be maintained unless Moscow remained adamant.[6] The onus was now on Soviet leaders to demonstrate their wish for a further association with Germany by liquidating the crisis.

The Foreign Ministry pursued two objectives in its interminable

[1] Stresemann to Rantzau, March 16, 1928, 5265/E319198–202.

[2] Memorandum regarding a session of the Foreign Affairs Committee of the Reichstag, March 21, 1928, L617/L195160–1.

[3] Stresemann to Rantzau regarding conversation with Litvinov, March 15, 1928, 5265/E319203–5.

[4] Hilger and Meyer, op. cit., 221.

[5] Rantzau to the Foreign Ministry regarding German press treatment of the Shakhty case, March 18, 1928, 2860/D559765–8; article by Rheinbaben, close friend of Stresemann, in *Europäische Gespräche*, July 1928, cited in Fischer, op. cit., II, 773.

[6] Notes by Dirksen for a speech by Stresemann to the Foreign Affairs Committee of the Reichstag on March 21, 1928. March 20, 1928, 5265/E319195–7.

pourparlers with Moscow that continued until the conclusion of the Shakhty trial early in July. First of all, German interests required an exoneration of the imprisoned German engineers and a clearing of the names of the German firms that had been dragged into the trial. To this end Rantzau applied considerable pressure on the Narkomindel. He showed lively interest in the case by attending the trial and repeatedly warning that a verdict of guilty would evoke in Germany a hue and cry that would bar further collaboration.[1]

His efforts were fruitfully augmented by the diplomacy of the Lithuanian Minister to Moscow, who served as spokesman for the Baltic states. A negative outcome to the Shakhty case, he felt, would disturb relations in eastern Europe by driving a wedge between Berlin and Moscow. So as to forestall this development he undertook an important *démarche* with Stomoniakov, a leading member of the Narkomindel, warning that the great powers would terminate their contacts with Russia if Germany concluded that collaboration with her had become too difficult. In that event, he noted, the border states would also be cut adrift. Previously they had been drawn to the Russo-German combination because they recognized in it a stabilizing factor for Soviet policy. If that partnership were to crumble 'the small powers would be compelled to throw themselves at the mercy of the west'. At this point a flustered Stomoniakov was said to have blurted out that the Foreign Commissariat was aware of the potentially grave implications of the situation but had only marginal influence on the chauvinists who were now forming policy.[2]

Such representations seem nevertheless to have had some effect. The first sign of a change took the form of a speech by Kalinin, the Soviet President, on June 2, in which he opened a path for an orderly retreat with a long statement containing the key words: 'we do not wish to discredit German industry for we value it very highly', and 'only three people stand accused'.[3] A month later the verdict was announced. Of the three Germans who had been tried

[1] Rantzau to Foreign Ministry regarding conversation with Shtein, June 22, 1928, 2860/D559575–80; Rantzau to Foreign Ministry, June 30, 1928, 2860/D559586–9; Rantzau to Foreign Ministry regarding conversation with Stomoniakov, July 3, 1928, 2860/D559592–5.

[2] Rantzau to Foreign Ministry regarding conversation with the Lithuanian Minister, Baltrusihaitis, May 22, 1928, 2860/D559935–9.

[3] *Izvestiia*, June 2, 8, 1928; Rantzau to Foreign Ministry, June 2, 1928, 2860/D559546–7.

– two others had already been freed – two were acquitted, and the third was given a one-year sentence and then released.[1] Moscow had accepted the hard truth that the domestic scapegoat advantages to be gained from a conviction of the German engineers were easily outweighed by the expected baneful foreign policy repercussions. The Wilhelmstrasse had fully achieved its first objective.

Its second goal, however, was more ambitious, but more ambiguous as well. Moscow was to recognize the fundamental incompatibility between one policy favoring strong ties with Germany and another that spilled over in provocations at Germany's expense. Had Germany's unyielding stand during the crisis already achieved this objective? Should more be attempted? Schlesinger for one believed so, urging the view on Hencke, Dirksen, and Rantzau, that the conclusion of the trial should be used as the occasion to talk the matter out fully with the Soviets in a 'serious, bitterly serious discussion. . . . Soviet policy is now so dishonest and mendacious that we cannot possibly get out of this blind alley unless we clarify matters for the immediate future.'[2] Matters, if allowed to drift, would entangle Germany in another cycle of incidents, similar to those that had burdened relations since late in 1927.

Dirksen, as usual, supported Schlesinger's proposal and seems to have persuaded Schubert of its widsom. Since it vindicated his own views, Rantzau eagerly concurred in Schlesinger's policy, and consented to his further proposal that the German position be detailed in an *aide-mémoire*: 'Neither for them nor for us can things continue as before.'[3] In short, the comment 'no information' would no longer serve Soviet officials as an excuse for evading fundamental issues.

Schlesinger also submitted to Dirksen the draft of such a note, composed, he said, after much reflection and in collaboration with 'our mutual friend',[4] probably Scheffer. The evidence suggests that the proposed *démarche* was undertaken, but the details cannot be established from the Wilhelmstrasse files. All we have is the record from mid-September of an angry exchange between Chicherin and Köpke in Berlin, in which the Foreign Commissar

[1] Rantzau to the Foreign Ministry, July 6, 1928, 2860/D559599–601.
[2] Schlesinger to Dirksen, July 14, 1928, 6698/H110685–7.
[3] Schlesinger to Dirksen, July 20, 1928, 6698/H110696, 97, 705, 706.
[4] Ibid.

spoke heatedly of the German 'press bandits' who had poisoned relations by their coverage of the Shakhty trial, and of the aggravation of this touchy situation by the recent 'note' from the German government.[1]

But regardless of whether Schlesinger's draft[2] formed the basis of the German representations, it serves as a convenient summary of the judgements of Wilhelmstrasse officials on the Soviet problem. On the surface the note, a trial balance of German-Soviet relations, spoke of the lessons of Shakhty, but only in order to develop two themes: *Leistung* without *Gegenleistung*, and 'cominternization'. On the one side, it alleged that Germany had served Russia well through economic concessions and unwavering political support in difficult times. In return her good faith had been questioned, her industry attacked, and her leaders slandered. Recently, moreover, the domestic problem had been raised by the encouragement from Moscow – in the Hölz and Voroshilov incidents – of conspiratorial elements in Germany.

The Soviet government, the note pointed out, stated officially that it valued collaboration with Germany in political and economic matters. Yet during the Shakhty trial Stalin had argued that help from abroad could be bought only at the prohibitive price of the USSR's transformation into a capitalist state.[3] Thus, the CPSU, the decision-making center, denied the possibility of the cooperation which the Soviet government publicly espoused. Such ambivalence, the note continued, was intolerable, and here the limits of German patience had been reached. The Soviet regime was given notice that further provocations would be apt to release forces in Germany beyond the control of the government. In concluding, Schlesinger posed the very same question that Rantzau had left open in his memorandum of the previous October: did Soviet priorities militate against collaboration of any kind?

[1] Memorandum by Köpke regarding conversation with Chicherin and Bratman-Brodovskii, September 17, 1928, K281/K097619–26.

[2] Draft by Schlesinger for note to be submitted to the Soviet government, undated, 6698/H110698–704; also 5462/E280222–8. The Geheimakten of the Eastern Department contain the draft of a telegram signed by Schubert addressed to Rantzau in Moscow instructing him to undertake a *démarche* roughly along the lines sketched by the Schlesinger draft (Draft telegram by Schubert, July, 6698/H110710–4).

[3] Extract from a report by Stalin on the Shakhty trial to a meeting of Moscow Communists, April 13, 1928, cited in Degras, op. cit., II, 300–2.

If in the meantime Soviet policy, for reasons that are unknown to the Reich government, were to proceed from the assumption that the revolutionary tendency must, or could be allowed to take precedence over the tendency towards normal relations from state to state, then this development would create an entirely new situation for the Reich government.[1]

It was this question that constituted the 'lesson' of the Shakhty episode. Long after the trial had ended what survived to bedevil German thinking was the slogan 'cominternization'. Not since the dark days of 1923 had this word crossed German lips so often. Since October 1927 Rantzau had viewed Soviet policy in these terms. But gradually his supposition became generalized in German thinking. Three developments were subsumed under one heading: the transition from NEP to the Five-Year Plan; the resolutions of the Sixth Comintern Congress (July–August)—that were thought determining for Soviet foreign policy; and recent electoral gains of the KPD in the Reichstag elections.[2] It was assumed that Soviet tactics were general and not particular and that they applied equally to domestic and to foreign affairs. There was, to be sure, a causal linkage between the Shakhty case and the Five-Year Plan, but not of the nature established by the Foreign Ministry. The proper conclusion to have drawn from both was that Soviet domestic policy was taking priority over both foreign and Comintern policy. Above all the Shakhty case was tailored for Russia's domestic needs; it was intended to demonstrate that the burdens of forced industrialization were attributable to international capitalist intrigues, and it did so at the cost of an international incident.

But amidst a medley of startlingly new developments in the Soviet Union so sophisticated a conclusion would have required extraordinary German prescience. It was therefore not surprising that the Wilhelmstrasse became ensnared in its slogans. Typical of this was an incident involving Dirksen. Sometime after the conclusion of the Shakhty trial Dirksen found himself in conversation with Boris Shtein on a train returning from Geneva. Their attention turned naturally to the recent crisis whose inflation the Soviet

[1] Draft by Schlesinger for note to be submitted to the Soviet government, undated, 6698/H110698–704.

[2] The KPD increased its number of Reichstag deputies from forty-five to fifty-four (Pinson, op. cit., 574–5).

official related to irresponsible German journalism. Dirksen, however, viewed it as a symptom: 'This general phenomenon is the ever growing interference of the tactical maneuvers of the party in Soviet policy as such; in other words, the growing influence of the Third International on foreign policy.'[1] Little did Germany's future Ambassador to the USSR realize that for the coming years not his words but Geneva would symbolize the direction of Soviet foreign policy.

5. A RECURRING HINDRANCE

ALTHOUGH most studies of the subject regard 1929 as the year in which KPD-Moscow ties reappeared for the first time after 1923 as a complicating factor in German-Soviet relations, it would seem better to begin treating the subject with the Hölz incident; this incident marked the beginning of a change in the German interpretation of Soviet policy. Since about 1924 the KPD had hardly featured in mutual relations. In 1925, for instance, the propaganda clause, which had formed an essential part of the first German-Soviet trade agreement of 1921, was included in the October agreements without any discussion. The German negotiators paid little attention to it, treating it routinely in order to avoid 'every misunderstanding'.[2] From 1925 to 1927 German protests regarding 'Comintern activity' were restricted to marginal episodes in which officers of the Third International impugned German policy. The propaganda use made of the '*Excelsior* interview' by Comintern publications was one such example.

But the public identification of Soviet leaders with the revolutionary purposes of the KPD after 1927 created a new situation. Rantzau, who reacted most strongly, went so far as to urge a general revision of military relations. He had been willing, he wrote

[1] Memorandum by Dirksen regarding conversation with Boris Shtein, July 11, 1928, K281/K097593–9. A few weeks later Dirksen expressed a similar view to Krestinskii and Litvinov (Memorandum by Dirksen, July 30, 1928, K281/K097606–15). General Blomberg in a talk with Voroshilov referred to the 'activities of the Third International' as the most immediate threat to further military collaboration (Report of Blomberg, November 17, 1928, 9480/H276183–236).

[2] Unsigned memorandum regarding the German-Soviet treaties of October 12, 1925: March 3, 1926, 5265/E317091–102.

Stresemann, to assume the foreign policy risks involved in continuing the clandestine contacts, until the

> domestic problem in Germany had been raised with such cynicism . . . by the *War Minister* of the Soviet government. For this reason I consider the situation to be incomparably more serious and a reevaluation of the entire complex of questions unavoidable, if, after the events of the last months, it will even be possible to continue collaboration in the area in question.[1]

(Stresemann's reluctance to back Rantzau as strongly as he wished led to a crisis in their personal relations that was still unresolved when Rantzau died in the autumn.)

The Ambassador's suspicion that Moscow was preparing a new revolutionary initiative for Germany was strengthened in April by a curious Soviet request that Blyukher, Moscow's ubiquitous proconsul in China in 1927, be accepted as military attaché in Berlin.[2] Reichswehr officials were apparently ready to agree, so as not to affront Voroshilov and the War Commissariat.[3] Rantzau, however, objected and the question was resolved to his satisfaction only when the Wilhelmstrasse informed the Soviet Embassy that such an appointment would 'really be very suspicious' in view of Blyukher's earlier activities as one of the 'chief propagandists and organizers of the uprising in China'.[4]

In 1927–8 German officials were still divided about the nature and gravity of a revolutionary threat. They were, however, becoming increasingly interested in the concatenation of problems of domestic security and relations with the USSR. This became evident from the treatment in Germany of Trotsky's exile. In January 1928, following Trotsky's banishment to Central Asia, Chicherin asked Rantzau to dissuade German news media from arousing sympathies for the exiled leader. The Ambassador agreed—viewed realistically, he said, a government headed by Trotsky was more dangerous for Germany than one led by Stalin[5]

[1] Draft, Rantzau to Stresemann, April 12, 1928, L337/L100723–30.

[2] Memorandum by Rantzau entitled: 'Richtlinien für Leg. Sekrt. Hencke zur Vorbesprechung im A.A.', April 23, 1928, L340/L101049–52.

[3] Memorandum by Rantzau, April 23, 1928, L340/L101048–52.

[4] Memorandum by Dirksen regarding conversation with Bratman-Brodovskii, April 23, 1928, 9480/H276341. On May 1 Blomberg agreed that Blyukher was unacceptable (Memorandum by Dirksen, 4564/E163937–40).

[5] Rantzau to Foreign Ministry, January 13, 1928, 2860/D559401–4.

—and the press was accordingly informed.[1] German reporters generally followed these guidelines, with one exception, Paul Scheffer, the knowledgeable correspondent of the *Berliner Tageblatt*. In a series of articles he described Trotsky's odyssey with passion and in great detail,[2] for which Rantzau chided him.[3]

Only Schlesinger, a Social-Democrat, considered the matter from the compelling perspective of domestic politics. His defense of Scheffer was that the exaggerated claims of the KPD could best be countered by exposing the dark flaws in the Soviet model. It would be foolish, he wrote, to 'desist from using those means which Soviet Russia offers us in again exiling Trotsky to Siberia, to show German workers the true situation in the Soviet Union'. That 'in matters of foreign policy we are all accomplices of Bolshevism, does not justify our becoming so also in domestic policy'.[4] One year later, on the eve of Trotsky's expulsion from the Soviet Union, Soviet diplomats requested that he be allowed to take up residence in Germany. The German government refused, fearful that he might imbue German Communism with a more militant spirit. Questions of domestic security were clearly beginning to take some precedence over interests of foreign policy.[5]

In 1928 resolutions of the Sixth Comintern Congress and electoral gains by the KPD were taken as evidence that Germany's social fabric and ties with Moscow were in for a period of hard testing. Accordingly the Wilhelmstrasse advised Interior officials that recent Comintern decisions would probably result in Soviet agents increasing their activities in Germany.[6] This expectation, together with the success of the KPD in increasing its representation in the Reichstag by nine deputies,[7] prompted members of the Eastern Department to explore two related questions: what reper-

[1] Schubert to Rantzau, January 16, 1928, 2860/D559405.

[2] Rantzau to Schubert, January 17, 1928, 2860/D559409–10.

[3] *Berliner Tageblatt*, January 15, 1928; Paul Scheffer, *Seven Years in Soviet Russia*, trans. A. Livingston (New York: Macmillan, 1932), 186–214. Cf. Schlesinger to Scheffer, January 21, 1928 (Schlesinger–Scheffer correspondence).

[4] Schlesinger to Hilger, January 28, 1928, 4829/E242600–2.

[5] 2860/D560141 ff.; see also Isaac Deutscher, *The Prophet Outcast* (London: Oxford University Press, 1963), 15–16.

[6] Unsigned directive of the Eastern Department, 'IV Ru 3675', to Rantzau, June 22, 1928, K281/K097580–3.

[7] Pinson, op. cit., 574–5.

cussions was the inexorable struggle against Communism in Germany likely to have on relations with Moscow? Through what measures could the Foreign Ministry aid in this struggle without impairing Germany's eastern policy? These questions were not yet acute, although, of course, they were to become explosive.

A directive to the Moscow Embassy containing these questions assumed that the material and tactical support given the KPD by Moscow was important for its growth. But it warned against making this into a monistic interpretation by explaining that the drawing power of the KPD was more directly tied to the existence of the Soviet Union as its prototype. Here was the rub. Since the elimination of the model was barred by 'general factors' and the need to continue the Rapallo line, it would have to be discredited through steps that would not have an 'undesirable influence on the foreign policy followed until now'.

One step suggested was an informational effort to counteract a situation in which Germans 'placed their votes at the disposal of the KPD because they had been led astray by the total misrepresentation of conditions in Soviet Russia'. It was proposed that the Wilhelmstrasse covertly establish an office to collect extracts from the Soviet press that reflected working conditions and living standards in the USSR, and distribute them to German news media.

The tone of this directive as well as its harmless proposal suggest that the Wilhelmstrasse officials who drafted it feared that German security agencies might demand such extreme measures to counter the influence of the KPD as to endanger the German-Soviet connection. Thus the information effort was to satisfy those groups without jeopardizing Germany's foreign policy. Within a year the problem anticipated here was to become a lively threat to the continuation of German-Soviet relations.

6. BRIDGES RESTORED

FROM February to November 1928 the Narkomindel seems to have taken seriously the possibility that the pressure of business and press opinion might compel the German government to turn its back on the USSR. The visit to Germany in April of the Russophobic British Minister Birkenhead was seen, for instance, as a renewed British effort at alliance building.[1] Stresemann's

[1] Rantzau to the Foreign Ministry, April 28, 1928, 2860/D559521.

studied failure to mention the subject of relations with the Soviet Union in a programmatic foreign policy statement was taken to mean that the 'Rapallo line was being traded in for the Locarno line'.[1] In November a similar omission in an important foreign policy address was cited by *Izvestiia* as supporting evidence that a 'western orientation was gaining ever more ground'.[2]

In addition to liquidating the Shakhty affair as efficiently as possible, one tactic used by Soviet officials to check the alleged 'drift' in German policy was to celebrate the 'fiasco of the Locarno policy'[3] in the areas of reparations, disarmament and the question of the evacuation of the Rhineland. This was to document a continued need for the line to Moscow. And though rankling for the Wilhelmstrasse, this approach was not ineffective because it supported the contention of growing numbers of Germans that Locarno was in bankruptcy.

A typical Soviet appeal was an *Izvestiia* article dealing with the questions of disarmament and, obliquely, Poland. In anticipation of the slogan 'appetite grows on feeding', it was maintained that German concessions to the west led down the one-way street to further exactions. Stresemann's calculation at Locarno that concessions to France would open the way to the east (Poland) had proved illusory; and Germany's entry into the League had gotten for her only the bitter fruit of setbacks in the disarmament question.[4] Some months later these arguments were reiterated with an apt sense of timing on the occasion of the tenth anniversary of the Versailles treaty:

> . . . in the tenth year of its existence Versailles remains in power. The western policy of Germany has not opened any possibilities for overcoming the Versailles system. For that reason the importance of Germany's eastern policy, her friendly relations with the Soviet Union, is enhanced. The development of relations with the Soviet Union is the only area of Germany's foreign policy that opens political as well as economic possibilities for her. German interests indicate that German

---

[1] German consulate in Kharkov to the Foreign Ministry, April 10, 1928, L622 (not filmed).

[2] *Izvestiia*, November 28, 1928.

[3] For examples of the use of this phrase see: *Ekonomitcheskaia Zhizn'*, September 14, 1928; *Pravda*, September 19; *Rabochaia Gazeta*, September 19, 1928.

[4] *Izvestiia*, April 3, 1928.

politicians recognize the necessity to treat this problem soberly. For our part, we would warmly welcome such treatment of the question from the German side; it would give both sides, to their mutual advantage, the possibility of moving from general statements to practical measures.[1]

By the summer of 1928 Soviet officials realized that honeyed words like these about shared interests would not suffice to restore the weakened bridges between Berlin and Moscow. More positive and more concrete measures were needed. And the first need was to assure that the maligned Social Democrats (who in May 1928 were to enter a coalition government for the first time since 1923 and provide its Chancellor in the person of Hermann Müller) would continue previous German foreign policy.

A government led by a Social Democrat was cause for real concern. Since Versailles the SPD had pleaded for a western orientation, had been unremitting in its attack on the KPD, and had seized the initiative in demanding a disengagement from the Red Army. To establish a claim of leadership in the German working class it had refuted the counter claim of the KPD by denying the legitimacy of Soviet Russia as Germany's model. Partly for this reason the SPD's press had consistently denounced domestic Soviet developments more vociferously than bourgeois papers. During the Shakhty trial *Pravda* was correct in noting that *Vorwärts* had heaped greater abuse on the Soviet Union in covering the event than the rest of the German press.[2] Consequently with the imminent assumption of governmental responsibilities by the Social Democrats, Soviet policy makers were anxious that their military and diplomatic bonds with Germany be separated from the increasingly acrimonious struggle between the SPD and the KPD.

The attempt to do this took the form of an important, obviously official, and rather cryptic *Izvestiia* editorial, which appeared eleven days before the SPD was scheduled to enter the government; the editorial spoke of Social Democracy's accession to power as marking a 'new stage' in mutual relations.[3] The previous six years of cooperation, it observed, had brought advantages to both sides because it had been based on shared interests that would also persist in the future. The Soviet government hoped that bonds with

[1] *Izvestiia*, July 11, 1928.

[2] *Pravda*, March 18, 1928.

[3] *Izvestiia*, June 17, 1928.

Germany could be strengthened during this second stage, perhaps by means of a new treaty.

The proposal for a new treaty, contained in a key passage that must be considered an official Soviet initiative,[1] read: 'The Soviet government and public believe that the treaties linking Germany and the Soviet Union are, to be sure, necessary but not sufficient for the next stage in German-Soviet relations.' The intention of this remark is difficult to establish because it was not followed by a diplomatic initiative, nor attended to in consultations in Berlin. Perhaps the Soviet government was hoping for a cheap international success that another agreement with Germany over peripheral matters would represent. Another possibility is that Soviet officials had concluded from the disastrous course of the economic negotiations in February and March that only a renegotiation of the principles of the 1925 economic and trade agreements could revivify the bond with Berlin.

A final explanation is suggested by a conversation in the summer of 1928 between General Blomberg, the *Chef des Truppenamts*, and Commissar of War Voroshilov. In it the latter was reported to have proposed a kind of defensive alliance against Poland: 'Not only in the name of the Red Army, but also in the name of the government of the Soviet Union, I wish to declare that in the case of a Polish attack on Germany, Russia is ready for every assistance. In the event of a Polish attack could the Soviet Union count on Germany?'[2] Blomberg declined to answer this question on the grounds that he was not competent to deal with such a highly political matter. And because the Wilhelmstrasse, as far as we know, did not respond, the riddle of the *Izvestiia* editorial of June 17 remains. But whatever its specific objectives, it succeeded in documenting Russia's will to continue collaboration with an SPD-led Germany. Perhaps that was its whole purpose.

The editorial found a broad echo in the German press, which augured well for the future. Papers close to the Wilhelmstrasse like the *Kölnische Zeitung* and the *Berliner Tageblatt* reaffirmed Stresemann's program of Germany maintaining a balance in her contacts

[1] *Kölnische Zeitung*, June 18, 1928; *Berliner Tageblatt*, June 18, 1928; *Deutsche Tageszeitung*, June 18, 1928.

[2] Report by Blomberg entitled: 'Reise des Chefs des Truppenamts nach Russland, August/September 1928', November 17, 1928, 9480/H276183–236.

to the east and west; they also pleaded that the internecine war within the socialist world be kept separate from relations with Moscow.[1] *Vorwärts* and *Germania*, the two newspapers representing the leading parties of the new coalition, also responded positively, but with reservations. The Center organ *Germania* welcomed the idea of reviving relations but warned that it not be at the expense of Poland—ties with Russia were valuable for their own sake.[2] The reply of *Vorwärts* similarly mirrored the peculiarities of the SPD position—at war domestically with the KPD and yet in need of Soviet support for the achievement of Germany's foreign policy goals. The SPD, it affirmed, wanted to continue Germany's neutral foreign policy but would have to take defensive measures if the KPD continued to represent Soviet Russia as the 'motherland of Socialism'.[3]

Despite this slightly jarring note, a political consensus had emerged favoring an end to the passivity in relations with Moscow. That Germany ought to preface important negotiations in the west with a demonstration of the vigor of her eastern connection had become a deeply rooted Wilhelmstrasse belief. Stresemann had elevated the technique of doing this into an art. In the coming winter, with a new season of bargaining over reparations and the Rhineland in the offing, the Foreign Ministry was determined to lead from a strongly buttressed position. (Some observers like Schlesinger noted that a predilection for quick successes at specified times led to needless concessions to the Soviets; the result was a momentary tactical advantage in the west, but a long-term disadvantage in the east.) For its part the Soviet government shared the eagerness of the Wilhelmstrasse to accent the USSR's limited maneuverability by again advertising the 'spirit of Rapallo'.

Consequently from July 1928 until the spring of 1929 the trend in German-Soviet relations was generally upwards. This upturn has led one historian to the erroneous opinion that this marked the 'heyday' of mutual cooperation in the 1920s.[4] It was much less than that, but it did mark an improvement. The period was heralded, as we have noted, by three events: tactical cooperation between Litvinov and Bernstorff at Geneva, the admission (implicit

[1] *Kölnische Zeitung*, June 18, 1928; *Berliner Tageblatt*, June 18, 1928.

[2] *Germania*, 'Ein "Silberstreifen" am deutschen-russischen Horizont', June 23, 1928.

[3] *Vorwärts*, June 19, 1928.

[4] Kochan, op. cit., 120–37.

in the release of the accused Germans) that the Shakhty episode had been a grave political error, and Russia's adherence to the Kellogg pact through German mediation. On his deathbed even Rantzau, who had become disillusioned about working with the USSR, contributed to the relaxation by dictating a note to Chicherin appealing for a strengthening of Rapallo.[1] In this same key were the orations at his funeral and the subsequent press commentaries in Moscow and Berlin.[2] These were straws in the wind.

The liquidation of the Shakhty affair also paved the way for intensified military collaboration. Indeed the expectation of this result, i.e. military considerations, may have weighed heavily in the Soviet decision to exonerate the German firms. Soviet officials may, for instance, have been familiar with Rantzau's repeated demands for a military disengagement following the incidents involving Voroshilov, Hölz, and the German engineers at Shakhty; in addition they may have sensed the studied reluctance of the Foreign Ministry to approve the sending of German personnel to the airdrome at Lipetsk, a decision repeatedly postponed during the months March–June. In mid-June Schubert confessed to Blomberg and Major Behschnitt that he had grave reservations about the wisdom of further activating the air base because recent Soviet behavior would prevent a maintenance of the formerly close ties with Moscow.[3]

This mood in Wilhelmstrasse circles changed only after the Soviet government had indicated a favorable resolution of the incident. On June 29 Dirksen bore witness to this change when he informed Reichswehr representatives that they could now make their plans on the assumption that relations with the Soviet Union would remain stable during the coming years. This prediction, he added, was based on his own belief that the new SPD-led govern-

[1] Helbig, op. cit., 148.

[2] Hey to Foreign Ministry, December 12, 1928, 2860/D559686.

[3] Memorandum of conference of Schubert, Köpke, Blomberg, Behschnitt, June 14, 1928, 9480/H276283–6. For discussions about the sending of personnel to Lipetsk see: Schubert regarding talk with Blomberg, December 29, 1927, 4564/E163921–3; Schubert regarding talk of Stresemann with Gessler and Blomberg, February 6, 1928, 4564/E163924–925; Schubert regarding talk with Behschnitt, April 19, 1928, 4564/E163930–1; Dirksen regarding talk with Blomberg and others, May 1, 1928, 4564/E163937–40.

ment would continue former policies.[1] On that same day the new Chancellor, Hermann Müller, gave an earnest of this intention by approving the long-standing Reichswehr request for the dispatch of forty-three pilots to Lipetsk for training.[2]

Military relations now developed without hindrance as the training and testing stations were gradually brought into full operation and the contacts between the two military commands grew more intimate. This trend was amply illustrated in the autumn of 1928 by a visit to Russia of a military mission headed by General Blomberg, head of the Truppenamt. Both during an inspection tour of the German stations and at the autumn exercises of the Red Army the German visitors were solicitously received by their Soviet hosts. Voroshilov, it was reported, had given instructions that nothing was to be concealed from the guests; and little was, to gather from the detailed fifty-four-page report in which Blomberg summed up his impressions.[3]

The German general characterized the Red Army as a distinguished force, tightly-knit, still technically deficient, but in the process of systematic modernization under the command of superior men. These leaders, he wrote, 'recognize their objectives and are pursuing them assiduously. . . . A further strengthening is to be expected.' Moreover, they recognized that close ties with the Reichswehr were essential to their rearmament program. Thus conditions for the further undisturbed functioning of the German bases were favorable, and the maintenance of those conditions was termed vital to the success of the Reichswehr's armament plans. The immediate need, he added, was to bring the three German enterprises into full operation as rapidly as possible: '[We] must pursue this goal in 1929 with all possible means.'

Despite his general optimism, Blomberg concluded his report on an apprehensive note. The clandestine dealings, he cautioned, would in future be productive for both sides only if they could be separated from the conflicts which were sure to arise from the

[1] Behschnitt regarding talk with Dirksen, June 29, 1928, 9480/H276256–7.

[2] Schubert regarding talk with Groener and Hermann Müller, June 29, 1928, 4564/E163941–2.

[3] Report by Blomberg: 'Reise des Chefs des Truppenamts nach Russland. (August/September 1928)', November 17, 1928, 9480/H276183–236. For details see: Erickson, *Soviet High Command*, 263–8; Carsten, *Reichswehr und Politik*, 307–9.

disparate political and social systems of the two sides.[1] This very same problem troubled Voroshilov; during the Shakhty affair he had appealed to Colonel Mittelberger, another Reichswehr officer, that occasional dissension between their countries not be carried over into the relations between the two armies.[2] Striking success crowned these wishes. During the years 1929–31 it was the great achievement of the two military commands to preserve stability in their contacts amidst mounting strife on the diplomatic level. During a period in which German-Soviet political relations were threatening to sink to their nadir the joint military operations reached their high-water mark. Indeed the strength of the military bond was probably instrumental in preventing a break in relations during the great crisis of 1929–30 even as it had earlier hastened an end to the Shakhty incident.

Two more public demonstrations of the 'revival' of friendship occurred at the turn of the year (1928–9). The first concerned economic and trade relations, a subject bitterly in dispute since the preceding autumn. The release of the three German engineers implicated in the Shakhty case led in November to a resumption of the economic negotiations in a much more salubrious bargaining climate. Both sides were now committed to an agreement. The formerly 'ultimatumist' mood of German industry—much tempered by mounting figures of unemployment—had given way to a conviction that trade with the Soviet Union, however meager, should not be jeopardized. Aggregate trade figures for 1927–8 had become available as well, and contrary to claims made in February, they showed a modest rise in Germany's exports to the Soviet Union over the preceding year. Finally, the German leadership, with one eye cocked on the impending negotiations that were to lead to the Young plan, was also in a bargaining mood.

Soviet policy makers were in a more conciliatory mood as well. With appetites for foreign capital whetted by mammoth industrialization plans they were anxious to avoid another public clash with Germany over loans that could damage their credit. At a moment when their energies were about to be engaged in an unprecedented domestic social revolution, they also wanted to forestall a negotiating failure that might further strain their already

[1] Report by Blomberg, November 17, 1928, 9480/H276183–236.

[2] Report by Mittelberger concerning military mission in the Soviet Union, May 7, 1928, 9481/H276305–9.

precarious international standing. For all these reasons the talks lasted only a short four weeks, ending on December 21 with a detailed protocol citing agreement on all important issues.

This outcome was all the more surprising because of two developments in Germany in the autumn of 1928 that challenged Soviet economic interests. In September a variety of German associations engaged in commercial relations with the USSR combined in one organization called the *Russlandsausschuss der deutschen Industrie*.[1] Its purpose was to concentrate German energies for dealings with the ubiquitous Soviet trade monopoly; as such it enjoyed the support of the German government which accorded it recognition as the sole representative of German industry in economic talks with the USSR.

The Soviet press responded with unconcealed misgivings. In an editorial entitled 'The German Monopolists oppose the Foreign Trade Monopoly', *Pravda* described the new committee as a 'syndicate for trade with the Soviet Union that would not permit the lowering of prices for Soviet orders – a united front of German capital to oppose the Soviet Russian monopoly buyer . . .'.[2] After Germany had served to legitimize the activities of the foreign trade monopoly on the international scene, Soviet leaders were unwilling to have her play a like role in pruning back their scope.

In London on October 23 a second development occurred fraught with greater menace. A consortium of German banks representing the owners of pre-war Russian securities adhered to a new association, the International Protective Committee of the Creditors of Russia.[3] Although the *Russlandsausschuss* could be defended as a stimulator of trade because it would serve to create equality at the bargaining table, the creditors' committee was patently more aggressive. Recognizing this, German Foreign Ministry officials had earlier tried to prevent such a development by threatening a public stand against it.[4] Now, so as to cushion the blow for Moscow, they stood by their word and issued a

[1] Unsigned memorandum: 'Schwebende Russen-Fragen', November 7, 1928, L622 (not filmed).

[2] *Pravda*, September 19, 1928.

[3] Schubert to Moscow Embassy, October 12, 1928, 2860/D559669–70.

[4] Memorandum by Dirksen regarding conference in the Foreign Ministry, May 1, 1928, 2860/D559877–9.

communiqué announcing that the creditors' committee had been set up against the express wishes of the government.[1]

Because this event marked the first occasion on which Germany was associated with an international anti-Soviet organization on even an unofficial level, Moscow reacted sharply. Litvinov warned of a possible clouding of relations and for a number of days the Soviet press played on the theme, 'a united front of European finance capital against the Soviet Union'.[2] The Soviets alleged that the initiative of the German banks violated a section of the Rapallo treaty in which Germany had renounced her claims to pre-war debts except in those cases where the claims of other states were recognized. Potentially the issue was an explosive one.

Yet in the protocol of December 22, which concluded the economic negotiations, these issues hardly featured amid a host of phrases such as 'unanimously agree', 'continued cooperation', and so on. The *Russlandsausschuss der deutschen Industrie*, for instance, was mentioned only obliquely in a statement which barred 'discrimination' by economic organizations of one country against those of the other. The path was thus cleared for this association of German industry to undertake a broad sweep of activities.

The question of the creditor committee proved to be somewhat less tractable. Till late in the negotiations Soviet representatives clung to their demand that the bank consortium be forced to withdraw from the international committee. This the German authorities refused to do, pleading that such action went counter to their non-interventionist role in domestic economic affairs. The matter was finally settled by a statement in the protocol which again dissociated the German government from the bankers' action and reaffirmed the validity of those provisions in the Rapallo treaty pertaining to pre-war debts.

For the rest, the protocol recorded agreement on all disputed points. Article One of the trade treaty, which in February had formed the basis of German complaints about Soviet discriminatory purchasing policy, was said to have been fulfilled to the letter. (What *quid pro quo* the German delegation received for withdrawing from its previously held position—one that German commercial circles adhered to for many years—is not clear.) Another

[1] Hey to Foreign Ministry regarding conversation with Litvinov, October 17, 1928, 4484/E197043-4.

[2] *Pravda*, October 26, 1928. Cf. *Izvestiia*, October 26, 27, 1928.

damaging German charge was wiped from the slate in a statement affirming that commercial relations were evolving normally and that disputes concerning their regulation were infrequent.[1]

Without going into the details of the bargaining sessions one is tempted to conclude that the protocol of December 21 was less an economic than a political document. Subsequently, before 1931, trade increased very little, and soon a new series of incidents overcast the economic sky. But politically the protocol was of some importance. For Germany it heightened the bluff effect of ties with the Soviet Union on the eve of negotiations for the Young plan; Soviet officials, on the other side, were able to exploit it as an open letter refuting what had been rumored about the Soviet Union as a bad credit risk, her political use of trade, and the ungentlemanly bargaining habits of the foreign trade monopoly.[2] Indeed the Soviet press went so far in drawing favorable inferences from the document that a press squall concerning its interpretation was stirred up.[3] There is much truth in Paul Scheffer's observation that the dearth of trade in these years gave the German-Soviet partnership a 'certain content by continually requiring negotiations as to how the vacuum might be filled'.[4]

Within five weeks (January 25, 1929) the conclusion of a conciliation treaty accented political contacts a second time. The initiative for this agreement – a proposal for conciliation machinery to handle disputes about the October agreements – had come from the Wilhelmstrasse.[5] The matter had then taken on more of a political complexion when the Narkomindel urged that all existing German-Soviet agreements be brought within its purview,[6] a proposal accepted by Berlin. The resulting treaty provided that disputes which could not be settled by diplomatic means be

[1] Report of Krämer, head of the *Russlandsausschuss der deutschen Industrie*, to a meeting of the Ausschuss, undated, Trautmann Papers: Russia, Economic Relations (not filmed).

[2] *Izvestiia*, December 22, 1928; Hey to the Foreign Ministry, December 22, 1928, Trautmann Papers: Economic Relations (not filmed); *Kölnische Zeitung*, December 28, 1928.

[3] *Der Ost-Express*, January 19, February 1, 1929.

[4] Paul Scheffer, op. cit., 317.

[5] Memorandum by Stresemann regarding conversation with Krestinskii, December 5, 1928, 2860/D559675–80.

[6] Stresemann to Moscow Embassy, December 7, 1928, 2860/D559683–684.

submitted for mediation to a commission composed of an equal number of German and Soviet members. The commission was to form anew for each session, and was scheduled to meet regularly once a year or on the request of one of the parties.[1]

Because the new commission could only make recommendations to either government it represented no more than an appendage to diplomacy. Substantively it was therefore unimportant; but politically its meaning was enhanced by the interpretation placed on it by the Soviet, German, and international press. Soviet commentaries celebrated the new pact as an important international departure, as a model for the conclusion of analogous agreements with other capitalist states.[2] A Norwegian paper typified foreign reaction when it suggested that Stresemann was using the accord to maintain the Soviet Union as a trump for his talks in the west.[3] The SPD press, which shared this explanation, decried the agreement as a futile and dangerous effort to pressure the western countries on the matter of reparations.[4] The remainder of the German press, however, following Foreign Ministry guidelines, welcomed it as Dirksen's first diplomatic triumph as Ambassador to the Soviet Union.[5] It was one of the few to grace his service in Moscow.

Thus Dirksen's ambassadorship began on an auspicious note, in an atmosphere of conciliation, which he immediately enhanced by one of his first official acts. Two days after his arrival in the Soviet capital he opened a 'German technology week' with a speech promising Germany's full support for the Soviet Union's industrialization program.[6] These words struck an agreeable note for Soviet ears, accustomed to hearing dire forecasts from foreign businessmen about the threat posed to the complementarity of the Soviet and western economies by the development of an independent Soviet manufacturing industry. Looking to western financial interests, *Izvestiia* paraded these words, citing them as proof that the industrialization of the USSR ought not to impede economic contacts 'with the industrial countries of western Europe'.[7] A few days later Dirksen was received by Soviet

[1] *Kölnische Zeitung*, January 26, 1929.
[2] *Izvestiia*, January 26, 1929. [3] *Oslo Aftenavis*, February 12, 1929.
[4] *Hamburger Echo*, January 26, 1929.
[5] *Kölnische Zeitung*, January 26, 1929.
[6] Hilger and Meyer, op. cit., 226–7. [7] *Izvestiia*, January 9, 1929.

President Rykov who declared that the partnership between their countries was not a passing phenomenon but rested on 'historical necessity'.[1]

After the nadir of relations associated with the incidents of the preceding year, it seemed that at least this illusion had been dissipated. A much chastened Wilhelmstrasse had emerged from the disappointments of the Anglo-Soviet crisis and commercial relations, saddled with the slogan 'cominternization'. Its assumptions were fast vanishing that in its internal development the Soviet Union would evolve toward the right or that German policy makers possessed means to arrest her isolation. To be sure, partly to compensate for the 'disappointed hopes' of Germany's diplomacy and trade new areas of cooperation had been opened in the matter of disarmament. But alone they were not able to preserve the bond with Moscow.

That task was principally aided by military contacts and the conviction of men like Stresemann and Schubert that the support of Soviet Russia was essential to Germany's policy in the west and the eventual resolution of the 'Polish question'. *Whether* this was so, indeed *how* this was so, was not the subject of debate—it had become an axiom. Yet a new question loomed on the horizon that could cloud future relations with the Soviet Union. Would the upsurge in strength of German Communism, again as in 1923, create for Moscow an irresistible temptation to subordinate diplomacy to revolution, 'Socialism in one country' notwithstanding?

[1] Dirksen to the Foreign Ministry, January 16, 1929, 2860/D560713–15.

Part Four

THE GREAT CRISIS, 1929–1930

1. HARBINGER OF STRIFE

THE revival in relations presaged by the economic protocol of December 1928 and the mediation agreement of January 1929 was short-lived. In less than a year Germany and the USSR were caught up in a press war and diplomatic altercations that brought their relations close to a full breach in February and March 1930. 'In the Embassy,' a Soviet spokesman remarked at the time, 'questions were being asked about how long we would be able to remain in Berlin. To all appearances [the German government] was considering a break in relations.'[1] The crisis he referred to was probably the most tangled and serious between the Rapallo partners in the period of the Weimar Republic.

The international setting of the crisis was the almost total preoccupation of the German government with its western interests. For more than a year, from February 1929, when international financial experts assembled in Paris to work out a formula for a final settlement of the reparations problem, until March 1930, when the resulting Young plan was approved by the Reichstag, German diplomacy was tied down in every way. The numerous conferences in Paris, Geneva, and The Hague and the struggle to gain acceptance of the Young plan at home against the obstructionism of Hugenberg and others, left German statesmen little time to devote to relations with Russia.

Yet their neglect of Moscow was occasioned by more than overwork; the western negotiations placed considerable restraint on new initiatives towards Russia. Exchanges with Moscow ground to

[1] Memorandum by unidentified member of the Wilhelmstrasse concerning statement made to Mr. Wiley of American Embassy in Berlin by a Soviet diplomat, February 21, 1930, 2860/D561254–5.

a halt while word of the outcome of the Hague deliberations was awaited. Credit negotiations that were to have started early in the year were postponed[1] because Germany's argument in support of the Young plan was not to be frittered away: the western powers were not to conclude that she had a surfeit of wealth with which to bolster the Soviet economy. As a result relations tended to stagnate. For over a year Berlin and Moscow had little to show from their association that might have offset the strife caused by a chance interplay between the *social revolution* associated with collectivization in the USSR, and the deepening *social crisis* in Germany.

In this setting of inactivity on the levels of diplomacy and trade, fear of the gathering strength of the KPD came gradually to govern Germany's thinking about relations with the USSR. Already evident in 1928, this process was considerably accelerated by the celebrations of May Day in Berlin, which were marked by serious disturbances. In response to threats by the Communists that they would use the occasion to fight for control of the streets, the SPD police chief of Berlin, Zörgiebel, forbade any demonstrations. In direct defiance of this ban, KPD marchers nevertheless paraded through the streets and clashed with the police. Some twenty-five dead were counted at the end of the disturbances that continued for several days.[2]

As the first major domestic incident since 1923 involving the KPD, it provided a foretaste of the bloody street fighting that was to mark the following years. The affair was considered a modest success by the German Communists. Although the clashes did not mobilize the masses to the side of the KPD, they did unfurl the flag in the Communist struggle to fashion a 'united front from below'. Moscow seemed to be implicated in the incident; the Soviet press had predicted the bloodshed, creating the impression that a general strike was being planned.[3] And more vexing to the German government, Soviet leaders had egged on their German comrades with displays and proclamations in Moscow.

[1] Dirksen to the Foreign Ministry, June 11, 1929, 2860/D560323–4; Köpke to Dirksen, June 14, 1929, 2860/D560325.

[2] Flechtheim, op. cit., 154–6.

[3] Report by Dirksen to the Foreign Ministry, entitled: 'Berichterstattung der Konsularbehörden über Maifeier und Stellungnahme Sowjetöffentlichkeit zu Berliner Maiereignissen', May 17, 1929, L622 (not filmed); Hilger and Meyer, op. cit., 228.

In the May Day parade through Red Square floats had passed before the reviewing stand and the assembled diplomatic corps mocking SPD cabinet members in Prussia and Germany and Berlin's domestic and defense policies. And as in 1927–8 Voroshilov was again singled out by his peers to fulminate against the established order in Germany. In a combative speech he compared the repressive conditions under which the workers in the capitalist world were allegedly celebrating the day to conditions in Moscow; he referred pointedly to Germany: 'In so-called democratic Germany even the Social Democratic police chief, Zörgiebel, has gone so far as to ban public demonstrations. In spite of this ban the workers will go onto the streets to demonstrate for their principles.'[1] A week later workers, members of Soviet sports associations and some police units, staged a noisy protest demonstration in front of the German consulate in Leningrad. Slogans shouted in unison and raised placards expressed support for the Berlin workers and condemned German Socialists.[2]

For some weeks the May Day incident clouded German-Soviet relations. Whereas the earlier episodes involving Hölz and Voroshilov had been treated perfunctorily by the German press and evoked weak protests from the Wilhelmstrasse, this incident was widely reported and vigorously protested against.[3] Stresemann, who demanded full satisfaction from the Soviets, had to be restrained from making a real crisis of the affair. He ordered Dirksen to lodge a sharp protest on the grounds that the 'national flag had been impudently mocked and an official German minister had been rendered a laughing stock'. Above all 'Voroshilov's speech represents inadmissible interference in German domestic affairs by a responsible Soviet official.'[4]

Again as in 1927 and 1928 the Narkomindel attempted to limit the damage. The reports of Voroshilov's speech in *Izvestiia* and *Pravda* deleted the passages that were offensive to Germany;[5] Karakhan, of the Foreign Commissariat, expressed his govern-

[1] Dirksen to the Foreign Ministry, May 2, 1929, 2860/D560258–9.

[2] Dirksen to the Foreign Ministry, May 9, 1929, 2860/D560275–6.

[3] As examples see *Deutsche Allgemeine Zeitung*, May 4, 1929; *Tempo*, May 3, 1929.

[4] Stresemann to Dirksen, May 2, 1929, 2860/D560260.

[5] Dirksen to the Foreign Ministry, May 5, 1929, 4562/E160062.

ment's regrets and those of Voroshilov to Dirksen;[1] and to allay the impression that his speech had made in Reichswehr circles, Voroshilov made an accommodating gesture by suddenly fulfilling a number of requests made of him some time ago by the Reichswehrministerium, which he had hitherto rejected.[2] At the same time Krestinskii emphasized that Voroshilov's words had been directed more against the SPD than the German government.[3]

Indeed, it was as part of the SPD-KPD struggle that the incident continued to burden relations even after Soviet apologies had been accepted. Day after day resolutions from Soviet factories appeared in *Pravda* and other party organs encouraging the German 'fighters of the barricades' and members of the KPD to endure in their revolutionary struggle. Promises were given of moral and material support and funds were established to provide aid for the survivors of the May 'massacre'.[4] Blame for the unrest was invariably laid at the doorstep of the SPD. *Pravda* on May 15 called the Prussian Interior Minister a 'Social hangman', the German Interior Minister Severing a 'Social scoundrel', and Zörgiebel a 'Social policeman'.[5] The German government was not mentioned. As late as May 17 *Pravda* entitled a lead editorial, 'out of the free land of the Soviets we challenge the German proletariat to continue its fight for the revolutionary cause'.[6] In this manner the SPD press was put in even more of a fighting mood and provoked into parrying every Soviet thrust with further hostile comments about domestic developments in Russia.

It may be true that the tactics of the 'united front from below', announced at the Sixth Comintern Congress, were a reaction to the war scare of 1927 and were intended to mobilize foreign Communist parties for the defense of the Soviet Union, i.e. to support her industrialization. But in the special case of relations with Germany this approach did not have the desired effect of increasing Soviet security. For by sharpening the conflict between the KPD

[1] Dirksen to the Foreign Ministry regarding conversation with Karakhan, May 11, 1929, 2860/D560284–7.

[2] Dirksen to the Foreign Ministry, May 11, 1929, 2860/D560288–9.

[3] Memorandum by Stresemann regarding conversation with Krestinskii, May 6, 1929, 2860/D560267–70.

[4] Dirksen to the Foreign Ministry, May 11, 1929, 2860/D560283.

[5] Dirksen to the Foreign Ministry, May 17, 1929, L622 (not filmed).

[6] Ibid.

and the SPD it contributed to the general radicalization of German politics and led to the public denigration of the KPD's model – the USSR. As a result it became increasingly difficult for the German government, headed by the Social Democrat, Hermann Müller, to retain much party support for a continuation of the Rapallo line, or to keep in check the western predilections of the SPD and the Center. In the winter of 1929–30 this problem was to become acute.

2. ASIAN COMPLICATION

IF no other problems had intervened the May Day affair would probably have been forgotten in the warm glow attending the co-operation at Geneva between Germany and Russia on the disarmament question. Objectively, the emergence in this period of France as the Soviet Union's chief enemy[1] had established a firmer base for collaboration in such questions of international affairs. Dirksen, who wanted this new situation exploited to the hilt, urged Stresemann to play down the May Day affair so that developments at Geneva would not be jeopardized and French ire aroused.[2] By early June it seemed that Soviet apologies had smoothed over ruffled feelings in Berlin and that cooperation was proceeding smoothly.

But in July the break in diplomatic relations between Moscow and Peking over the control and operation of the Chinese Eastern Railway unexpectedly introduced a further strain into the partnership.[3] At first the alacrity with which Berlin agreed to assume the protection of Soviet interests in China served to accent the intimacy of the association.[4] But then Soviet action turned a promising demonstration of German-Soviet accord into an unseemly wrangle that delighted the western powers.

Soviet mistrust of Germany was first aroused when the German

[1] V. B. Ushakov, *Vneshniaia politika Germanii v period Veimarskoi Respubliki* (Moscow: IMO, 1958), 120–1.

[2] Dirksen to Stresemann, May 11, 1929, 2860/D560288–9.

[3] For the background to this controversy, which 'between July and December 1929 . . . was the focus of international politics', see: David J. Dallin, *The Rise of Russia in Asia* (New Haven: Yale University Press, 1939), 249–60.

[4] Schubert to the German Consul in Peitaiho, July 18, 1929, 2860/D560341–2.

government also assumed the representation of Chinese interests in Russia. This action, Stomoniakov complained to Dirksen, was not customary diplomatic practice, and 'did not accord with the general line of Russo-German friendship'.[1] Moreover, it was being linked in Soviet thinking with an unfriendly commentary questioning Moscow's willingness to resolve the railway dispute that had recently appeared in the semi-official *Deutsche diplomatisch-politisch Korrespondenz*.[2] Both actions were taken as signs that Germany was siding with China, a view that soon found its way into the Soviet press.[3]

In August the situation along the Russo-Chinese border worsened and sporadic fighting broke out. The Chinese interned some 1,000 Soviet citizens in a concentration camp near Harbin, and the Russians retaliated by arresting a like number of Chinese in Russia. Germany's protective function became onerous. Rumors circulated about atrocities in the Chinese camps, to which the Soviet government responded on September 6 by dashing off a note to the German government; the note reproached German consular officials in Harbin for failing to carry out their protective duties. It demanded that Germany 'take immediate steps to put an end to the inhuman actions of the Chinese government and Chinese authorities'.[4] These charges were immediately published in *Pravda* and accompanied by what the Wilhelmstrasse termed an insulting commentary.

Dirksen, who considered the matter serious enough to warrant something stronger than a diplomatic protest, asked for permission to leave his post.[5] This request was not granted. But in Berlin it was realized that Germany's technical role in the dispute as a protective power might soon find her lodged between two chairs. Schlesinger urged that Germany offer to mediate, a proposal similar to that made by him during the Anglo-Soviet dispute.[6] Otherwise she might soon find herself in an untenable position. If

[1] Dirksen to the Foreign Ministry, July 20, 1929, 2860/D560354–7.

[2] *Deutsche diplomatisch-politisch Korrespondenz*, July 15, 1929.

[3] *Izvestiia*, July 20, 1929; Schubert to Dirksen, July 22, 1929, 2860/D550393–5.

[4] Köpke to Embassy Peiping, September 7, 1929, 2860/D560552–4.

[5] Dirksen to the Foreign Ministry, September 9, 1929, 2860/D560568–569.

[6] Memorandum by Schlesinger entitled: 'Russisch-Chinesischer Konflikt', September 24, 1929, 2860/D560746–9.

her mediation offer was rejected she should withdraw as a protective power: 'In spite of the fact that until now we have actually rendered good services to both sides, we have been repaid badly . . . .'[1] The Soviet's intolerable treatment of Germany as a protective power, he concluded, was unique in the annals of diplomacy.

Such a frontal approach to the problem, however, was rejected by Berlin because it would have been construed as inspired by the western powers.[2] Yet decisive action to relieve Germany's ticklish position was nevertheless taken. On October 9 the German government in an important *aide-mémoire* called on the Russians and Chinese to desist from further hostile acts and to release any prisoners interned since May 1.[3] Now it was Litvinov's turn to protest. He characterized the German *démarche* as a *fait accompli*, made without consulting Moscow, which could have unpleasant repercussions for mutual relations.[4] The German Chargé in Moscow reported that the *démarche* was being interpreted there as an effort by Germany to rob the USSR of the fruits of her victory in the Far-Eastern dispute. Yet even though the *aide-mémoire* was rejected by both sides, the Foreign Ministry felt that it had eased the work of its representatives in China and had insulated them against further Soviet reproach.[5]

This episode again demonstrated that when its own interests were involved, the German government was ready to act independently to promote a settlement between the USSR and third states, but would not do so in concert with other powers. Despite the rebuffs received for her services, Germany still valued the Soviet partnership enough not to endanger it by cooperating with other states in measures that the USSR considered inimical to her security. Germany was still the breach in any 'anti-Soviet front'—and she knew it.

In July Germany had rejected a first American initiative in the dispute, and in December she declined a second time to associate

[1] Memorandum by Schlesinger entitled: 'Russisch-Chinesischer Konflikt', September 24, 1929, 2860/D560746–9.

[2] Memorandum by Dienstmann concerning Schlesinger's suggestion, September 24, 1929, 6698/H116811–12.

[3] Schubert to Embassy Peiping, October 7, 1929, 2860/D560781–4.

[4] Twardowski to the Foreign Ministry regarding conversation with Litvinov, October 9, 1929, 2860/D560786–9.

[5] Twardowski to the Foreign Ministry, October 17, 1929, 2860/D560805–6.

herself with Stimson's efforts to force a settlement on the basis of the Kellogg pact. But the Wilhelmstrasse found it awkward to have to reject western proposals, particularly when they were directed to the pacific settlement of disputes. It was therefore greatly relieved when the dispute was finally, in late December, resolved in Moscow's favor with the establishment of the *status quo ante.*[1]

3. BALANCE SHEET OF PARTNERSHIP

THE chief reasons for Moscow's perverse treatment of Germany during the Chinese imbroglio are probably to be found outside of the immediate situation. By September the Russians had become sensitive to Germany's dealings with the western powers in connection with the Young plan; their suspicion was heightened by the repeated postponement of the promised credit negotiations with Berlin. Furthermore, the cheerful economic protocol of December 1928 had not had the intended effect of halting pessimistic commentaries by the German press about the viability of the Soviet economy.

And, finally, the repeated discussion in the German press of the touchy subject of Germany bartering her ties with Russia for concessions in the west was far from reassuring. This contingency, an old Soviet nightmare that revived as soon as Germany became active in her western negotiations, had recently been broached by the German press as a result of the May Day disturbances in Berlin. On May 23 *Izvestiia* replied that such talk was a sign of political immaturity. Germany's social problems had not been created by the Soviet regime but by the exploitive reparations policy of the Versailles powers.[2]

Nor were German-Soviet relations a realistic bargaining object, the editorial continued, for Russia's friendship could only be sold once; any imaginable bargain would not place Germany on the same level with England and France. The divisions between Germany and her former enemies required that Germany maintain her eastern ties as a necessary counterweight to the west. Soviet 'public

[1] Memorandum by Michelsen entitled: 'Die gegenwärtige Stellung der deutschen Politik im russisch-chinesischen Konflikt', October 22, 1929, 6698/H117147–50.

[2] *Izvestiia*, May 23, 1929.

opinion' was persuaded of the 'correctness, vitality and utter suitability of the Rapallo policy for the interests of both countries . . .'. Was Germany?

Uncertainty about the direction of German policy thus helps to explain the preposterous Soviet charges from July onward that Germany was taking sides with China in the Manchurian dispute. It led, as we have seen, to the Soviet note of September 6, that was re-enforced two days later by a jarring article in *Izvestiia* entitled: 'A Heart to Heart Conversation'.[1] It raised fundamental Soviet views too hot for diplomatic channels to handle and led in September and October to a series of exchanges between the German and the Soviet governments that appeared in the columns of their press as a war of editorials.

For the first time since 1925 a Soviet commentary spoke of a Rapallo 'crisis'. The symptoms were legion: recently Schubert had shaken the hand of the Chinese representative at the League of Nations; *Vorwärts*, Chancellor Müller's paper, had conducted an 'unheard of, systematic, and shameless campaign against the Soviet Union . . . '; and the German press had adopted an attitude towards Soviet interests in the Far-Eastern conflict that was not compatible with the Berlin treaty. The cause was that 'Germany is dying for a chance to step into the imperialistic arena and is daily showing new evidence that the German bourgeoisie is ready to pay any price for the "imperialistic birthright" '.

Considering Germany as a reviving *imperialist* power was a fundamentally new interpretation that was advanced increasingly in the following years to explain any upsets in mutual relations. Proceeding from the assumption that foreign policy is the policy of the governing minority in a bourgeois state, Germany's alleged drift away from the Soviet Union was explained in terms of economic processes. Germany had succeeded in meeting her reparations payments not through increased exports but through an alienation of the capital of German industry to foreign entrepreneurs, mainly American. In this way an independent international economic policy had been abandoned by German industry.

This was also the explanation for Germany's waning interest in economic relations with the Soviet Union. Implicit in this somewhat contradictory article, was the warning that if Germany tried

[1] *Izvestiia*, September 8, 1929; *Kölnische Zeitung*, September 9, 1929.

to bargain her friendship with Russia for equality with the western powers she would only become more dependent on them. Its immediate purpose was to draw attention to the allegedly widening gap between actual relations and the terms of the existing treaties.[1] In this spirit *Izvestiia* marked the first anniversary of Rantzau's death.

'Spiteful and badly damaging for mutual relations', was Dirksen's description of the article to Litvinov.[2] He attributed the declining interest of German businessmen in trade relations with the USSR to the shrinking buying power of the Soviet economy, the sharp practices of the trade monopoly, and the favoritism shown American industry in the placing of orders. Charges of Soviet intervention in German home affairs – May 1, the reception of the May Day 'barricade fighters' as heroes in the USSR, a new series of incidents on August 1 – were revived to explain any fraying of the relationship. Litvinov, in response to a request from Dirksen that the Soviet government denounce the article if it disagreed with it, explained that it was not official and did not reflect government views. He was only familiar with a 'depressed tone' in 'certain' circles over the long delayed credit negotiations, which was only aggravated when the German government cited the Young plan *pourparlers* as the cause.

Dirksen asked for a sharp reply to the affront, something more than a diplomatic protest.[3] But Stresemann was fully engaged with the Young plan at home and abroad and reluctant to add to his worries or to depreciate what he regarded as his Russian trump. He therefore turned down Dirksen's request to leave Moscow and questioned whether a polemical exchange with *Izvestiia* would serve any purpose.[4] Eventually a government inspired reply utilizing some of Dirksen's ideas appeared in the *Kölnische Zeitung*.[5]

But it was tepid. More than anything it revealed that the Wilhelmstrasse wanted the discussion terminated: 'We do not

[1] Ibid.

[2] Dirksen to the Foreign Ministry, September 10, 1929, 2860/D560574–581.

[3] Dirksen to Stresemann, September 9, 1929, 2860/D560568–9; September 12, 1929, 2860/D560631–8.

[4] Stresemann to Köpke, September 11, 1929, 2860/D560618.

[5] *Kölnische Zeitung*, September 13, 1929.

believe that there is a crisis in Russo-German relations . . . but even a worsening of relations is completely undesirable.' Though the matter was kept alive for some time by articles that cropped up in the German press and were answered by *Izvestiia*,[1] it was officially closed. Litvinov was reported relieved at the course of the polemics, while Dirksen, who felt that Germany should have gone further in order properly to secure the Soviet tie, was pessimistic. It was a familiar Soviet tactic, he complained, 'first to poison relations and when there had been a public reaction, to withdraw and again put on a friendly face'.[2]

It should be noted, in summary, that the initiative for this press exchange had come from Moscow and that the carefully modulated German reaction to it was under the firm control of the Wilhelmstrasse. This sets it apart in character from the crisis that soon followed.

4. A CHANCE INTERPLAY

THE disturbances of May Day in Berlin had shown that the Rapallo partnership was badly insulated against the deepening social crisis in Germany. Chance circumstances in October–December determined that it would also be gravely affected by the social revolution in the USSR associated with forced industrialization and the collectivization of agriculture. An incident of domestic Soviet politics came unexpectedly to interact with the growing instability of German politics and fanned mounting anti-Soviet sentiment until the structure of German-Soviet relations was threatened with dissolution.

The incident, although dramatic, seemed politically insignificant. In the second half of 1929 the collectivization of rural Russia entered its first critical phase. It was an 'intermediary stage' in which plans were laid for the all-out drive of 1930. In some regions, however, experiments in total collectivization were begun, and everywhere the campaign against the kulaks moved into medium

[1] See, for example, *Berliner Börsen Zeitung*, September 14; *Berliner Tageblatt*, October 12, 1929; *Pravda*, October 18, 1929; *Izvestiia*, October 12, 1929; *Berliner Tageblatt*, November 9, 1929; *Izvestiia*, November 11, 1929.

[2] Dirksen to the Foreign Ministry, September 20, 1929, 6698/H116843–6.

gear.[1] In the autumn of 1929, in response to the increasing pressures on their economic position and traditional way of life, some 13,000 to 18,000 peasants of German stock abandoned their terrorized villages and fled to Moscow. Their sole object was to leave Soviet Russia.

The difficult circumstances of their flight and the vicissitudes of their stay in the capital were widely publicized in Germany, where the press reacted with a volcanic anti-Soviet campaign that was neither part of the Wilhelmstrasse's policy nor susceptible to its control. Indeed the response of German public opinion was such that the German government had no choice but to become entangled in the fate of these people. What had begun as a domestic Soviet incident was thereby transformed into a highly charged question of German-Soviet relations.

The flight of Russo-German colonists (the term used to identify them in Moscow) started in early 1929 with the arrival in the capital of a few families from Siberia, the place of origin of most of the refugees in the later movement. Others followed and after three months some sixty families had successfully petitioned the Soviet government for exit permits.[2] On their departure for Europe these emigrants sent word of their fortune to remaining relatives and friends, kindling hopes among them that an escape from the onerous collectivization measures was possible also for them in Moscow.

What had begun in early 1929 as the departure of individual families was transformed in the summer and autumn into a mass movement as the collectivization campaign gained momentum. According to German figures the number of colonists in Moscow at the end of September stood at 2,000,[3] 5,000 on October 23, 10,000 on November 9, and 13,000 a few days later.[4] The colonists themselves estimated their final number at 18,000. By

[1] A detailed treatment of the stages of collectivization is given in, I. P. Halpern, 'Stalin's Revolution: The Struggle to Collectivize Rural Russia, 1927–1933' (unpublished Ph.D. dissertation, Columbia University, 1965).

[2] C. C. Peters (ed.), *Vor den Toren Moskaus: Gottes gnaedige Durchhilfe in einer schweren Zeit* (Yarrow: Columbia Press, 1960), 11–17.

[3] Ibid.

[4] Memorandum by Trautmann, November 25, 1929, 4562/E160405–10; Twardowski to the Foreign Ministry, November 11, 1929, 4562/E160304.

mid-November Soviet officials had sealed off those German villages involved, thereby slowing and then halting the head-long exodus from the countryside. At the time, of course, persons abroad did not realize this and acted on the belief that the stream of colonists had subsided only temporarily.

Of the 13,000 refugees to reach Moscow (to use the minimum figure cited in Foreign Ministry sources) 10,000 to 11,000 were members of the pacifist Mennonite sect. The rigors of their situation left few of them time to reflect on the irony of their plans—they hoped to leave Russia over roughly the same route on which their forefathers had entered a few generations earlier. From 1787 to 1866 some 8,000 Mennonites, affronted by the military policies of Prussia, which conflicted with their pacifist convictions, and drawn by the immunities and generous land grants promised by St. Petersburg, had fled the Danzig area to enter Russia as settlers.

Their first colonies had been planted on the rich virgin lands of southern Russia, which had only recently been seized from the Tartars. With the growth of their population in the second half of the 19th century they had established daughter colonies in the Kuban, the Caucasus, Samara, and beyond the Volga in Orenburg and Ufa. But population pressures had persisted and in the first years of the 20th century Mennonites had joined the movement of Russian settlers eastward to the broad unpopulated plains of south-western Siberia. By 1914 they had established about 100 villages in the regions of Omsk and Tomsk. It is estimated that the Mennonite population in Russia in 1926—much reduced by war, revolution, famine, and emigration—numbered about 120,000, or 10 percent of a total German population in the USSR of 1¼ million.[1]

The foreign connections of the Mennonite colonists which they had established earlier influenced their behavior in 1929. From 1923 to 1926 some 20,000 of their co-religionists had emigrated to the Canadian prairies.[2] They had prospered materially in their new environment and were put psychologically at ease by their success in organizing themselves into integral communities patterned on their villages in Imperial Russia. The remaining Mennonites in

[1] Adolf Ehrt, *Das Mennonitentum in Russland* (Langensalza: Julius Beltz, 1931); C. Henry Smith, *The Story of the Mennonites* (Newton: Mennonite Publishing Office, 1957).

[2] Ehrt, op. cit., 58.

Russia were aware of the Canadian situation; faced now with the inhospitable prospect of collectivization or even extinction they looked to North America for deliverance. About 3,000 of the colonists in Moscow were in possession of pre-paid steamship tickets to Canada, which their relatives had sent them.[1] All of the refugees believed that the obstinacy of the Soviet regime in denying them exit permits was all that stood in the way of their emigration. Initially, therefore, they directed their appeals to Soviet agencies, Soviet leaders, and luminaries of Soviet literature. None of these, however, gave the Mennonites any encouragement.[2]

Since their goal was Canada they did not at first approach German officials. But when their petitions in Moscow had been rejected and their position grew daily more desperate, they turned for help to the German Embassy. And willy-nilly they succeeded in mobilizing the Wilhelmstrasse to their cause. This involvement marked a sharp departure from the hands-off policy that Berlin had formulated earlier. In the summer of 1929 the German Red Cross and other groups had responded to the imminent tragedy of collectivization by asking the Foreign Ministry to use its considerable influence in Moscow to better the lot of the colonists and to ease their emigration. It was also suggested that German representations be given teeth through an inspired press campaign that would awaken Germans to the plight of their Soviet *Landsleute*.

The German Ambassador in Moscow, however, rejected all of these proposals in a lengthy memorandum dated August 1.[3] They

[1] Otto Auhagen, *Die Schicksalswende des Russland-deutschen Bauertums 1927/30* (Leipzig: S. Hirzel, 1942), 42.

[2] The colonists directed appeals to the Administration of the Moscow Region, to the Central Executive Committee of the RSFSR, and finally to the Central Executive Committee of the USSR (Auhagen, op. cit., 42). Towards the end of October a lengthy petition outlining their wish to emigrate was sent to six of the principal organs of the Soviet government. It concluded melodramatically with the threat that if exit permits were further refused, the colonists would go to the Red Square as one man and there die (Peters, op. cit., 51–60). Next they sought the advice of lower Party officials and of followers of Tolstoy in Moscow. A mass demonstration of women and children in President Kalinin's office was suggested. This was also done, but with indifferent results (Peters, op. cit., 51–60). Letters of appeal were then directed to Lenin's widow, and to Gorky (Auhagen, op. cit., 54).

[3] Dirksen to the Foreign Ministry, August 1, 1929, cited verbatim by *Rote Fahne*, November 14, 1929. The authenticity of this document is attested by Zechlin to Schubert, November 14, 1929, 4562/E160326–9; Trautmann to Embassy Moscow, November 14, 1929, 2860/D561141.

were both hazardous and doomed to failure, he wrote. The Soviets were unlikely to exclude from the socialization of agriculture thousands of peasants because their mother-tongue was German. And a directed press campaign would probably have the unintended effect of impelling the Soviets to wipe out any remnants of opposition among the colonists. Even if the USSR should open its frontiers to them, the securing of the necessary funds seemed to him 'impossibly problematical'.

Dirksen's final argument against a German initiative was that the poor and middle colonists had accepted the fact that peasant Russia was undergoing fundamental change; only the wealthy German peasants were anxious to leave. Instead of encouraging them in their hopes, Dirksen recommended that the colonists be informed through German consuls in the USSR that insuperable difficulties stood in the way of their emigration.[1] This dispatch, it should be remembered, was written at a time when the dachas on Moscow's northern outskirts were not yet crowded with thousands of cold and desperate colonists who would soon have their condition publicized abroad by an obliging international press.

German diplomacy's first involvement with the colonists was informal and fully in keeping with its obligations towards Moscow. Word of the exodus came from Professor B. H. Unruh, a Mennonite and confidante of the Russian Mennonites in Germany, who sketched the details of the situation for the Wilhelmstrasse in a memorandum that asked for government intervention in Moscow. If the colonists were brought to Germany he promised that their continued passage to Canada could be guaranteed.[2] From the Soviet capital came a similar appeal written by Otto Auhagen, the German Agricultural Attaché. He echoed Unruh's claim that the refugees would not burden the German government because their passage overseas was assured.[3]

The Wilhelmstrasse took quick action on this modest appeal. On October 12 Consul Dienstmann of the Russian desk was sent to Moscow to negotiate the emigration of the colonists with Boris Shtein of the Narkomindel. The Soviet response was extraordinary

[1] Dirksen to the Foreign Ministry, August 1, 1929, quoted in *Rote Fahne*, November 14, 1929.

[2] Peters, op. cit., 11, 112.

[3] Memorandum by Auhagen, October 11, 1929, in Auhagen, op. cit., 49–54.

—with little debate the promise was given Dienstmann that the refugees already in Moscow or in transit to the capital would be let out. The only condition attached was that transportation arrangements should begin immediately.[1]

So accommodating a Soviet response marked a precedent when seen against a background of the tenacity with which Russia had previously defended her sovereignty. It was a striking example of the value that Moscow continued to place on good relations with Berlin and of its fear that they were beginning to flag. The Dienstmann mission represented a clear-cut case of outside interference in Russia's domestic affairs, even though it was not characterized as such. And Moscow's cooperation could have been interpreted as the tacit admission of the principle that Germany had the right to exercise protection over German-speaking Soviet citizens.

To be sure several considerations prompted the Soviet response. With about 8,000 colonists already encamped in Moscow's suburbs and many more arriving weekly, the need was recognized to clean out the refugee center that was acting as a magnet on the remaining 1¼ million sensitized German colonists. Emigration may have seemed the easiest solution after the obvious one, the forcible return and exile of the colonists (reportedly favored by Interior officials),[2] was rejected because of the hostile reaction the Soviets expected from abroad.

Yet foreign policy considerations were more critical for Moscow's easy agreement. Shtein confided to Twardowski, the German Chargé in Moscow, that the peasant movement had surprised Moscow and the lively reporting of it by the foreign press had complicated matters; nonetheless the Narkomindel had 'supported emigration for foreign policy reasons, and had achieved a positive decision only over strenuous opposition'.[3]

The German Embassy staff worked feverishly to speed transportation arrangements; it operated on the assumption, as Unruh had reiterated, that existing agreements between Mennonite organizations and the Canadian government provided for the settlement of the colonists. The Wilhelmstrasse was only asked to issue

[1] Memorandum by Trautmann, November 25, 1929, 4562/E161405–10. Peters, op. cit., 112.

[2] Twardowski to the Foreign Ministry regarding conversation with Shtein, November 2, 1929, 4562/E160278–80.

[3] Ibid.

German identification papers for the emigrants – Ottawa refused to recognize their Soviet ones – and to receive any of them whom Canada might later deport.[1] The refugees were quickly divided into eleven groups and, in the quiet of night, so as not to disturb the capital's population,[2] the first trainload of them departed on October 27. Others were expected to follow shortly. On October 30, however, came news of a Canadian decision not to accept any of the colonists as settlers before at least the following spring.[3] Soviet authorities immediately halted all further planned transports. At this point the incident came to intrude on the high politics of German-Soviet relations.

The blocking of the escape route to the west by the Canadian development put Berlin and Moscow in a quandary. Because of the international spotlight that the incident had focused on the human costs of collectivization (and for domestic reasons) the Soviets wanted the refugee settlements dissolved at once. Earlier the Narkomindel had tried to accomplish this in concert with Germany; now, however, the Soviet Interior Commissariat might frustrate German policy by deporting the refugees to the east.

In the weeks following the Canadian decision of October 30 Narkomindel officials put the alternatives of emigration or forcible return squarely before German Embassy officials in Moscow. 'There were only [these] two possibilities', Shtein reminded the German Chargé.

> The Soviet government had no interest in what happened to the emigrants later. It was only concerned that the encampments of these unemployed and half-starved individuals in the environs of Moscow be dissolved. The trains are fired and ready to leave: if they do not journey to the west they will be routed to the east.[4]

A few days later, apparently under great pressure from Soviet interior officials, the Soviet government issued its stiffest warning. The Narkomindel, the Chargé was told, would be unable to post-

[1] Memorandum by Trautmann, November 25, 1929, 4562/E161405–10.

[2] Peters, op. cit., 57–9.

[3] Memorandum by Trautmann, November 25, 1929, 4562/E161405–10.

[4] Twardowski to the Foreign Ministry, November 2, 1929, 4562/E160278–80.

pone the deportation beyond the end of the anniversary celebrations of the October Revolution. If Germany's borders were not opened to the colonists the worst could be expected. And if the German government exploited the incident propagandistically it would have to assume the blame for its tragic conclusion.[1]

The certainty that these threats would be implemented placed the German government before uncomfortable alternatives. It could shrug off the blame for the deportation of the colonists or open its doors to them and provide for their transportation and care until they were settled permanently. Actually, however, this was only a theoretical choice: the government no longer had the freedom that would have made it real. Since October German public opinion had crystallized into an adamant mood that would not tolerate having the colonists condemned to Siberia.

This is suggested both by the tenor of the German press during those weeks and by the concerted attempt made by the Wilhelmstrasse to win the government's support for a pro-colonist policy. Against a background of threats by Moscow and charges of spinelessness by the domestic press the Foreign Ministry was active in the Soviet, German, and Canadian capitals. In Moscow it appealed for a delay in the deportations until a decision could be ground out in Berlin. At the same time it tried on its own to throttle the flow of colonists into Moscow; Auhagen, who had in the preceding weeks won the trust of the colonists,[2] urged them to dissuade other Mennonites still in the villages from joining the trek. These efforts probably helped to stem the flow of refugees.

On another front the German Consul in Montreal sounded Mennonite and government authorities in Canada about the possibility of having some of the refugees accepted immediately as immigrants.[3] The Canadian picture was befogged by mounting unemployment and a tug-of-war between the federal and provincial governments; nevertheless on November 9 the federal Department of Immigration informed the German government that it

[1] Twardowski to the Foreign Ministry, November 8, 1929, 4562/E160296.

[2] Twardowski to the Foreign Ministry, November 5, 1929, 2860/D561098–100.

[3] Kempff, German Consul in Montreal, to the Foreign Ministry: November 5, 1929, 4562/E160281; November 6, 4562/E160289; November 8, 1929, 4562/E160295.

would try to accept about 1,000 families early in 1930. In the meantime, however, Germany would have to act on her own.[1]

The decision about the future of the 13,000 colonists was now in the hands of the German government alone. Postponement was hazardous. Yet the task of framing a policy that was viable within the narrow limits imposed by budgetary considerations, the demands of a fickle public, and the needs of foreign policy was highly complicated. A number of cabinet meetings in early November explored the question at issue: should Germany accept the refugees even if Canada could later take none? The first, on November 9, heard a brief from the Foreign Ministry that answered 'Yes.'[2]

Foreign Minister Curtius recommended that funds to the value of 3 million marks be appropriated to help the colonists. There were two arguments for such action, he said: 'Germany's public opinion is very interested and would not understand if peasants of German origin who had decided to leave the Soviet Union because of the strain of unbearable physical and mental distress, were to be left in the lurch and exposed to certain death.' And if Germany dallied the Soviets would 'saddle us with the blame for the fate of these people in the eyes of all of Europe'.[3] Implicit in this reasoning was the recognition that Germany's political instability did not permit her mercurial public to be flouted. Curtius was aware that helping the colonists might start a chain reaction in the USSR—he had little faith in the ability of Soviet authorities to seal off the countryside. But he saw no alternative for Germany.

The cabinet, however, preoccupied at the time with the pinched state of the budget, temporized. Although Germany had yet to feel the total impact of the economic crisis, she already counted more than one million unemployed in September. Could a further drain on the treasury be defended? The Finance Minister, Hilferding, found ready acceptance in the cabinet for his view that Germany should not assume the indefinite obligations that support for the colonist movement in the USSR would entail: 'Eighty thousand people of German origin are in transit in Central Russia.' A deci-

[1] Kempff to the Foreign Ministry regarding conversation with Canadian Minister of Immigration, November 9, 1929, 2860/D561101.

[2] Extract from minutes of a cabinet meeting, November 9, 1929, L617/L196168–9.

[3] Memorandum by Curtius, November 6, 1929, 4562/E160290–4.

sion on Curtius' recommendation was therefore postponed until the leaders of the coalition parties and the Budgetary Committee of the Reichstag could be consulted.[1]

In the meantime the dramatic story unfolding in Moscow was being given top billing in the leader sections and editorial columns of most German newspapers. By November 14, when the Chancellor conferred with his coalition leaders, the mounting pressure of party and public opinion in favor of the colonists forced the abandonment of financial considerations. The party leaders shrank back from a posture that would have stigmatized them as *Volksverräter* in the municipal elections being held throughout Germany.

Appeals for funds had been issued by the Red Cross and other charitable organizations;[2] President Hindenburg himself had donated 200,000 marks from a special account to a fund, 'Brüder in Not',[3] which action he defended in spirited terms: 'The German public will not understand why these people should be abandoned to certain starvation when we admitted to Germany after the war many thousands of aliens, often of very undesirable quality.'[4] So bitterly anti-Soviet was the tone of the press that Twardowski feared it would provoke the Soviets into implementing their threatened deportations.[5]

The party chiefs succumbed to the pressure of public opinion and agreed that funds to a limit of 6 million marks should be provided for the transportation and care of the 13,000 colonists 'then in Moscow'.[6] But the Foreign Ministry disputed this decision because it was made subject to the approval of the Budgetary Committee of the Reichstag that was not scheduled to meet until November 25.[7] On November 15 Litvinov again warned that the Narkomindel lacked authority to postpone the deportations beyond

[1] Extract from minutes of a cabinet meeting, November 9, 1929, L617/L196168–9.

[2] *Frankfurter Zeitung*, November 13, 1929; *Berliner Tageblatt*, November 13, 1929.

[3] *Berliner Tageblatt*, November 19, 20, 1929.

[4] Otto Meissner to Pünder, State Secretary in the Reichs Chancellery, November 12, 1929, L617/L196165–6.

[5] Twardowski to the Foreign Ministry, November 13, 1929, 2860/D561129.

[6] Extract from minutes of a cabinet meeting, November 14, 1929, L617/L196192–6.

[7] Memorandum by Curtius, November 15, 1929, 4562/E160333–6.

the end of 'this week'.[1] Twardowski was instructed to tell the Deputy Commissar of the steps taken so far and to ask that any further action await another German cabinet meeting.[2] This cabinet session, summoned on November 18, finally approved the use of state funds independently of the Budgetary Committee.[3] But tragically its action was one day too late for most of the refugees. On the previous evening interior officials had started the deportations. And within a week about 8,000 of the colonists were forcibly removed from their cramped dachas, loaded onto freight cars and returned to their disoriented villages or sent into a northern exile.[4]

This action subjected German-Soviet relations to considerable strain. The German press reported it fully, and amid a storm of public protest the German government interceded in behalf of the colonists. During the first days of the mass arrests the Moscow Embassy warned of the mischief for mutual relations if the deportation order were not rescinded. As a gesture of its good faith it offered to issue at once 1,000 German entry visas.[5] Shtein tried, half-apologetically, to defend the conduct of his Commissariat; he asked Twardowski how any government could act otherwise when masses of hungry and half-frozen peasants flocked into cramped quarters in the capital's suburbs. At first, he added, the Narkomindel had braved conflict with the Commissariat of the Interior to support German wishes. The German press, however, had treated the story demogogically—Interior officials had now taken the matter out of the Narkomindel's hands by acting on their own.[6]

Relations were burdened still further when two days after the start of the forcible exiles Soviet officials formally withdrew the

[1] Twardowski to the Foreign Ministry, November 15, 1929, 4562/E160350.

[2] Trautmann to Embassy Moscow, November 16, 1929, 4562/E160347; Memorandum by Curtius regarding conversation with Krestinskii, November 15, 1929, 4562/E160331.

[3] Extract from the minutes of a cabinet meeting, November 18, 1929, L617/L196228.

[4] Auhagen, op. cit., 79; Peters, op. cit., 119–22; Memorandum by Trautmann, November 25, 1929, 4562/E160405–10; Twardowski to the Foreign Ministry, November 18, 1929, 4562/E160358–60.

[5] Twardowski to the Foreign Ministry, November 18, 1929, 4562/E160361.

[6] Twardowski to the Foreign Ministry, November 19, 1929, 4562/E160362–4, E160365–6.

agreement of October, which had promised the release of the colonists.[1] This action had earlier been predicted by Shtein, who volunteered that 'highly important' Soviet leaders wanted Soviet press organs to reciprocate the calumnies against the USSR of Germany's newspapers: 'demagogic outbursts can only lead to a withdrawal of the permission to emigrate'.[2] He reported that the decision would be reviewed on November 24 or 25 by the Council of People's Commissars but that its reversal should not be expected. The German government, which had been lackadaisical in its decision to support the colonists, now reacted abruptly. 'The action', Twardowski remonstrated, 'would be understood neither in Germany nor in the rest of the world. German public opinion had taken a lively interest in the fate of the emigrants. This belated action would serve only to burden German-Soviet relations.'[3] On a higher level, Curtius entered as sharp a caveat as diplomatic usage permitted:

> The German government is compelled to regard the Russian decision as an unfriendly act. If the Russian government is seriously interested in maintaining normal relations which are free from the polemics of a hostile press, then the emigration may not be refused. The German government is no longer in a position to control the press. If this request should be denied then the German press would be justified in unleashing a storm of indignation.[4]

To support the *démarche*, Dirksen, who was himself of Mennonite extraction, was called from vacation and sent back to Moscow. By this time Litvinov recognized the gravity of the situation and decided to intervene personally. He promised to ask the Council of Commissars to reverse its earlier decision.[5] Nevertheless the round-up of the colonists in Moscow was not immediately stopped and the diplomatic temperature remained critical. Finally, on

[1] Twardowski to the Foreign Ministry, November 21, 1929, 4562/E160381–3.

[2] Twardowski to the Foreign Ministry regarding conversation with Shtein, November 19, 1929, 2860/D560873–4.

[3] Twardowski to the Foreign Ministry, November 21, 1929, 4562/E160381–3.

[4] Memorandum by Curtius regarding conversation with Krestinskii, November 22, 1929, 4562/E160387–8.

[5] Twardowski to the Foreign Ministry, November 23, 1929, 4562/E160402.

November 25 it was announced by the Soviets that the remaining refugees, whose numbers had by then dwindled to about 5,600, might leave for Germany.[1] This time transport was immediately ready and within two weeks the incident was officially closed when the last of nine trains bearing the colonists crossed the Soviet frontier into Latvia.[2] But far from having the intended effect, Moscow's reversal only confirmed the German press in its conspiratorial view: the decision had been purposely delayed in order that the 'deportation of the unfortunate colonists could in the meantime be carried out'.[3]

5. SURGE OF INDIGNATION

THE most significant result of the colonist affair for German-Soviet relations was the marked increase of anti-Soviet animus it occasioned in Germany. The outside world was first introduced to the story on October 11, when three American and two German correspondents accompanied the German Agricultural Attaché on a visit to the colonists' quarters.[4]

But the episode aroused little interest in Germany until the end of that month when Canada's refusal to open its frontiers transformed it into a controversy. Soon thereafter the KPD organ, *Rote Fahne*, expressed bitterness about a new anti-Soviet crusade. It described the entire German 'bourgeois press', from the Nazi to the SPD, as devoting unusual attention to the fate of '10,000 Russian kulaks of German origin'.[5]

The news story was widely reported indeed. It had the elements of a 'thriller'—suspense, a villain, the betrayed—and soon it occupied a prominent place in every German paper. In the critical period from November 7–27, the soberly democratic *Berliner Tageblatt* and *Frankfurter Zeitung* covered the story in leader articles about one-third of the time and in detailed news stories on the remaining days. Important international developments such as the clash between Soviet and Chinese troops in the Far East were driven from the front pages.[6] And long after the incident had ended, interest in it in Germany was kept alive by reports of interviews

[1] Dirksen to the Foreign Ministry, November 25, 1929, 4562/E160413–15.
[2] Peters, op. cit., 76.
[3] *Berliner Tageblatt*, November 26, 1929.
[4] Auhagen, op. cit., 85.
[5] *Rote Fahne*, November 9, 1929.
[6] *Frankfurter Zeitung*, November 21, 1929.

with the escaped colonists, or, when an epidemic of measles struck a refugee center, by daily reports of its toll.

The episode was inflated in Germany both by humanitarian and political interests. Early in November the Red Cross and other charitable groups revived their appeal to the German government for intervention. At the same time Hindenburg privately recommended that a drive for funds be launched throughout Germany.[1] Indeed, an appeal for such a drive was drafted in the aged President's name, but it was issued without his signature: in order to evoke a wide response it would have had to describe Soviet conditions realistically and implicitly indict the Soviet system.[2]

On November 13 the German press carried a highly emotional proclamation, sponsored by the charitable societies, under the suggestive caption, 'Brüder in Not': 'A catastrophe for Germans abroad has begun. Thousands of German peasants have been driven from their homes by hunger, economic need and the circumstances of the times! A German hunger migration in Russia has begun.' The colonists were said to have preserved their race, speech, and customs for centuries; now, however, they had been uprooted in body and soul and 'abandoned to despair'. The nation was asked to help despite her own economic malaise: 'The fate of every German is the concern of every other German.'[3]

The first deportation a week later goaded Hindenburg out of anonymity to add his voice to the public clamor. He made a statement in which he described support of the relief fund by government offices and private organizations as a 'duty of honor'; it was at this time also that he underwrote it with a 200,000-mark contribution.[4] Now the German postal service was authorized to accept money for the colonists, private banks volunteered to do the same,[5] and the state rail lines were empowered to carry gifts of clothing and food without charge.

It is noteworthy that the German public was stimulated to

[1] Extract from the minutes of a meeting of the cabinet, November 9, 1929, L617/L196168–9.

[2] Meissner to Pünder, November 12, 1929, L617/L196164–6.

[3] *Frankfurter Zeitung*, November 13, 1929; *Berliner Tageblatt*, November 13, 1929; *Vorwärts*, November 13, 1929.

[4] *Berliner Tageblatt*, November 19, 20, 1929.

[5] The participation of the banks was cited by the KPD as proof that the drive was part of 'the imperialistic preparation for the war against Russia' (*Rote Fahne*, November 16, 1929).

become so highly involved in this question by the journalistic efforts of individuals whose primary concerns were not foreign policy. Chief among them was Otto Auhagen, Germany's Agricultural Attaché in the Soviet Union, a leading expert on Soviet agriculture who was widely respected in academic circles for his reports that appeared regularly in the informed journal, *Osteuropa*. During the refugee entanglement he occupied a central position in the Moscow Embassy: Ambassador Dirksen was away on leave and the remaining Embassy officials reasoned strangely that it was of first concern to him because it had grown out of Soviet agrarian policies. For this reason many of the reports to Berlin above the name of Twardowski were actually his. And when he wrote them his mind was not on international politics, but, as he later put it in his own defense, on the 'life and death of thousands and the existence or non-existence of German peasantry (*Bauertum*) in the Soviet Union. . . .'[1]

Auhagen, who had been in touch with the refugee colonists daily since early October, had won their confidence[2] and, as a highly sensitive person, was deeply moved by their tragic circumstances. Consequently when his own government responded irresolutely to the Soviet deportation threats he decided to go outside of his own office in an effort to sway German policy through the press. This attempt took the form of a lengthy article for the November issue of *Osteuropa*,[3] which Auhagen sent to the most powerful of Germany's newspapers before publication. It had purposely not been cleared with either the Embassy or the Wilhelmstrasse.

The article was moderate in tone but its impact was nonetheless devastating. It described the colonists' flight as being of great 'symptomatic importance'; it was an 'outcry of Russian public opinion unequalled since the winter of 1921–1922 . . .'. The article further detailed the prohibitive tax burdens, grain delivery quotas, and forced auction sales that would end with the colonists being

[1] Twardowski to Trautmann regarding conversation with Auhagen, November 19, 1929, 4562/E160374–5.

[2] In 1961 the writer had the occasion to speak with some former Mennonite refugees, now resettled in the Fraser Valley, Canada. They still referred to Auhagen as the 'German Ambassador'. In Paraguay, whither some of the colonists finally emigrated, one Mennonite village still bears his name.

[3] Otto Auhagen, 'Wirtschaftsumschau', *Osteuropa*, V (November 1929), 137–48.

'driven out onto the steppes and abandoned to the wolves'. Auhagen also made and documented the claim that the 'vast majority' of refugees in Moscow were not 'kulaks', as Soviet sources alleged, but poor and middling peasants. And his added observation that the Russian peasant found himself in similar straits was tantamount to indicting collectivization *in toto*.

As the work of a specialist on Soviet agriculture, reputedly of moderate views, the article in *Osteuropa* caused a sensation in Germany. On November 16–18 lengthy excerpts from it were printed in most non-Communist papers, accompanied by editorials and headlines demanding governmental action on behalf of the colonists. Domestically, of course, all non-Communist parties, but especially the SPD and Center, saw that a playing-up of the story accorded both with their moral and political interests—a combination happy as it is rare. Humanitarian considerations and the struggle with the KPD were the general reasons for publicizing it; the municipal elections scheduled for November 17 added an immediate one. More potent material with which to discredit the KPD was hard to find.

The KPD was markedly embarrassed by the episode and tried, by labelling the colonists 'kulaks' and 'exploiters',[1] to conceal the human toll of collectivization. The Communists were well aware that the episode might hurt them at the polls. But the treatment of the incident by the Communist press indicates that the KPD and the Soviet regime were even more alarmed about its international implications. Was the incident, they asked, being used to start a crusade against the USSR? The KPD searched for evidence to substantiate its charge that the refugees were kulaks and that the outcry of the German press was officially inspired.

On November 14 the *Rote Fahne* was able to print an unusual stolen dispatch, Dirksen's secret report of August 1;[2] that report, it will be remembered, had warned against encouraging the colonists through the German press and had stated that most of them were accepting collectivization. This was choice grist for the Communist mills in Berlin and Moscow. The pointed confronting of Dirksen's earlier analysis with the strident voice of the German press had the effect of putting German government officials on the spot. Could

[1] *Rote Fahne*, November 24, 29, 1929; December 1, 7, 1929.

[2] Ibid., November 14, 1929; *supra*, 165; the dispatch was reprinted in *Pravda* and *Izvestiia* on November 16, 1929.

they still deny that the colonists had not been incited against their government by the Wilhelmstrasse's 'official and irresponsible representatives' in Moscow? Was the German press not playing under a single baton?[1]

These charges were considered so serious that they were answered publicly by a German government spokesman. He admitted that the stolen document was genuine, but denied that it was at all relevant because it no longer related to the changed situation. The Ambassador and the Foreign Ministry were described as holding identical views. This statement, accepted at face-value by the non-Communist press, was widely distributed.[2]

Although the colonist story was cut to the political needs of the National Socialists (government indecision, Soviet bestiality), their organ, the *Völkischer Beobachter*, was too busy at first attacking the 'Young plan criminals' to use it. But when it did it acted with vigor. Arthur Rosenberg defined the Nazi line on November 24 in an article with the ponderous title: 'The German Peasantry in Russia, a Parable of the Incompetence of the Parasitic Moscow Government: A Warning to the Enthusiasts for Russia in Germany'. It developed standard Nazi themes about Communism and concluded with a warning to the German Nationalists and National-Bolsheviks that an alliance with Russia was not possible.[3]

While the radical and SPD press treated the colonist story by merely playing old tunes more loudly, a politically significant change was at the same time occurring in the tone of the more moderate press. Earlier its conciliatory attitude towards the USSR had been undeniable. In July the *Frankfurter Zeitung*, for instance, had written that even the appearance of a shift in Germany's policy should be avoided for the sake of the Rapallo connection.[4] In September the *Kölnische Zeitung* had expressed similar views.[5] Such sentiments were not once repeated during the months of rising anti-Sovietism in Germany that followed.

The democratic press at first concentrated on the human aspects of the story; it urged government action and warned Moscow

[1] *Rote Fahne*, November 16, 1929.

[2] *Frankfurter Zeitung*, November 15, 1929; Trautmann to Embassy Moscow, November 14, 1929, 4562/E160319–20.

[3] *Völkischer Beobachter*, November 24, 1929.

[4] *Frankfurter Zeitung*, July 1, 1929.

[5] *Kölnische Zeitung*, September 13, 1929.

against carrying through the threatened deportations. But by degrees the spotlight shifted from the colonists to the system that had prompted their flight. Eventually the whole non-Communist press came to regard the refugee incident as part of a general paroxysm that had seized Soviet society and could plunge it into the abyss. *Vorwärts* spoke of the affair as having opened the eyes of the world to the brutal campaign that the Soviets had mounted against their own peasants.[1] The *Berliner Tageblatt* pointed to it as evidence of the tyranny on which the Soviet system rested.[2] A visit to one of the camps housing the colonists on their arrival in Germany was described as 'providing deeper insight into peasant Russia than a hundred lead articles or novels'.[3]

In short, the incident, for some Germans, had emerged as a kind of symbol. No longer was the USSR viewed as a remote and politically useful monolith that occasionally derided the German system; she had become a brutal system that trafficked in the lives of German *Landsleute*. The German press had been partly successful in making Germans vicariously experience the wounds of the Soviet class struggle. And the impact of the incident on popular psychology takes on an added dimension when it is recalled that the number of normal diplomatic dealings with Moscow had been reduced during the preceding months by the Young plan negotiations. Much energy was to be expended by both governments in the following months before Germany's run-away public indignation could be brought under control.

The Soviet government, irritated and then disturbed, tried to interpret the raised voice of the German press. It was sure that the 'colonist question was being used as the occasion to slander the Soviet Union'.[4] An *Izvestiia* editorial entitled 'Whose Fault?' blamed Germany's press and men like Auhagen for having injected the refugee incident into German-Soviet relations by intervening in Russia's domestic affairs.[5] Another Soviet press commentary characterized Auhagen as the 'kulak ideologist with the diplomatic passport', who had used the colonists to launch an unconscionable attack on Russia's agrarian program.[6] One mark of the attention

[1] *Vorwärts*, November 29, 1929.

[2] *Berliner Tageblatt*, November 25, 1929.

[3] *Vorwärts*, December 25, 1929.

[4] *Izvestiia*, November 28, 1929.

[5] Ibid., November 22, 1929.

[6] *Pravda*, November 28, 1929.

paid the story in the USSR was that *Pravda* and *Izvestiia* together devoted four articles to it on November 28.[1]

Yet more prominent in Soviet commentaries than impatience with Germany's press was a sense of bewilderment over what its conduct might denote: 'It is necessary to question whether this concern is over the fate of the German emigrants, or whether [the incident] is being used as a pretext to slander the Soviet Union in the eyes of the German public and the eyes of the whole world.'[2] Auhagen's conduct, Hindenburg's public appeal, and Dirksen's dispatch of August 1,[3] were all alleged to be indicators of the centralized inspiration and direction of Germany's newspapers.[4] This interpretation helped confirm the view that the German Republic's Young plan talks were speeding her orientation westward.

In brief, the diplomatic crisis was viewed from conflicting perspectives. Soviet officials saw it as another 'Locarno'; they believed that Germany was again threatening a *volte-face* to the west. German leaders and public opinion, on the other hand, were convinced that they stood on the threshold of another 1923. They suspected that Moscow was laying the groundwork for a new revolutionary initiative in Germany. Both sides, by acting on their equally erroneous assumptions, prolonged the crisis.

6. ANIMUS AT HIGH TIDE

AFTER mid-October the Soviet government tried repeatedly to improve its strained relations with Germany. It continued, as before, to celebrate the 'failures' of Berlin's negotiations in the west; as *Izvestiia* explained, it was necessary to 'clarify the political inexpediency of a one-sided orientation to the west under the conditions of Versailles'.[5] But more affirmatively it sought a public demonstration of the continued vitality of Rapallo. After the conclusion of a German-Polish commercial agreement in October, Shtein suggested that a German trade delegation composed of prominent persons visit the USSR. This would serve as a gesture

[1] *Izvestiia*, November 28, 1929; *Pravda*, November 28, 1929.

[2] *Izvestiia*, November 27, 1929.

[3] Reprinted in *Pravda* and *Izvestiia* on November 16, 1929.

[4] *Izvestiia*, November 27, 1929.

[5] Ibid., November 14, 1929.

to strengthen the hands of Germany's friends against a 'tendency' in the USSR that was feeding on 'mistrust of Germany's attitude'.[1] The Politburo was reportedly behind this initiative which was repeated several times in diplomatic exchanges and by the Soviet press.[2] The Narkomindel's ready agreement in October to permit the colonist refugees to emigrate was a further unsuccessful effort to breathe life into what remained of the Rapallo bond.

A final attempt to mend relations was a speech by Litvinov to the Central Executive Committee on December 4, 1929, a few days before the departure of the last refugee trains. The basic line of these relations, he reported, had not changed despite recent efforts by 'persons, groups, organizations, and even parties' to draw Berlin into an anti-Soviet orbit.[3] Dirksen was jubilant over these conciliatory words and asked for a positive German response as a way of ending the 'tension created by the colonist question'.[4] As a result two favorable commentaries appeared in Germany,[5] one avowing that the Wilhelmstrasse wanted Rapallo continued,[6] and the other voicing official optimism with the banner: 'Litvinov's Speech Welcomed in Berlin: The Start of an Actual Relaxation?'[7] Within a few weeks this question was given an unequivocally negative answer.

A marked change had occurred on the German scene. Earlier, a speech as accommodating as Litvinov's would probably have revivified the Rapallo connection. Although the Foreign Ministry and business circles had frequently been disappointed with the fruits of their eastern association in the past, they had always managed to maintain about it a façade of intimacy. When other German interest groups had lost their enthusiasm the Wilhelmstrasse had always reserved to itself the final words about relations with the USSR.

And those words, 'continue as before', had repeatedly been

[1] Twardowski to the Foreign Ministry, October 31, 1929, 2860/D560818.

[2] Schlesinger to Curtius and Schubert, November 2, 1929, 4562/E160178–9.

[3] Degras, op. cit., II, 408–32.

[4] Dirksen to the Foreign Ministry, December 5, 1929, 2860/D560998–9.

[5] Saucken to Kaufmann, December 5, 1929, 4562/E160998–9.

[6] *Deutsche Allgemeine Zeitung*, December 6, 1929.

[7] *Kölnische Zeitung*, December 6, 1929.

based on the recognized needs of foreign policy, often to the detriment of Germany's bargaining position on economic and trade matters. Now, partly because of Stresemann's death in the autumn of 1929, and more directly because of the deepening of the social crisis in Germany, the political environment had changed. Consequently, in foreign policy the initiative rested more with the parties and the press, whose mood was vengeful.

Increasingly Wilhelmstrasse officials were caught in the fire of press attacks, which maintained that their defense of Germany's domestic and foreign interests against the Soviets was woefully inadequate.[1] From January to May 1930 few commentators in Germany were able to preserve a sense of perspective about developments involving the USSR. In January and February the German press erupted in a spate of charges that the CPSU and the Comintern were inciting the KPD to revolution. Only Otto Hoetzsch, who had just returned from a visit to Russia, suggested that Stalinism in the form of the Five-Year Plan signified the downgrading of the revolutionary arm of Soviet policy.[2] The rest of the non-Communist press, however, was agreed that the KPD had become more militant, sufficient 'proof of a reversal in Comintern policy that had gone hand-in-hand with the leftist development in Soviet policy generally'.[3]

There were indeed many indications that the KDP was becoming more active, but they did not point to imminent revolution. The KPD sponsored mammoth meetings in 'defense of the Soviet Union';[4] German factory workers concluded 'Socialist competition' agreements with Soviet trade unions to defend the Soviet Union, form Communist cells in their factories, and fight Social Democracy; German 'barricade fighters of May 1' were received as heroes in the USSR; and KPD workers' delegations, members of the *Rotfrontkämpferbund*, and men like Max Hölz toured the Soviet Union.[5] From this flurry of activity the German press concluded that the CPSU was responsible for the 'criminal policy of

[1] *Sozialdemokratischer Pressedienst*, November 14, 1929.

[2] *Deutsche Allgemeine Zeitung*, December 22–31, 1929; January 5, 21, 1930.

[3] *Börsenzeitung*, January 21, 1930.

[4] *Berliner Tageblatt*, January 25, 1930.

[5] Hilger and Meyer, op. cit., 228–9; *Berliner Tageblatt*, January 25, 1930.

the German Communists despite the efforts of diplomacy to conceal this fact'.[1]

The anti-Soviet crusade of the German press, fed by new incidents, began to spread uncontrollably in the first months of 1930. The Russian network of service stations in Germany – Derop – for example, was accused of spreading revolutionary agitation.[2] More seriously, the Soviet Embassy and trade delegation were described as centers of 'bolshevistic-communistic propaganda for the whole of Germany'.[3] *Vorwärts* reported that the *Rote Fahne* was receiving a handsome subvention from the Soviet Embassy,[4] and the *Berliner Tageblatt* accused Moscow of supporting the KPD with funds and agents: 'It is manifest that in Moscow the present situation in Germany is viewed as a revolutionary one.'[5] None of these charges, however, was documented. In the heightened atmosphere of German politics early in 1930 rumor was made to serve as fact.

The German press also continued to follow the changing fate of the German colonists in Russia, reporting large numbers of deportations. Often such stories were puffed up through rumor. In late February, for example, the *Deutsche Zeitung* carried information about a decree ordering all German peasants in the Ukraine, some 1,000 villages and 50,000 families, to evacuate their homes.[6] Partly erroneous reports such as these were then taken up and publicized by the rest of the press. At the same time many *Reichsdeutsche* from the USSR, mainly individual peasants and artisans, entered Germany after losing their possessions and means of livelihood through the collectivization decrees; in a penniless state, they would add to the flood of anti-Soviet press releases about the 'fruits of Socialism'.[7]

Another issue raised by Soviet efforts to transform their economy was the fate of the remaining German concessions in the USSR. By 1930 the Soviet government had given up hope of attracting outside capital through foreign concessions and began harassing the remaining ones. In mid-February the influential

[1] *Vorwärts*, January 28, 1930.
[2] *Berliner Tageblatt*, January 25, 1930.
[3] *Düsseldorfer Nachrichten*, February 7, 1930.
[4] *Vorwärts*, January 28, 1930.
[5] *Berliner Tageblatt*, January 25, 1930.
[6] *Deutsche Zeitung*, February 28, 1930.
[7] *Kölnische Zeitung*, March 3, 1930.

Berliner Tageblatt took up the cause of the German agricultural concession Drusag (*Deutsch-Russische Saatbau-Aktiengesellschaft*),[1] a state-supported model agricultural enterprise in the northern Caucasus, that had recently been subjected to some collectivization measures. This sent a further anti-Soviet ripple through the German press.

The existing commercial treaties with the Soviet Union, the *Sozialdemokratischer Pressedienst* concluded, were no longer adequate to protect German interests. The emigration of the colonists, the collapse of the German concessions, and the expulsion of the *Reichsdeutsche* were evidence that the Soviet government was not willing to keep its contractual agreements. The SPD sounded the alarm bell: 'There can no longer be any doubt that German-Soviet relations have now reached their lowest point.'[2]

7. URGENT APPRAISALS

THE German government shared the view of the Social Democrats. The interaction between problems of domestic security, an enraged public opinion, and the hiatus in German-Soviet relations, called for a departure in Germany's policy. Since the previous summer, Dirksen—who was most immediately concerned about the problem—had bombarded the Foreign Ministry with a medley of reports suggesting measures to rescue the Russo-German partnership. A viable relationship with Moscow, he felt, was threatened by two political circumstances: a Soviet commitment to revolution as an historical imperative (which he thought could best be broken by stringent measures on the home front rather than by diplomacy) and the Soviet belief that Germany was joining an anti-Soviet alignment of states.

Because this latter assumption was politically crucial Dirksen suggested concerted measures to demonstrate to the Soviets how illusory it was. He recommended, therefore, placing the 300-million-mark credit on a revolving basis, upping German technical aid to Russia, and expanding cultural relations with the USSR. This policy was broached by him on August 28,[3] repeated in a

[1] *Berliner Tageblatt*, February 16, 1930.

[2] *Sozialdemokratischer Pressedienst*, February 12, 1930.

[3] Dirksen to Schlesinger, January 17, 1930, 4562/D162269–74.

lengthy memorandum on October 31,[1] and urged without interruption as relations worsened in early 1930.

But even Schlesinger, who generally favored meliorative policies of an economic kind, rejected the Dirksen plan as economically unnecessary and politically dangerous. The credit, he informed Dirksen, had already been put on a revolving basis early in 1929 after the suspension of credit negotiations with the USSR. If this action were now made public to placate Moscow, it would probably have the opposite effect, merely provoking a further acrimonious debate in Germany about her eastern policy. And even if this were not the result, such action would serve only to win for the USSR the economic support of other states and mute unfavorable reports in the world press about the viability of her economy.[2] The Ambassador nevertheless repeated his proposal on January 29, 1930: 'The question of credits is the key that will open the way to a further development of Russo-German relations'.[3]

Dirksen's impassioned advocacy of one-sided concessions to Russia in early 1930 must be attributed to his distance from the German scene. It showed his scant appreciation of the close limits that the new popular anti-Soviet psychology in Germany had placed on the freedom of German diplomats to decide issues on the basis of foreign policy criteria alone. In this matter Foreign Minister Curtius took the Ambassador's education personally in hand. After receiving from him a further proposal that he send a prominent politician to Moscow as a goodwill token and make a statement to the Reichstag about Germany's fidelity to her Soviet partnership,[4] Curtius informed him of the changed situation in Germany.

Without a Soviet *quid pro quo* for the suggested concessions to Moscow, he wrote, the Comintern would be encouraged only to increase its support of the KPD. Moreover, inflamed German public opinion would not tolerate such a lopsided exchange. He reproached Dirksen for not being more sober about the justified hostility of the press toward the USSR. He added that it was

[1] Dirksen to Curtius, October 31, 1929, 2860/D560829–34.

[2] Schlesinger to Dirksen, January 25, 1930, 4562/E162275–8.

[3] Dirksen to Curtius, January 29, 1930, 2860/D561074–81.

[4] Dirksen to Curtius, February 14, 1930, 4562/E160614–23; another dispatch similar in content but more urgent in tone was sent to Curtius one week later (Dirksen to Curtius, February 21, 1930, 4562/E160703–8).

impudent of Moscow to ask for *evidence* of Germany's friendship after burdening relations with numerous provocations. Nevertheless his government was willing to repair the bonds if this was not made too difficult by the 'attitude of the Soviet government and the Comintern or through the repercussions of this attitude upon the political factors in Germany'. Curtius promised to take up the question after the conclusion of the Young plan debate; preparations in this direction, he noted, were already under way in the Foreign Ministry.[1]

These preparations consisted partly in the examination of a crucial question: should a conciliatory policy toward the USSR be continued in view of the burgeoning of KPD strength and the insistently anti-Soviet tone of German public opinion? Was such a policy defensible on prudential grounds? Put differently, were intimate ties with the USSR being bought at the price of Germany's internal security, or were they serving to inhibit the revolutionary predilections of the KPD? An assessment of the internal German situation and of Soviet priorities would largely determine the answer to that question.

In February and March the Wilhelmstrasse attributed KPD militancy to Soviet directives distributed in anticipation of a revolutionary situation in Germany.[2] Yet security officials downgraded the gravity of this threat; they were confident that timely precautions would keep the Communists in check until a building boom in spring reduced the ranks of the unemployed.[3] What stance should the Foreign Ministry therefore take? Since, to his mind, diplomacy was a blunt tool for use against the KPD, the more so because Interior officials had not succeeded in documenting a link between German Communism and Soviet agents, Dirksen felt that relations with the USSR should be judged independently of considerations of domestic politics.[4]

Trautmann, Director of the Wilhelmstrasse's Eastern Department, was inclined to share this view. The assumption of the Rapallo relationship, he stated, was that Germany had the resources to hold in check any revolutionary tendencies within her

[1] Curtius to Dirksen, February 15, 1930, 2860/D561210–13.

[2] Memorandum by Trautmann, March 5, 1930, 4562/E162322–4.

[3] Memorandum by Trautmann, February 15, 1930, 4562/E160561–78.

[4] Dirksen to Curtius, February 14, 1930, 4562/E160614–23; Dirksen to the Foreign Ministry, February 7, 1930, 4562/E162314–17.

own frontiers. Since the German government was still master of the situation there was no reason yet to alter basically the relationship because of 'our domestic circumstances'.[1] And a more affirmative view in the Wilhelmstrasse was that close relations with Moscow were actually a stabilizing factor within Germany. In the words of Schubert, whenever Germany maintained cordial relations with the USSR the 'activities of our domestic Communists became somewhat weaker and vice-versa'.[2]

If considerations of internal security did not militate against restoring some intimacy to relations in the east, were the reasons that had dictated the former intimacy still valid? Dirksen, a rather colorless bureaucrat with a static view of inter-state relations (constants derived from clearly recognized 'national interests'), thought that little had changed since 1922: 'The prerequisites for the political friendship that led to Rapallo and the Berlin treaty have remained the same'.[3] These he identified as common interests in eastern Europe (especially Poland and Lithuania), broader international questions, and economic and trade matters.[4] This interpretation was shared by the even less imaginative occupant of the Russian desk, Consul Dienstmann.[5]

Trautmann, however, was more systematic and astute in his assessment, summing up his ideas in a seventeen-page memorandum addressed to the Foreign Minister. After describing the setting of the crisis he examined the assumptions that German policy makers had hitherto made about the utility of the Russian tie. He rejected as outdated the notion that Moscow still served Germany as a counterweight to the west; to the European powers, he observed, Russia had become a cloud on the eastern horizon that evoked curiosity but not fear. Economic and trade relations with the USSR had proved equally disappointing.

But despite these negative conclusions about *Gesamtpolitik* and *Wirtschaftspolitik*, Trautmann was still hopeful concerning *Ostpolitik*. A shared interest in the questions of Lithuania and Poland,

[1] Memorandum by Trautmann, February 15, 1930, 4562/E160561–78.

[2] Memorandum by Schubert regarding conversation with the King of Sweden, January 28, 1930, 2860/D561059–66.

[3] Memorandum by Dirksen entitled: 'Sowjetrussland in 1929', December 27, 1929, 2860/D561042–50.

[4] Dirksen to Curtius, October 31, 1929, 2860/D560289.

[5] Memorandum by Dienstmann: 'Die deutsch-sowjetischen Beziehungen seit 1918', February 20, 1930, 4562/E160640–55.

he observed, was 'finally the only positive factor that has remained as an active moment (Aktivum) in Russo-German relations despite all mutual incidents'. And for this reason, if for no other, the special link with Moscow would have to be retained. But it would have to be secured so as to ensure that Germany would not again be exploited.[1] A few days later Curtius expressed similar sentiments when he informed the cabinet that Germany's grievances against the USSR would be negotiated in an effort to salvage mutual relations, but only in such a way as to protect German domestic interests: 'One need only recall the Polish question in order to be convinced of the need [for such negotiations].' Germany, he concluded, must be careful not to let herself be drawn into the anti-Soviet front that seemed to be forming throughout the world.[2]

Finally Germany's military interests had to be weighed in the balance as well. Thus the same cabinet session addressed by Curtius received a strong warning from Reichswehr Minister Groener that a political disengagement from the Soviet Union was militarily indefensible. 'Only relations with Russia', he informed his colleagues, 'give the army the opportunity to familiarize itself with the most modern weapons and to keep abreast of [new] manufacturing processes.' The minister reported that the means for doing so, the German bases—just fully coming into their own as training and testing sites—were completely staffed and performing all of their assigned functions.[3] The most compelling reason for maintaining them (one not mentioned by Groener) was that the Reichswehr had just entered a new phase in its rearmament program whose success hinged on the continued use of Kazan and Lipetsk for the testing of prototypes of new aircraft, tanks, and other weapons.[4]

Groener further noted that certain branches of German industry had recently also developed a vital stake in the maintenance of the military tie. This interest marked a revival of an earlier military-technical phase of German-Soviet collaboration, although on a

[1] Memorandum by Trautmann, February 15, 1930, 4562/E160561–78.

[2] Extract from minutes of cabinet meeting, February 20, 1930, 4562/E160629–38. [3] Ibid.

[4] Völker, 'Die Entwicklung der militärischen Luftfahrt in Deutschland', 227. For details of this phase see: Carsten, op. cit., 306–11; Erickson, op. cit., 271–7.

new basis. In the autumn of 1928 Soviet officials began approaching German firms with proposals for technical assistance in the creation of a modern native war industry; these were made after the Deputy Commissar of War had twice been rebuffed (in March 1926 and again in July 1927) in his appeal to the German government for similar technical aid as well as financial assistance.[1] During 1929 a first agreement was concluded with Krupp for technical help in the production of high grade steels.

But after long talks the same German firm turned down a further proposal that it provide the War Commissariat with some of its military production secrets and undertake to staff a 'construction bureau' that would carry out specified technical and design assignments for the buildup of the Soviet armaments industry.[2] A similar overture was then made to the firm of Rheinmetall, another large German steel enterprise, which resulted in a tentative contract that was ready for initialing early in February—at the height of the winter crisis. The sixty-page agreement provided for the establishment in the environs of Moscow of the requested 'construction bureau' staffed by twenty German engineers from Rheinmetall and the delivery to the Red Army of artillery pieces and other equipment produced in Germany or by affiliates of German firms in neutral states.[3] While these talks were proceeding the Soviet government was also negotiating subsidiary agreements with a number of German firms—including Zeiss—for the production of related pieces of specialized equipment.[4]

Foreign Ministry officials viewed this new line of military collaboration with unconcealed disfavor and tried to block it by dissuading Rheinmetall from initialing the pending agreement.

[1] *Supra*, 25–7, 96–7.

[2] Unsigned memorandum, probably by Moltke, May 1, 1929, 4564/E163956–8; Dirksen to Trautmann, May 7, 1929, 4564/E163960–1; Memorandum by Trautmann regarding talk with General Ludwig, former head of the *Truppenamt*, at the time adviser on armament questions to Uborevich of the Soviet War Commissariat, January 3, 1930, 4564/E163984–9; Memorandum by Moltke regarding conversation with representatives of Krupp, January 30, 1930, 4564/E164006–8.

[3] Memorandum by Moltke regarding conversation with Eltze, director and chief negotiator for Rheinmetall, February 12, 1930, 4564/E164052–4.

[4] Memorandum by Trautmann, January 3, 1930, 4564/E163984–9; Memorandum by Schubert regarding talk with General Hammerstein, February 10, 1930, 4564/E164022–9.

Schubert, Trautmann, and Köpke were able to recognize its employment potential for Germany's unemployed engineers and idle factories and also acknowledged its possible military importance for the Reichswehr. But they nevertheless opposed it because their eyes were on the threat of revolutionary Communism. Further military ties were fraught with the gravest risks, Trautmann wrote. They would keep Germany from exploring alternate political alignments, and, of greater concern, they would support the efforts of the Bolsheviks to create a modern armaments industry precisely at a moment when they were pressing for a revolutionary initiative in Germany.[1]

Early in February a conference of leading Foreign Ministry officials decided to intervene in Rheinmetall's dealings in Moscow. Accordingly a telegram was drafted for Eltze, the firm's chief negotiator, informing him that the Wilhelmstrasse would 'refuse to give its express consent to the transaction'. At this critical juncture General von Hammerstein, Head of the *Truppenamt*, approached Schubert with an urgent plea that he not disrupt the negotiations; such action, he remonstrated, would have unacceptable military and political consequences for Germany. Voroshilov and Uborevich, he reported, had both threatened a termination of the military contacts if the talks with Rheinmetall were to shatter over German governmental reservations.[2] (These clear words served to accent earlier warnings by Dirksen that the German stations in Russia would 'atrophy' if the proposed military-industrial cooperation were refused.)[3] Schubert again pointed to the danger of Soviet cannons being used against Germany in a future military attack or revolutionary attempt; finally, however, he relented, and in a telegram to Moscow withdrew his categorical opposition to the agreement.[4]

[1] Memorandum by Trautmann: 'Votum', January 30, 1930, 4564/E164009–10.

[2] Memorandum by Schubert regarding conversation with Hammerstein, February 10, 1930, 4564/E164022–9.

[3] Dirksen to Moltke, February 3, 1930, 4564/E164019–21; Memorandum by Schubert citing letter from Dirksen of December 19: December 23, 1929, 4564/E163974–7.

[4] This followed a further conference with Gaus, Trautmann, and Moltke (memorandum by Schubert, February 10, 1930, 4564/E164044; Schubert to Dirksen, February 10, 1930, 4564/E164032). The negotiations with Rheinmetall were not successfully terminated until July. The reasons for the delay are obscure. We know, however, that they originated

Despite the political and military arguments favoring negotiations to end the winter crisis with the Soviet Union the decision to bargain with the Narkomindel required considerable courage on the part of the Wilhelmstrasse. For as the press increasingly portrayed Moscow as the source of Germany's domestic difficulties the risks of pursuing a conciliatory policy increased accordingly for the government. Frequently the Wilhelmstrasse now came under fire from a number of directions – including parties of the government coalition – for not defending Germany from militant Bolshevism. Such criticism was first voiced by the Socialist press in connection with the colonist affair.[1] Then in February some papers charged the Foreign Ministry with keeping security officials from taking resolute action against KPD machinations: 'It is high time that the Foreign Ministry realize the seriousness of the situation and drop its opposition to necessary measures by the police.'[2] On February 12 the SPD *Pressedienst* went so far as to attribute the fiasco involving the colonists, the plight of Russia's *Reichsdeutsche*, the collapse of Germany's concessions, and the domestic excesses of the KPD, to the Wilhelmstrasse's velvet-gloved treatment of Moscow during previous incidents. At a time when Hermann Müller still headed the government it asked: 'What does the Foreign Ministry plan to do?'[3] Even the *Berliner Tageblatt*, which frequently served as a voice for the Wilhelmstrasse, commented in connection with the Drusag episode that German interests were being sacrificed to the 'great line of our Russian policy'.[4]

During the subsequent fourteen weeks of German-Soviet negotiations (from March to mid-May), the anti-Soviet press 'crusade' not only failed to abate, it spread to new inflammatory subjects. Of these Soviet religious persecution raised a hue and cry in Germany from March to May that was more intense than that raised by previous issues. This was particularly true in the Catholic press and among the rank-and-file of the Center Party. Attention was

---

with Rheinmetall and not the Foreign Ministry (Dirksen to Curtius, June 7, 1930, 2860/D561674–5; Dirksen to Curtius, July 30, 1930, 2860/D561791–3).

[1] *Sozialdemokratischer Pressedienst*, November 14, 1929.

[2] *Düsseldorfer Nachrichten*, February 7, 1930.

[3] *Sozialdemokratischer Pressedienst*, February 12, 1930.

[4] *Berliner Tageblatt*, February 11, 1930.

first drawn to this subject by the religious persecution of the colonists.

The Catholic press, however, only took it up after the Pope recommended prayer for the Russian Christians (March 2)[1] and staged a pontifical mass in Rome (attended by the diplomatic corps but not the German representative) for the atonement of wrongs committed against Christianity in Russia (March 19).[2] Thereafter well-attended meetings in all parts of Germany, but particularly in the Rhineland and southern Germany, decried the mounting Soviet anti-religious crusade in petitions calling for governmental intervention in Moscow. The leaders of the Center and numerous private citizens issued similar appeals, which flooded the Chancellery and Foreign Ministry.[3]

The Wilhelmstrasse was in an awkward position; it intervened where it could, but with little fanfare. Where cases of persecution involved *Reichsdeutsche* it entered *démarches* on the basis of the German-Soviet treaties of 1925, often with positive results. In other cases it cautioned Moscow informally that a resumption of intimate relations would be psychologically difficult if the anti-church measures were not halted.[4] In public, however, the Wilhelmstrasse tried to dissociate itself from anti-Soviet demonstrations that were beginning to take on an organized international character. 'Out of consideration for the official relations between Germany and Russia,' the German Ambassador to the Vatican explained, he had declined to join in the pontifical mass for Russian Christianity.[5] And when the Soviets protested the participation of Dr. Held, the head of the Bavarian regime, in an anti-Soviet gathering, the Wilhelmstrasse forwarded the *démarche* to his government.[6] Again the Foreign Ministry was charged with timidity: 'In its Russian policy the Foreign Ministry is completely out of touch with the overwhelming majority of the German people.'[7]

[1] *Germania*, March 3, 1930. [2] *Vossische Zeitung*, March 19, 1930.

[3] Some examples of appeals addressed to the Chancellor and the President may be found in files of the Reichs Chancellery: L617/L195670, L195690–1.

[4] Unsigned memorandum, April 4, 1930, L617/L195704–36.

[5] Bergen to the Foreign Ministry, March 21, 1930, 4562/E161023–5.

[6] Schubert to Dirksen, March 27, 1930, 2860/D561463.

[7] *Dresdner Neueste Nachrichten*, May 28, 1930. See further: *Bayerischer Kurier*, March 27, 1930; *Schlesische Volkszeitung*, March 27, 1930.

Of greater concern to the Wilhelmstrasse than these repeated accusations was an episode involving leading members of the coalition parties. On March 14 the prestigious Herrenklub was the scene of a secret meeting of about eighty persons; its purpose was to consider the threat to religion posed by Moscow's assault on the Russian church. The group, which included a few Russian *émigrés*, consisted mainly of leaders in the religious, political, and economic life of Germany. It was summoned and chaired by Franz von Papen and addressed by an illustrious roster of speakers: Catholic Bishop Schreiber, General Superintendents Karow and Dibelius of the Evangelical-Lutheran Church, members of the Center Party (but not Brüning), Graf Westarp of the Nationalists, former cabinet members Gessler and Raumer of the People's Party, and former Chancellor Luther.[1]

The deliberations quickly established a consensus that action was necessary against the threat of Bolshevism. When the Catholic and Protestant notables signified their intention to join hands against a common enemy, von Papen was beside himself with hope. It was, he announced, a moment of 'world historical importance'. But the debate about possible measures to counter the recognized threat showed the meeting to be of somewhat less significance. Some participants suggested the possibility of revamping Rapallo, boycotting Russia economically, or launching a military invasion. The timid majority, however, wanted only to voice their opprobrium of Moscow's war on the Russian Church. The assembly's only concrete step was to set up an action committee composed of the rabid Soviet haters, the von Alvensleben brothers, the more innocuous von Papen, von Raumer, and others.

On first learning of the Herrenklub episode from reports that had leaked to the press and after receiving a Soviet diplomatic inquiry about the meeting a short time later,[2] Foreign Ministry officials became active. If reports carried in the *Rote Fahne*[3] and intelligence reaching the Wilhelmstrasse by more reliable channels were true, then a well-financed anti-Soviet group was being organized that had as its goal nothing short of a revolution in

[1] Minutes of a confidential discussion concerning the religious persecutions in Soviet Russia, March 14, 1930, Nachlass Schleicher, 73–9.

[2] Memorandum by Schubert concerning conversation with Krestinskii, March 20, 1930, 4562/E161007–1008.

[3] *Rote Fahne*, March 22, 23, 1930.

Germany's foreign policy and the secession of the Ukraine from the USSR.[1] A special cause for discomfort was the fact that the initiative for the meeting had apparently come from the Center Party, one of whose leaders, Brüning, was already known to have been chosen by Hindenburg as Germany's next Chancellor.

To inhibit anti-Soviet currents in the Center Party, Curtius asked about the attitude of Brüning and received an encouraging report: at a recent Catholic meeting the next Chancellor had allegedly expressed support for a continuation of the Rapallo policy. He then contacted members of his own party, some of whom, like Raumer, had been elected to the action committee of the Herrenklub gathering. Finally he scheduled appointments with both von Papen and Brüning. Through these channels the Foreign Minister apparently underscored the fundamental conflict between the government's policy and the measures envisioned by some participants at the meeting on March 14.[2] It has not been possible to establish Curtius' action in each case, but in sum they probably helped to extract the political teeth from the Herrenklub affair.

This is also suggested by the first progress report of the action committee appointed at the March 14 meeting,[3] and a covering letter from Werner von Alvensleben, its secretary, to Schleicher.[4] Von Alvensleben requested that the report be transmitted to Curtius to reassure him about the goals of the Herrenklub group. And as now described those goals were indeed modest when contrasted with the more extreme demands expressed on March 14. The report reflected the restraining hand of Curtius as well as the practical difficulties involved in giving programmatic form to the anti-Soviet revulsion of a medley of interests. It concluded that the program of the action committee would have to be restricted to the lowest common denominator of the eighty persons in attendance—informational work in the areas of religion and *Weltan-*

[1] Redlhammer to Curtius, March 20, 1930, 2860/D561418–20; Memorandum by Trautmann, March 22, 1930, 4562/E161035–6.

[2] Curtius to Schubert, March 22, 1930, 2860/D561430–3.

[3] Report by Werner von Alvensleben, April 23, 1930, Nachlass Schleicher, 73–9.

[4] Werner von Alvensleben to Schleicher, April 23, 1930, Nachlass Schleicher, 72; See also the letter forwarding the report to Curtius, Schleicher to Curtius, April 25, 1930, Nachlass Schleicher, 80.

schauung.[1] The Herrenklub initiative, it seemed, was running out in the sands.

But coupled with recurring press accusations of timidity directed against the Foreign Ministry (notably by Center and SPD papers), and a spate of editorials calling for a revision of the German-Soviet treaties,[2] this incident demonstrated that the solid party support which had earlier supported German-Soviet cooperation was eroding quickly. These were difficulties at home that the Wilhelmstrasse would have to weigh carefully in taking up negotiations with the USSR.

It would also have to take into account the mood in Germany's business community. At the time it could be characterized as anger about the cavalier manner in which Germany's economic interests (concessions, *Reichsdeutsche*) had been violated by measures stemming from Russia's industrialization and collectivization programs. Symptomatic of this mood were the virulently anti-Soviet columns of the *Börsen-Courier*[3] and a peremptory resolution of the *Russlandsausschuss der deutschen Industrie*. This resolution demanded Soviet guarantees that the rights of German enterprises anchored in the October treaties would in future be recognized.[4]

Moreover, at the time German industrial opinion was not optimistic about the Soviet regime's chances of survival. Leading opinion in the Wilhelmstrasse held that the Bolsheviks would survive collectivization because there was no visible alternative to their rule.[5] Many of Germany's industrial leaders, however, had come to the conclusion that Soviet rule was on the verge of collapse. In February one of I.G. Farben's directors told Schubert, Trautmann, and the German Finance Minister, that he expected unsettled conditions in the USSR for a number of years. It would therefore be wise to keep one's fingers out of business relations with her: 'One should not encourage German industry to engage

[1] Ibid.

[2] *Sozialdemokratischer Pressedienst*, February 12, 1930; *Vorwärts*, March 18, 1930; *Kölnische Zeitung*, March 18, 1930; *Berliner Börsen-Zeitung*, April 4, 1930; *Sozialdemokratischer Pressedienst*, April 15, 1930; *Berliner Börsen-Courier*, April 17, 1930.

[3] *Berliner Börsen-Courier*, April 17, 1930.

[4] *Berliner Tageblatt*, April 8, 1930.

[5] Dirksen to the Foreign Ministry, February 15, 1930, 4562/E160559–60; Memorandum by Trautmann, February 15, 1930, 4562/E160561–78.

itself more deeply in Russia'.[1] And in his memorandum to the Foreign Minister on the eve of the clarification talks with the Soviets, Trautmann described the outlook of German industry in these words:

[Our industry] does not want us to break off our connections with Moscow. It expects German policy to remain involved in business relations with Russia with at least one foot, but it warns against acting too hurriedly (*Überstürzung*). A large credit action which would arouse a great deal of public attention is not considered desirable by our business leaders at this time.[2]

Given, on the one hand, the resolve of the Wilhelmstrasse—for compelling political reasons—to restore the frayed bond with the USSR and, on the other, a press hostile to the Soviet Union, political parties wavering in their sentiments towards her, and a business community wary of deepening its involvement in the USSR, the bargaining objectives of Curtius were easily definable. Germany would agree to warm up again the 'spirit of Rapallo' only if she were given visible concessions that would soothe German public opinion. It would be necessary to demonstrate that close relations with Moscow were not being bought at the prohibitive price of Germany's foreign interests or her internal security.

Meanwhile the uneasiness felt in Moscow in December had mounted into near-panic by January. The entire German press, from *Vorwärts* to the *Deutsche Allgemeine Zeitung*, commented *Izvestiia*, had been integrated into a single anti-Soviet front.[3] Shtein observed that one upshot of the unrestrained press offensive was that German requests which he passed on to Soviet departments were being consistently rejected. 'Outside of the Narkomindel no person believes in German friendship any more; everyone is convinced that Germany no longer stands on the side of the Soviet Union.'[4]

Another warning was addressed to German industry. Its choice,

[1] Memorandum by Schubert regarding conversation between members of the German government and representatives of I.G. Farben, February 21, 1930, 2860/D561237–49.

[2] Memorandum by Trautmann, February 15, 1930, 4562/E160561–78.

[3] *Izvestiia*, January 27, 1930; February 4, 1930.

[4] Twardowski to the Foreign Ministry, January 30, 1930, 4562/E162262–5; M318/M013296–8.

Izvestiia stated, was either to continue its polemics against Soviet developments or desist from them and profit from the Five-Year Plan.[1] But the polemics continued. By late February the discord was so marked that a member of the Soviet Embassy in Berlin confided to an American diplomatic official that he and his colleagues would soon be leaving the German capital; it was apparent that the German government was considering a 'break in relations'.[2]

Such baneful Soviet expectations were heightened in February by the acquittal in a German court of a group of counterfeiters charged with printing and distributing large quantities of Soviet *chervonets* notes.[3] The accused, five Germans and two stateless Georgians, had a ready defense; they asked for the application of the German amnesty law of July 14, 1928, which provided for the amnesty of persons charged with politically motivated crimes. Their sole goal, they said, had been to topple the Soviet regime, strike a blow at the KPD, and free Georgia. The prosecution, strongly supported by the Foreign Ministry, tried to prove that the accused had acted from base motives. There were stormy court scenes in which the defendants and defense counsel vilified the Soviet government and tried to implicate influential German politicians in their conspiracy.

Already political because of the nature of the offense, the trial was given a still sharper political relief by an *Izvestiia* editorial on the eve of the verdict. It called the defendants 'tools in the hands of political adventurers who had sought, together with the aid of a far-flung organization, to organize a war of intervention against the Soviet Union'.[4] *Izvestiia*'s response to the verdict was blunt: 'The court has proven that Germany is going over into the camp of our

[1] *Izvestiia*, February 16, 1930.

[2] Memorandum by a member of the Foreign Ministry regarding conversation with Wiley of the American Embassy, February 21, 1930, 2860/D561254–5.

[3] Unsigned memorandum about the case of the *chervonets* counterfeiters, February 11, 1930, 4562/E162356–60; Hilger and Meyer, op. cit., 230–1. An East German account, colored and intensely anti-Weimar, is given in: Albert Norden, *Fälscher: Zur Geschichte der deutsch-sowjetischen Beziehungen* (Berlin: Dietz Verlag, 1960), 86–123. The *chervonets* was a gold-backed note issued by the State Bank to stabilize the currency after the inflation of 1921–2.

[4] *Izvestiia*, February 7, 1930.

enemies.'[1] Soon thereafter Dirksen came away from a trying conversation with Litvinov. Never before, he reported, had he seen the Commissar so downcast and pessimistic: 'He spoke repeatedly of a catastrophe that had now broken in upon our mutual relations.'[2] German-Soviet relations had reached an impasse.

The Narkomindel saw the breaking of that impasse as an important diplomatic goal. Although diplomatic relations with Britain had recently been resumed,[3] that development had not served to strengthen Russia's international position.[4] For in Great Britain, as in Germany, the social and religious war accompanying collectivization in the USSR had released a strong current of anti-Sovietism. In the House of Commons the government had equated the Comintern and the Soviet regime. In Poland and France as well anti-Sovietism remained at high tide. Under such conditions of international isolation the Soviet government recognized that it would have to tread more gingerly on German interests if the feared anti-Soviet alliance were not to crystallize. In addition the needs of a modernizing Red Army had to be considered.

At any rate after mid-February the Soviet government began paving the way to a reconciliation with Berlin through a series of accommodating gestures. On February 26 Litvinov informed Dirksen that he was now able to guarantee the continued existence and undisturbed functioning of the Drusag concession, a gesture, he added, that was politically motivated.[5] Two days later Shtein announced that all *Reichsdeutsche* in Russia would be excluded from the provisions of the anti-kulak confiscation decrees.[6] On March 8 Dirksen reported a speech by the Comintern official Manuilskii to its Presidium; it was marked by an unusually restrained tone, deflating hopes about revolutionary possibilities for Communism in the bourgeois world.[7] Of more anecdotal interest

[1] *Izvestiia*, February 9, 1930. The *Frankfurter Zeitung*, February 9, 1930, discussed the verdict under the headline 'Eine rein juristische Entscheidung'.

[2] Dirksen to the Foreign Ministry, February 9, 1930, 2860/D561159–62.

[3] V. G. Trukhanovskii (ed.), *Istoriia mezhdunarodnikh otnoshenii i vneshnei politiki SSSR, 1917–1939 gg.* (Moscow: IMO, 1961), 330–3.

[4] See the Soviet study: A. N. Krasil'nikov, *Politika Anglii v otnoshenii SSSR 1929–1922 gg.* (Moscow: Gospolitizdat, 1959).

[5] Dirksen to the Foreign Ministry, February 26, 1930, 2860/D561277–80.

[6] Dirksen to the Foreign Ministry, February 28, 1930, 4562/E162301.

[7] Dirksen to the Foreign Ministry, March 8, 1930, 2860/D561318–19.

was a report in early March from the German Consul in Tiflis that local officials had removed the bells from all of the city's edifices except the ones from the German-Evangelical church.[1]

And within Germany itself a marked decline in Communist militancy was noted. May Day in Berlin, which had ended bloodily the year before, passed without incident in 1930.[2] Without considering Russia's objectives in Germany during this time, surface evidence suggests that Moscow concluded from the truculence of Germany's press that further incidents could separate the badly ravelled fabric of German-Soviet relations. And while the deceleration of the collectivization program heralded by Stalin's 'dizzy with success' statement of March 2 must be explained principally in terms of domestic Soviet politics, an ancillary cause was unquestionably the added strain that Russia's radical domestic course had had on her delicate international position. But whatever the explanation of these measures of accommodation, without them a revival of cooperation between Moscow and Berlin, however modest in form, would have been psychologically barred.

8. A TOLERABLE BASIS

IN this setting Curtius and Krestinskii met on March 5 for the first of an interminable series of conversations that were intended to reduce tensions.[3] At the outset the German Foreign Minister made clear his bargaining objective. Germany, he said, wanted the Soviet government to create conditions suitable to the resumption of intimate relations. It would however be necessary to do so step by step—matters should not be rushed. The negotiations, he suggested, should first treat specific complaints, then move on to political questions, and in a final stage deal with disputed economic issues. More than likely this approach was chosen to arm the Wilhelmstrasse against charges by its press that German interests were being bartered away without any *Gegenleistung*. As a minimum *Gegenleistung* Curtius asked for a Soviet pledge not to interfere in Germany's domestic affairs.

On March 17 a long and detailed list of German grievances was

[1] Dirksen to the Foreign Ministry, March 12, 1930, 4562/E161388.

[2] Dirksen to the Foreign Ministry, March 8, 1930, 2860/D561320–1.

[3] Memorandum by Schubert, March 5, 1930, 4562/E160797–821.

submitted to Krestinskii;[1] this was intended to initiate the first stage of the negotiations. Two days later Litvinov replied, outlining the Soviet approach. The incidents cited in the German note, he said, were of peripheral interest only. Their treatment would leave untouched the recalcitrant root of the crisis – the anti-Soviet temper of the German press: 'The Soviet government wanted a declaration [by the Wilhelmstrasse] that it was or was not adhering to the Rapallo line.'[2] Implicit in these words was the Soviet negotiating objective: a pledge of allegiance to the 'Rapallo spirit' was to be elicited at minimum cost while the incidents that had stirred up the German press were to be treated casually as accidental and atypical.

Dirksen adamantly reiterated that the prior satisfaction of Germany's conditions would be the condition to any such public statement. Faced with so unyielding a German position the Soviets, as was their custom, raised the Polish question in a manner calculated to enhance their bargaining stand. On March 19 *Izvestiia* renewed the earlier Soviet proposal for a Polish-Soviet non-aggression pact.[3] At the same time *Pravda* warned that any inclination by Germany to identify the Comintern with the Soviet government, as the British had, would be judged a sign that Germany was closing ranks against the USSR.[4]

Goaded by the Polish threat and repeated Soviet pleas for a statement on German-Soviet relations, the Wilhelmstrasse altered its bargaining style. Political questions, it was decided, would be treated simultaneously with the gravamina of both sides.[5] Such a change in approach was all the more prudent because Brüning's elevation to the Chancellorship, in late March, raised justified questions in Moscow concerning the new government's policies. The new Chancellor was, after all, a leader in the Center Party, whose wavering attitude towards the USSR was widely known.

Curtius therefore took the first opportunity to encourage Moscow's confidence in the new government. His own continuance in office, he told Krestinskii, was one indication of its resolve not to

[1] Memorandum by Schubert regarding conversation with Bratman-Brodovskii, March 17, 1930, 2860/D561342–61.

[2] Dirksen to Schubert, March 19, 1930, 2860/D561399–403.

[3] *Izvestiia*, March 19, 1930.

[4] *Pravda*, March 19, 1930.

[5] Curtius to Schubert, March 23, 1930, 2860/D561434–5.

deviate from former policies; an even weightier one, however, was a statement to him by Brüning that he planned no alteration in the Rapallo policy: 'surely this declaration of his was of great importance'.[1] Krestinskii admitted that the statement was reassuring, but only its publication would help to restrain Germany's press. These repeated Soviet pleas led Dirksen in mid-April to recommend that the Wilhelmstrasse be chary in making concessions. The Soviets, he wrote, were seizing the initiative in the negotiations and might maneuver the Foreign Ministry into a position where 'we one-sidedly declare our fidelity to Rapallo and otherwise the debate runs out in the sand'.[2]

It was high time for Germany to become active, place her demands on the table, and discuss the more critical political side of the crisis. This was achieved in three lengthy conversations, one between Curtius and Krestinskii in Berlin on April 16,[3] and the second and third between Dirksen and Litvinov in Moscow on May 13,[4] and May 16.[5] In all three the German aim was to establish Moscow's main responsibility for the crisis.

Both Curtius and Dirksen traced its origins back to two sources and characterized the petulance of the German press as a symptom not the cause of the crisis. The first source was identified as the heightened militancy of Soviet 'Communist organizations' (the term Comintern was purposely not used) and the support of a similarly militant German Communism by the Soviet party and press. The second source was no less important. It was Moscow's domestic revolution, that had erupted in war against the kulaks and war against the church. Soviet violence against the colonists had first aroused the rancor of the German press, Curtius explained; thereafter a like treatment of Russian religious groups had inflamed the sensibilities of the religious in Germany. The consequences were so grave, he added, precisely because the staunchest friends of Rapallo were, as a result, 'beginning to waver'.

The exchange became heated as Krestinskii rejected what he

[1] Memorandum by Schubert, March 31, 1930, 2860/D561471–5.

[2] Dirksen to the Foreign Ministry, April 14, 1930, 4562/E161615.

[3] Memorandum by Schubert, April 16, 1930, 2860/D561532–51.

[4] Memorandum by Dirksen, May 13, 1930, Trautmann Papers: Russia, Politics, General (not filmed).

[5] Memorandum by Dirksen, May 16, 1930, Trautmann Papers: Russia, Politics, General (not filmed).

described as complaints about the repercussions of Russia's domestic policies on the feelings of Rightist circles in Germany. The assumption at the base of their relations, he said, was that cooperation was possible despite the differing systems within their states. Their partnership was not based on sentiment but on shared interests and, perhaps, shared enemies. But Curtius pressed his initiative. 'The first agitation arose in Germany', he repeated, 'through the persons of German origin in Russia.' It was a matter of justified concern to the government if thousands of fleeing colonists knocked at Germany's gates. But of even greater concern was Moscow's encouragement and support of the KPD.

At this point Krestinskii interrupted the Foreign Minister and the conversation took a happier turn. 'He would', he said, 'like to officially declare that the Russian government certainly did not wish to interfere in German domestic affairs.' And although he dulled his announcement by repeating that the Comintern was a subject he was not competent to discuss, Curtius felt that progress had been made.[1]

The meeting between Dirksen and Litvinov almost a month later covered similar ground, but the atmosphere was much more relaxed. This, in part, reflected the changed circumstances within Russia since Stalin's statement of March 2. The drive to collectivize had been somewhat decelerated and the anti-religious tide had ebbed enough to permit a crowding of the churches by the faithful for Easter services (a fact noted with satisfaction in the German press, by Center cabinet members, and by Dirksen).[2] And, as we have seen, May Day in Berlin was celebrated without any breaches of the peace. A continuation of this milder course, Dirksen commented, was thought by political opinion in Germany to constitute *the* condition to the termination of the negotiations and the resumption of normal relations.[3]

In a further exchange on May 16 Litvinov summarized the Soviet case. The German explanation of the roots of the crisis was illogical, he said. Not Soviet policy but the 'press campaign' and hostile utterances of German statesmen, business groups, and

[1] Memorandum by Schubert, April 16, 1930, 2860/D561532–51.

[2] Memorandum by Pünder for the information of the Chancellor, May 16, 1930, L617/L195795–7.

[3] Memorandum by Dirksen, May 13, 1930, Trautmann Papers: Russia, Politics, General (not filmed).

political parties had encouraged 'public opinion' in the USSR to conclude that Germany was slipping into a hostile political orbit and turning against Russia. He realized that Wilhelmstrasse officials rejected this view, but they had only done so privately: 'For that reason the Soviet government had repeatedly suggested that . . . Curtius make a public declaration concerning the state of their mutual relations; this would reassure Soviet public opinion and mitigate the anti-Russian campaign in Germany.'

He had thought, he added, that Krestinskii's previous statement about the Soviet resolve not to meddle in German affairs and his government's action in issuing supporting ordinances to Soviet departments would hasten an accommodating gesture by the Wilhelmstrasse. The incidents, Dirksen replied, had not, however, stopped; recently members of the militant arm of the KPD, the *Rotfrontkämpferbund*, had been publicly feted in the USSR by many groups, including the Red Army. Litvinov granted that such cases constituted violations of the non-intervention principle: 'the Soviet government condemned them'.[1]

The 'either–or' alternatives put to the Soviets by the German press and the Foreign Ministry were having an unmistakable impact on Soviet policy. Krestinskii's non-intervention pledge, reiterated by Litvinov, was the first indication of this; a quiet May Day was the second. Others followed, as action was taken in specific cases. In Berlin, for instance, a second secretary of the Soviet Embassy was hastily recalled after his participation in the spreading of Communist propaganda had been documented.[2]

The Narkomindel, similarly demonstrative, promised that politically active party members would no longer find employment in Soviet trade delegations within Germany.[3] At the same time a circular to members of the *Rotfrontkämpferbund* inviting them to join in maneuvers of the Red Army was withdrawn by the Soviet government with an apology to the Foreign Minister. As a last gesture, Litvinov responded to a German *démarche* by vowing that all radio transmitters under his government's control would be ordered to stop propaganda broadcasts beamed to Germany. He refused to accept responsibility for the trade union transmitters–

[1] Memorandum by Dirksen, May 16, 1930, Trautmann Papers: Russia, Politics, General (not filmed).

[2] Extract from the minutes of a cabinet meeting, May 22, 1930, L617/L195802–5. [3] Ibid.

if he did so, he argued, a precedent would have been created that would revive talk about the government's responsibility for the Comintern's activities—but hinted that he would 'unofficially' try to influence them as well.[1]

These measures, Dirksen felt, had gone far to meet Germany's political grievances, and he recommended that the negotiations be concluded. More far-reaching demands might serve to reverse the presently favorable trend in Soviet policy. Dirksen's impatience was related in part to the particular angle from which he viewed diplomacy. Unlike Trautmann, who defined the *raison d'être* of the Rapallo partnership in terms of the Polish question, Dirksen argued:

> At this moment I consider as imperative the continuation of good relations as the only force which we have that is completely independent of the Western Powers. This is necessary in view of the fact that the disarmament conference has in the main been shattered, an Anglo-American bloc disinterested in Europe is forming, and Europe is coming more and more under the influence of French hegemonic wishes. . . .[2]

The Wilhelmstrasse, too, was by this time ready to terminate the political discussions if a satisfactory agreement could be made. (The unresolved individual grievances, juridical and economic issues were to be considered at a first session of the conciliation commission scheduled to assemble in mid-June.) In Berlin, Soviet promises together with Krestinskii's non-intervention pledge of April 16 were considered major although inadequate steps toward subduing German public opinion. Only a public statement equally positive was regarded as adequate. Since the Soviets demanded that the German government make public its resolve to continue Rapallo, the Foreign Ministry decided on a maneuver: it would seek to combine such an affirmation with a non-intervention statement in a bilateral communiqué announcing the end of the political conversations and the assembling of the Conciliation Commission.[3]

During the course of the talks the idea of some kind of communiqué was raised several times by both sides. On May 16 a

[1] Dirksen to the Foreign Ministry, May 26, 1930, 2860/D561640–50.

[2] Dirksen to the Foreign Ministry, May 28, 1930, 2860/D561628–31.

[3] Extract from the minutes of a cabinet meeting, May 22, 1930, L617/L195802–5.

German draft communiqué was submitted to Litvinov for study.[1] The non-intervention section noted that the two governments agreed to 'refrain from all attempts actively to influence the domestic affairs of the other country'.[2] The preamble of the draft communiqué referred to the mutual gravamina that had already been discussed, and otherwise exuded a warm conciliatory spirit.

Litvinov commended the fraternal tone of the draft but immediately took issue with the non-intervention declaration and the reference to the conciliation commission. The former, he claimed, was a tacit admission by the Soviet government that it had previously interfered in German affairs, while the latter suggested that Russia had violated the Russo-German treaties and that they were now being revised. This exchange again indicated that Berlin wanted the stress of the communiqué placed on obligations which the Soviets had assumed in order to prevent a recurrence of a similar crisis, while Moscow wanted to pass over the differences as 'isolated incidents' and accent its declaratory side.

Negotiations about the text of the communiqué, which almost broke down several times, continued for more than three weeks. At first the Narkomindel proposed an excision of both the non-intervention statement and the reference to the preceding negotiations over grievances.[3]

On this point the Wilhelmstrasse, however, was adamant. To have entertained the proposal would have placed it in an untenable position *vis-à-vis* the cabinet, the Reichstag, and the German press. Brüning, for one, felt that the communiqué in even its original form went too far and might arouse the impression that Germany was opting for Russia. His abhorrence of the Soviet system was voiced in a suggestion that the term 'friendly relations' be replaced by the more neutral 'treaty relations'.[4]

Moreover, the press again reproached the Foreign Ministry for being too lenient in agreeing to send a German conciliation delegation *to* Moscow, instead of vice-versa.[5] If the communiqué was to serve as the capstone to the negotiations and herald a revival of the former intimacy it would have to satisfy disparate interests in

[1] Memorandum by Dirksen, May 16, 1930, Trautmann Papers: Russia, Politics, General (not filmed). [2] Ibid.

[3] Dirksen to the Foreign Ministry, June 1, 1930, 2860/D561654–7.

[4] Curtius to Dirksen, May 23, 1930, Trautmann Papers: Russia, Politics, General (not filmed). [5] Ibid.

Germany of Soviet good faith. For that reason Curtius wired Dirksen that he would not 'consider making significant changes or weakening those sections of the communiqué that interest us especially'.[1]

Faced with such unaccustomed inflexibility and the possibility that the Wilhelmstrasse would leak word of its vow of non-intervention to the press, the Soviet government agreed to accept the German draft in its entirety. The one condition was that it be amended in two places through the insertion of four 'innocuous' words.[2]

For one thing, the Narkomindel wanted the preamble edited to include the adverb 'naturally (*naturgemäss*)': 'In the relations between Germany and the Soviet Union a number of questions have arisen *naturally* in the course of time. . . .' The effect of this change, however, would have been to represent the differences of the preceding months as routine rather than fundamental. But more consequential it asked that three decisive words be inserted in the non-intervention undertaking to read: 'Both governments are agreed that, *just as heretofore* (*nach wie vor*), they will refrain from any attempts actively to influence the internal affairs of the other country.'[3]

Who in Germany would accept this unambiguous affidavit of Soviet innocence? What Curtius wanted instead was an indictment of past Soviet conduct and a promise of good behavior for the future. He knew that he would be laughed out of the Reichstag if he presented such a communiqué, and instead of placating the parties and the press it would only incite them to further anti-Soviet outbursts.[4] The 'editorial' recommendation was therefore rejected without discussion.

By this time more than three weeks had elapsed. The conciliation commission was scheduled to begin work in the middle of the month and no announcement concerning the confidential discussions of the preceding fourteen weeks had yet been made. The impasse was only broken on June 12 by a United Press scoop

[1] Curtius to Dirksen, May 23, 1930, Trautmann Papers: Russia, Politics, General (not filmed).

[2] Dirksen to the Foreign Ministry, June 7, 1930, Trautmann Papers: Russia, Politics, General (not filmed). [3] Ibid.

[4] Curtius to Dirksen, June 10, 1930, Trautmann Papers: Russia, Politics, General (not filmed); Curtius to Dirksen, June 12, 1930, 2860/D561704–7.

reporting the summoning of the conciliation commission.[1] Litvinov, under great pressure from Berlin, now withdrew his reservations, the offending four words were stricken, and with the addition of a phrase emphasizing the routine nature of the conciliators' tasks and some rearrangement to enhance the prominence of 'Rapallo treaty' the communiqué was released to the press on June 13.[2]

The pivotal question which remained was whether the non-intervention clause of the communiqué would have the intended effect on German public opinion. Curtius had some anxious moments at first. On the eve of the communiqué's publication a number of papers greeted rumors that a Russo-German conciliation commission was about to assemble with unpromising headlines: 'Why to Moscow?'[3] 'Withdrawal Upon Withdrawal.'[4] This tone was initially maintained by *Vorwärts* even after the contents of the communiqué were made known: 'Everything remains as it was.'[5]

But happily for the Foreign Ministry the rest of the press, with few exceptions, received the communiqué cautiously and soberly; it was described as a tolerable basis for cooperative relations, given Soviet good faith. The accent in most of the commentaries was understandably on the non-intervention clause. *Vorwärts* and *Germania* were most reserved,[6] while the *Vossische Zeitung* was the most ebullient.[7] *Izvestiia* noted optimistically that after months of unrelieved Soviet-baiting the *Berliner Tageblatt* had resumed its former conciliatory stand.[8]

Both Russia's modification of the Stalinist program in March and the publication of the joint communiqué in June helped prepare German party and public opinion for a rapprochement with the USSR. Such a restoration of strained bonds was considered all the more necessary in Berlin because of France's drive towards European hegemony under the banner of 'pan Europe'. The *Bereinigungsaktion* was terminated with Curtius' long-awaited speech to the Reichstag about German-Soviet relations, and some

[1] *Deutsche Allgemeine Zeitung*, June 12, 1930.

[2] Dirksen to the Foreign Ministry, June 13, 1930, 4562/E162074–5.

[3] *Berliner Tageblatt*, June 12, 1930.

[4] *Sozialdemokratischer Pressedienst*, June 12, 1930.

[5] *Vorwärts*, June 14, 1930.

[6] *Germania*, June 14, 1930.

[7] *Vossische Zeitung*, June 13, 14, 1930.

[8] *Izvestiia*, June 16, 1930; *Berliner Tageblatt*, June 15, 1930.

positive results from the work of the Conciliation Commission. Looking back on the long and tortuous course of the crisis and on the protracted negotiations Dirksen concluded that tensions were relaxing which would help 'reestablish the earlier friendly atmosphere'.[1]

[1] Dirksen to the Foreign Minister, July 10, 1930, 2860/D561777–83.

Part Five

REVIVAL AND DECLINE, 1930–1933

1. *SALON DES REFUSES*

THE publication of the joint Russo-German communiqué and the setting up of the conciliation machinery in the spring of 1930, introduced a year of cooperation in German-Soviet relations that was as substantial as it was demonstrative. On one side, military collaboration reached its high-water mark and trade relations achieved the impressive levels that had long been anticipated, while, on the other, the anti-Versailles theme came to dominate the shared utterances and actions of German and Soviet diplomacy. To be sure, this substantial revival did not eliminate from the partnership disturbing elements that had caused the suspicion, instability and crisis during the previous year, nor were new disturbing elements kept from arising. But temporarily common enmity to France and mutual interest in trade (depression, Five-Year Plan) were able to keep these elements from forming the keynote of German-Soviet relations.

The gradual substitution after 1927–8 of France for Britain as Russia's chief enemy in Europe also served to enhance the community of interests between Berlin and Moscow that had been threatened by the Anglo-Soviet dispute; although at first it seemed that this development might inhibit rather than invigorate the relationship. The conclusion of the Young plan and the agreement for the evacuation of the Rhineland suggested for a flickering moment that Germany and France might be resolving their differences at last.

Yet contrary to general expectations, the withdrawal of Allied troops from the Rhineland on July 3, 1930, marked the beginning of increased tensions rather than amity in Franco-German relations. Part of the cause was the deepening economic crisis in

Germany which produced broad public support for demands by the parties of the Right and the Left that reparations payments be stopped.

Similarly, the slight improvement in German-Polish relations during the winter of 1929–30, marked by the conclusion of a comprehensive liquidation agreement in October 1929 and by the signature of a commercial agreement in March 1930, was the prelude to renewed hostility;[1] it reached its first culmination in the Reichstag elections of September 1930, when the Nazi Party and political militancy made substantial gains. This election, which a Soviet official correctly described as a victory for the idea of 'revanchism',[2] evoked a feeling of concern in France and Poland and made them work strenuously to maintain their military superiority over Germany. Provocation and retaliation came to constitute a vicious and seemingly unbreakable circle.

Such an exacerbation of tensions with Warsaw and Paris from the summer of 1930, on the one hand, and the partial restoration of Russia's prestige (a result of her success in weathering the worst dislocations of collectivization and its worst excesses), on the other, put German leaders in a frame of mind where they eagerly welcomed Soviet support against the despised 'Versailles system'. Typical of this attitude was a remark attributed to Chancellor Brüning, a devout Catholic who found everything associated with Soviet relations almost physically repugnant. 'We will only release Russia's finger, which we now hold,' he told Bülow, the new State Secretary in the Foreign Ministry, 'when we feel the hand of France tightly in ours.'[3]

The Soviets welcomed the end of Germany's ephemeral rapprochement with France and Poland, which they had found so distressing during the preceding winter; at the time their own relations with all three states had been strained. Yet while they favored tension between Germany and her two neighbors, they did not in the long run want to see it carried to the point of armed conflict. Analogous to Germany's position in the period 1925–8, when Foreign Ministry officials had sought a mean position in

[1] *Survey of International Affairs*, 1932, 318–19.

[2] Renner, German Minister to Finland, to the Foreign Ministry concerning conversation with Maiskii, October 3, 1930, L622/L197522–5.

[3] Memorandum by Bülow, February 12, 1931, 2860/D562023–30.

their relations with Russia between *Ausschaltung* and *Alleinbleiben*, the Soviet government now also worked on two fronts (considering the whole period until the accession of Hitler). On one front it sought to prevent a Franco-German-Polish alignment at its expense (*Ausschaltung*); on the other it tried to avoid having its international relations restricted to an increasingly militant and unstable Germany, bent, perhaps, on war with Poland or France. Both of these extremes, Moscow realized, would impede Russia's immediate goal of forced industrialization through the Five-Year Plans.

But first things first. As a start French efforts to isolate the USSR by organizing a united economic front under the slogan 'anti-dumping campaign' would have to be stymied. Since early 1930 this endeavor, whose success would have meant the frustration of the Five-Year Plan, or, at best, a drastic limitation of its objectives, had assumed threatening proportions. To counter it, a broadly conceived political strategy was needed. From about July 1930, the date of Litvinov's elevation to the office of Foreign Commissar, to May 1931, Soviet diplomatic efforts concentrated on support of the revisionist states in Europe.

This policy, although not new, was given an unprecedented momentum in the year under review. Litvinov alluded to it frequently in his conversations with German statesmen. In a meeting with Curtius early in November he made the important programmatic statement that the 'bases of Russian foreign policy were friendship with Germany and Turkey, good relations with Italy and England and the struggle against French hegemony'.[1] He urged the Wilhelmstrasse to align its policy more closely with that of Italy. And some weeks later, in an exchange with Dirksen, he first expressed great interest in a rapprochement with Bulgaria and Hungary, and then stated that any efforts by Germany to improve Russia's relations with the latter country would be welcomed.[2] Dirksen concluded that the Narkomindel was accelerating its efforts to promote a 'certain degree of contact between these governments, which do not have any interest in a further extension of French hegemony'.[3]

[1] Memorandum by Curtius, November 3, 1930, 2860/D561876–82.
[2] Memorandum by Dirksen, December 22, 1930, 4620/E198404–17.
[3] Dirksen to Bülow, December 23, 1930, 4620/E198402–3.

Germany's and Russia's joint interest in preventing a 'further extension of French hegemony' on the European continent was visible in a number of areas. It could be observed at work in Geneva during the final sessions of the Preparatory Commission of the Disarmament Conference. There the policies of the Russian and German delegations were quite closely coordinated. On one occasion, Litvinov admitted candidly to the German Foreign Minister that he did not expect any practical measures to flow from the work of either the Preparatory Commission or the Disarmament Conference. Nevertheless the sessions should be continued: 'The important thing is to isolate France and her satraps.'[1]

Another question that found Berlin and Moscow as one in opposition to France was the Briand proposal for a European federation. The Wilhelmstrasse saw this suggestion as part of a drive by France to perpetuate Germany's inferiority by maintaining the territorial and military *status quo* in Europe. The Narkomindel interpreted Russia's pointed exclusion from the purview of the proposed federation as one more effort to weld together an anti-Soviet grouping.[2] To render the planned federation innocuous the revisionist quartet of Germany, Italy, Bulgaria, and Hungary advocated the inclusion of the Soviet Union. Finally, after numerous representations to the European Committee, a body in Geneva constituted to consider the matter, the Soviet government was invited to participate in its deliberations to a limited extent.[3] The invitation was accepted; Litvinov took the opportunity to demonstrate in a public forum the closeness of Russo-German ties[4] and, of greater moment to Russia's broader strategy, the futility of French efforts to isolate the USSR.

Soviet eagerness to support Germany in the disarmament question and in her efforts to frustrate the pan-Europe plan had its effect on the Foreign Ministry's judgement. When considering whether or not to renew the Berlin treaty that was about to expire,

[1] Dirksen to Bülow, December 23, 1930, 4620/E198402–3; Memorandum by Curtius, November 3, 1930, 1843/420300–4.

[2] Memorandum by Dirksen regarding conversations with Litvinov, May 26, 1930, Trautmann Papers: Russia, Politics, General (not filmed).

[3] Memorandum by Weizsäcker entitled: 'Betr. Beteiligung am Europa-Ausschuss', April 29, 1931, Trautmann Papers: Russia, Politics, General (not filmed).

[4] *Der Tag*, May 19, 1931.

Curtius in March 1931 cited the recent aid of Soviet diplomacy as one compelling reason for renewal:

In recent times it has been possible to work together more closely with the Russians in the disarmament question and the pan-Europe problem. This contact has, of its own accord, led to a certain degree of cooperation with Italy in a variety of questions. Since the summoning of Litvinov and Krestinskii to the leading posts of the Russian Foreign Service the Russian side has shown even greater understanding of the usefulness of this cooperation.[1]

During this year an unspoken agreement thus formed the basis of German-Soviet cooperation. The Soviet government tacitly undertook to support Germany's anti-Versailles demands, if Germany would, in exchange, remain aloof from the anti-dumping campaign of France and her client states. Since such a campaign would fail without Germany, the Narkomindel spared no efforts in upholding its side of the bargain. It documented its contempt for Versailles on all possible occasions, and at times with such gusto as to embarrass the Foreign Ministry.

Two weeks after the publication of the Russo-German communiqué of June 14, the evacuation of Allied forces from the Rhineland provided Litvinov with a further opportunity to underline the services that the USSR had given Germany in her past struggle against Versailles. 'The Union Government,' he stated in a congratulatory telegram to Curtius, 'having publicly protested on 13 January 1923 against the occupation of German territory, notes with particular satisfaction the restoration of the rights of the German people in the Rhineland.'[2]

Such references to past services were enhanced by vows of renewed support for Germany's revisionist claims. An *Izvestiia* editorial of November 18 spoke of French imperialism as a common threat to Germany and the Soviet Union. Such support 'by the Soviet press of our wishes regarding the revision of the Versailles treaty can only be welcomed by us', Dirksen noted.[3] And there were many such statements in the Soviet arsenal, the

[1] Memorandum by Curtius concerning the question of the Berlin treaty, March 16, 1931, German Embassy in the Soviet Union: A19a, Berlin treaty, Renewal (not filmed).

[2] Telegram from Litvinov to the German Foreign Minister, July 3, 1930, cited in Degras, *Soviet Documents on Foreign Policy*, II, 447.

[3] Dirksen to the Foreign Ministry, November 18, 1930, 2860/D561904–905.

strongest of which came from the vitriolic pen of Radek. After tracing the upward curve of tensions in Franco-German relations, he concluded:

French policy does not sufficiently consider the internal situation in Germany, which makes the Versailles yoke more unbearable every day. It does not consider sufficiently the circumstance that influences in England and America could increase with the passing of time, that in their own interests would support the revisionist efforts of Germany. It underestimates the possibility of the consolidation of German-Soviet relations. It underestimates the possibility that once the question of revision has been raised, it will force its way through all historical obstacles. It is impossible in the 20th century to keep one of the most cultured nations in the center of Europe in chains. If France does not recognize this, then it will be compelled by history to do so.[1]

The aim of Soviet diplomacy—to wean Germany of any economic or political combination with France by making itself indispensable to Germany's revisionist policy—was directed to a lively political danger. For while the Russian press was bolstering the German claims to revision, the Foreign Ministry was canvassed more than once by Paris about the possibility of supporting economic measures against the USSR. The German delegation at Geneva was first approached by the French in September 1930 with a proposal to collaborate in the formation of an anti-dumping combination. The suggestion was rejected out of hand by the German representatives as being inconsistent with their relations with the Soviet Union;[2] but rumors of successful negotiations between France and Germany reached Moscow, and were not quashed until an official German denial was released to the press.[3] French efforts, however, persisted. In late December Briand asked the German Ambassador to consider the frightening consequences for capitalist industry if Soviet dumping were not stopped.[4]

Although the matter was not pursued at the time about two months later French representations to Germany took on explicit political overtones. They were most pronounced in two conversations between Hoesch and François-Poncet in February. In the

[1] *Izvestiia*, November 28, 1930.

[2] Ritter to Trautmann, September 20, 1930, 2860/D561846–8.

[3] Ibid.

[4] Hoesch to the Foreign Ministry, December 31, 1930, L622/L197581–583.

first the French official referred to the problems that were sure to be at the center of discussions at the May session of the League. Among these would be the matter of Soviet business methods; 'the question would arise whether Germany planned to renew the Berlin treaty and whether it did not plan to alter somewhat its attitude towards Russia'. The startled German Ambassador replied that the French should stop reading more into German-Soviet relations than existed. As for trade relations with Russia, these were for Germany a sheer economic necessity.[1]

Three days later François-Poncet nevertheless returned to the topic. In a moment of candor, he confessed France's anxiety over the recent intimacy observable in Russo-German relations: 'At present France feared the dangers of Germany going-together with Russia despite the opposition to such a policy that was being raised in Germany itself.'[2] Such expressions of discomfort, when coupled with an avowal of the need for a 'comprehensive Franco-German understanding', as in this instance, represented a French invitation for a deal at Russia's expense.[3]

There is no reason to believe that the Brüning government would have scrupled to conclude such an agreement if it had been restricted to limited objectives and if it had been accompanied by an offer of adequate compensations to Germany. But to raise the question of *adequate* compensations is to dismiss a Franco-German understanding at this point as unfeasible. Given the demanding mood of German public opinion a rapprochement between Germany and France would have required France to admit not only the principle but the fact of equality. It would have required an end, or at least a sharp scaling down, of reparations. Finally it would have required France's support for Germany's revision demands on Poland. Brüning had earlier said that he would not be ready to release Russia's finger until the hand of France was securely in his.[4] In 1930–1 such a vigorous clasp was as remote a possibility as it had ever been.

[1] Hoesch to the Foreign Ministry, February 20, 1931, 2860/D562042–3.

[2] Hoesch to the Foreign Ministry, February 23, 1931, Trautmann Papers: Russia, Economics, General (not filmed).

[3] Ibid. [4] *Supra*, 210.

2. AFTER DISCONTENT, PROMISE

WHILE German-Soviet international cooperation was growing more demonstrative in 1930–1, military contacts were reaching their high-water mark. As before, the Soviet government continued to hire German specialists for help in the construction of a modern war-industry and negotiated further with German firms for the delivery of war materials, equipment for armament plans and licenses for war-industry purposes.[1] Furthermore, the exchange of visits at maneuvers by high-ranking Red Army and Reichswehr officers was repeated each summer and the German bases continued to function. Indeed, in the summer of 1931 the testing program at Lipetsk reached its high point. The significance of these military operations for the German military command was expressed in July 1931 in a Reichswehr Ministry memorandum which rejected the possibility of Brüning making any concessions to the British government in the matter of the joint military operations.[2]

The French, who were familiar with the broad outlines of these military ties, and further aggrieved by mounting German-Soviet cooperation in international questions, also brooded over the development of Russo-German trade. For while the French government had sought German support for anti-dumping measures and had established an embargo on the import of some goods from the Soviet Union, a prestigious German trade delegation was touring Soviet industry. In Moscow it had begun trade and credit negotiations with the Soviet government, which concluded in April 1931 with the signature of a substantial trade and credit agreement. Thereafter, in 1931, German exports to Russia rose steeply to almost double those of 1929; and in 1932 Germany provided an impressive 46 percent of Russia's total imports.[3]

This significant upsurge in economic traffic was the fulfillment of expectations for the growth of trade relations that German industry had cherished in 1925–6, but had since abandoned. This favorable turn, like the rest of the relationship, was in sharp contrast to conditions during the foregoing winter; at that time the

[1] Völker, 'Die Entwicklung der militärischen Luftfahrt in Deutschland', 142.

[2] Memorandum by Fischer, July 13, 1931, Groener Papers, 112.

[3] Alfred Anderle, 'Die deutsch-sowjetischen Verträge von 1925/26', 502.

Foreign Ministry had refused to act on a Soviet request that a German trade delegation visit the Soviet Union on the grounds that the invitation was only intended to attract credits and whet the trade appetites of other states. Furthermore, open credit negotiations had been stalled by the reparations talks in the west as well as by the resolve of the Wilhelmstrasse not to provide Moscow with the bait of a public agreement that could be used to enliven Russia's trade contacts with Germany's rivals.[1] Schlesinger, to be sure, had astutely maintained the conditions for the previous modest level of trade by quietly placing the 300-million-mark credit of 1926 on a revolving basis, that is, by plowing payments on it back into new loans. But, supported by the Foreign Ministry, he had persistently refused to give way to Dirksen's pleas that Germany try to reverse the downward trend in political relations by making the matter public. Such a course, he had warned, would be tactically unwise and difficult to carry through in the face of a hostile German public.[2]

The improvement in trade relations that began during the summer and autumn of 1930, was attributable to a variety of causes. On Germany's side shrinking foreign and domestic markets and a worsening employment situation drew renewed attention to the possibility of capturing a larger share of the remaining orders from the first Five-Year Plan. The apparent success of the Soviet regime in outliving the worst dislocations of collectivization also helped to put the German business community in a more cheerful mood regarding the viability and credit standing of the Russian economy.

It was remarkable how quickly the outlook of German businessmen about the wisdom of committing themselves to the Five-Year Plan was changing in the spring of 1930. This sudden shift can be traced in the behavior of von Raumer, a noted industrialist, a leading member of the People's Party and sometime cabinet minister. Von Raumer had participated in the Herrenklub meeting on March 14 (where, indeed, he was made a member of the Action Committee). In the summer of 1930 he was named German economic conciliator on the Russo-German Conciliation Commission that was to meet for the first time in Moscow. It is possible and highly instructive to compare the opinions that Raumer

[1] Ibid.

[2] Schlesinger to Dirksen, January 25, 1930, 4562/E162275–8.

uttered at the height of the winter crisis with those that he held on leaving Moscow at the end of June.

In March Raumer had warned the Herrenklub against German support for Russia's industrialization plans on the grounds that such aid would merely buttress the sagging strength of a potential business rival and provide the means that the Soviet regime would use to intensify its foreign dumping.[1] In keeping with views that were common currency at the time in the United States and Europe, Raumer assumed that the dumping campaign was a revolutionary technique designed to disorganize the capitalist economies and not a desperate measure by the Soviets to earn foreign exchange for the purchase of producer goods from abroad. The Communists, he said, were unleashing the 'Red Army of their goods'; Germany's credits to Russia 'can no longer be defended; they represent today a sin against common sense (*Sünde wider den Geist*)'.[2]

These somber words were in marked contrast to those which Raumer addressed to Chancellor Brüning in a private letter some three and a half months later on the eve of his departure from Moscow. While in the Soviet capital Raumer had gone beyond his official duties as economic conciliator to explore the possibilities of intensified economic intercourse in private conversations with Soviet leaders. Wherever he turned he invariably found the question of credits to be taking first priority. In his official work on the Conciliation Commission he was told by his Soviet opposite that additional German credits were a prerequisite to the satisfaction of German grievances.

In his unofficial consultations with, among others, Gurevich, the man chiefly responsible for the execution of the Five-Year Plan, and Mikoyan, the Soviet Commissar for Trade, he discovered further credits being characterized as *the* key to an increase of German exports to the Soviet Union. From these conversations and the portentous snowballing of unemployment at home, Raumer concluded, as had Dirksen, that new German credits should be granted immediately.[3]

[1] Minutes of a confidential discussion concerning the religious persecutions in Soviet Russia, March 14, 1931, Nachlass Schleicher, 73–9.

[2] Ibid.

[3] For a renewed plea by Dirksen for the resumption of credit negotiations see: Dirksen to Bülow, June 20, 1930, 4620/E198322–35.

In a lengthy letter to Brüning he urged action; it was possible 'to penetrate the Russian market and to obtain a substantial part of the orders in the Five-Year Plan, if [Germany] meets the credit needs of the Russians halfway'. As for the risks, he felt that the Soviet economy was in a much stronger position than it had been a few months earlier. In any case, 'a continuation of unemployment in Germany constitutes a far greater risk than business with Russia (*Russengeschäft*)'.[1] Such views were probably fairly representative of the trend of thinking in the German business world in June 1930.

During July, August, and September the question of stimulating trade with the USSR by means of increased credits was considered at length in Berlin. Two points of view were in sharp conflict. The one (Dirksen) favored an entirely new credit agreement to be negotiated with the Soviet government, as the Narkomindel wished. The other (Schlesinger) asked merely for an increase in the 300-million-mark credit for which the Reich government and the Länder had assumed a guarantee. Finally the latter course was adopted and sometime in mid-October the Foreign Commissariat was so informed.

The reasons that dictated enlarging the existing credit rather than seeking a new one were delineated at length in a conversation between Dirksen and Krestinskii in late October.[2] In reply to Krestinskii's complaint that his government would have preferred new negotiations with the chance of winning new credit terms, Dirksen urged greater appreciation for what Germany was offering. In addition to placing the 300-million-mark credit on a revolving basis, he said, a further 300 to 400 million marks were now being freed for Russia's use: 'Therewith credits in the total value of 600–700 million marks have been guaranteed by Germany—which really speaks for a far-reaching accommodation on the part of the Reich government'. Unilateral action by Germany, he explained, was preferable because an acrimonious debate in the Reichstag and a discussion in the German press could thus be circumvented. Formal negotiations could have led to a postponement of the credit, and, more grievously, to the danger

[1] Von Raumer to Brüning, June 28, 1930, L617/L195882–92.

[2] Dirksen to the Foreign Ministry, October 28, 1930, Trautmann Papers: Russia, Politics, General (not filmed).

of 'unwelcome discussions of German-Russian economic relations. . . .'

There was a further consideration not cited by the Ambassador but one that, judging from past experience, must have argued strongly for a quiet, unilateral extension of credits; it was the deeply-rooted suspicion that the Soviets might try, as they had earlier with the 300-million-mark credit in 1926 and the Economic Protocol of December 1928, to use a further public agreement to pace-set their economic relations with France, England, and the United States. The Foreign Ministry and the German business community were approaching the possibility of increased trade with the Soviet Union hopefully but with a good measure of caution.

Until the autumn of 1931 the Soviets had publicized the prospects of their market for German imports, but otherwise had remained quite passive. Early in November, however, after the German government had announced its decision in the credit question, they assumed and maintained the initiative until the Piatakov Agreement was signed a little more than five months later. This spurt of activity must probably be traced back to a fundamental decision regarding Soviet purchasing policy (that the principal orders remaining from the first Five-Year Plan be placed in Germany) reached in Moscow sometime in late October or early November.

This conclusion emerges from a number of conversations between German and Soviet statesmen. On November 10 President Kalinin sounded the German Ambassador on the possibility of working out more suitable credit terms and increasing Germany's imports from the Soviet Union if Russia placed orders in Germany up to the sizeable limit of one billion rubles. As Krestinskii explained, 'a certain change had occurred in the economic policy of the Soviet government. It was less interested now in gaining credits than in increasing its exports, and, above all, in securing them [for a longer period of time].'

Dirksen answered by reiterating the familiar German lament. He cited the current fiscal year in which Soviet purchases from the United States were exceeding those from Germany. Yet in his report to the Foreign Ministry, Dirksen showed himself less skeptical of Soviet intentions than his listeners might have believed. For one thing he categorically denied that Soviet dumping was a revolutionary technique. Russia's eagerness to increase exports, he wrote, was proof that dumping was a means to earn foreign exchange and nothing else.[1]

The further course of the *pourparlers* between Berlin and Moscow provided further evidence that the Soviet government had revised its trade policies. Concerted efforts were made to revive the confidence of German business in the possibility of substantial trade with Russia. The Wilhelmstrasse was to be persuaded that Russia's political friends could expect a pay-off in increased trade. On November 29 Litvinov told Curtius that his government wanted to plan its imports and exports more carefully so that the earlier haphazard methods could be ended: 'it wished to concentrate [trade] more upon those countries with which Russia stood in friendly relations'.[2]

On December 22 the Foreign Commissar promised that trade with the United States would be sharply curtailed for reasons of *political* rationality. The Narkomindel, he added—admitting a further internal dispute over policy—had always taken the position that one should trade with those countries 'with which one got along well politically'. He had just discussed this question with Rosengolts, the new Commissar for Foreign Trade, who had accepted the viewpoint of the Foreign Commissariat: 'Rosengolts has a great deal more instinctive feeling for these foreign policy questions than his predecessor Mikoyan.'[3]

What *were* the political motives that may have induced the Soviet government to alter its purchasing policies in Germany's favor in the autumn of 1930? (We shall pass over purely economic considerations, such as proximity, familiarity, quality, and price, that may also have spoken for a redirection of Soviet trade.) The winter crisis of 1929–30 was clearly the background to the decision. The Soviet penchant for explaining foreign policy in terms of economic processes, as the reflection of the material and class interests of the ruling bourgeoisie, may well have persuaded Soviet theorists that the cooling of Germany towards Russia was partly

[1] Dirksen to the Foreign Ministry regarding conversations with Kalinin, Krestinskii, and Voroshilov, November 10, 1930, 1843 (not filmed).

[2] Memorandum by Bülow, November 29, 1930, 2860/D561923–6.

[3] Memorandum by Dirksen, December 22, 1930, 4620/E198404–17; Dirksen to the Foreign Ministry, December 23, 1930, 2860/D561951–2.

related to the bitterness of German industry over trade relations. What also tends to bear this out is that subsequent commentaries of the Soviet press were inclined to relate the improvement in relations to the greater optimism of the German business community about the Soviet market.

However, the *timing* of the shift in Soviet ordering policies in the weeks around the end of October and the beginning of November would suggest a more immediate cause. It was just at this time that the French were most active in trying to win German support for a common economic front against the USSR. The Narkomindel realized that repeated German refusals to entertain such proposals would seal the failure of French machinations. But there could be no certainty that Berlin would maintain her uncompromising stance. The German press, for instance, seemed to be more pro-French than pro-Soviet in its treatment of the dumping controversy; even the staunchly pro-Rapallo *DAZ* remarked that Germany was isolating herself by singly opposing anti-dumping measures that seemed to be universally favored throughout the rest of Europe and in America.[1]

Curtius, in a survey of the entire question, admitted that considerable domestic pressure was building up to counter dumping threats to the German match and wood products market. He asked Dirksen to take up the matter with the Soviet government.[2] The German Ambassador had already, on his own, warned Litvinov of strong currents in Germany 'that were directed against Russian dumping', and that 'could assume dangerous proportions for the Soviet government in the area of general politics'.[3] A few days later Curtius himself broached the matter to Litvinov.[4]

Significantly, all of this activity took place in the period from October 28 until November 3, lending weight to the view that there was a causal link between the anti-dumping campaign, which the Soviet government considered the principal threat facing it at this time, and the decision, announced a short while later, that Germany was to receive a lion's share of the remaining orders from the first Five-Year Plan.

Khinchuk, the Soviet Ambassador in Berlin, and a trade expert

[1] *DAZ*, November 1, 1930.

[2] Curtius to Dirksen, October 29, 1930, 1843/420468–74.

[3] Dirksen to the Foreign Ministry, October 28, 1930, 1843/420286–90.

[4] Memorandum by Curtius, November 3, 1930, 2860/D561876–82.

himself, extended the invitation asking a delegation of prominent German industrialists to visit the Soviet Union. He explained to Curtius that the Soviet government was drawing up its import and export schedules and wanted to discover whether German industry was in a position to satisfy Russia's industrial needs. Curtius indicated that he would personally support such a tour if it was not simply being sponsored as another political demonstration.[1] The deep-seated fear of being exploited was again evident a few days later when Dirksen asked Litvinov for a guarantee that the prospective negotiations in Moscow would have positive results; otherwise 'one might come to the conclusion that we were again being used as a pace-setter for America'.[2] Dirksen did not support the trip until Ordzhonikidze, the Chairman of the Supreme Economic Council, renewed a pledge to him that the invitation was not meant to play off Germany against England or the United States.[3]

The sequel of Russia's initiative was a manifestly successful visit to the USSR of Germany's leading industrialists from February 26 to March 11, 1931.[4] The German delegation was made up of many of the luminaries of German heavy industry. They represented enterprises such as Friedrich Krupp, Klöckner, Vereinigte Stahlwerke, Otto Wolff, Demag, Borsig, Siemens, AEG, Reinecker, and Shichau.[5] After two weeks of touring Soviet industry and of exploratory talks with Ordzhonikidze and his associates the group returned home with an attractive Soviet offer. German industry was given the firm promise of *additional* orders for 1931 alone of industrial goods worth 300 million marks on the condition that further credits of the same value would be provided on terms more favorable than those for the credit in 1926.[6]

Two searching questions had now to be answered in Germany

[1] Memorandum by Curtius, January 13, 1931, 2860/D561984–7.

[2] Dirksen to the Foreign Ministry regarding conversation with Krestinskii and Litvinov, January 17, 1931, 2860/D561993–4.

[3] Dirksen to the Foreign Ministry regarding conversation with Ordzhonikidze, January 24, 1931, 2860/D562002–3.

[4] See also: Hilger and Meyer, *The Incompatible Allies*, 239–42; Dirksen, *Moscow, Tokyo, London*, 89–96.

[5] Memorandum by Schlesinger regarding composition of the German delegation, February 13, 1931, 2860/D562031.

[6] Minutes of the various conversations between the German delegation and Soviet negotiators, entitled: 'Industriellen-Reise nach Moskau vom 26. February-Marz 1931', Trautmann Papers: Russia, Economics, General (not filmed).

before the conclusion of any agreement—could the orders be financed and would the Reich and the Länder assume an additional guarantee for such a credit? In their report to the German government, the industrialists recommended acceptance of the Soviet offer and asked for a 70 percent state default guarantee. The Soviet system, they reported, had stabilized itself to a degree far beyond any of their expectations; it was therefore a good risk. Furthermore, unemployment in Germany made the conclusion of the deal imperative: 'Given a contract in the value of 300 million, an additional 100,000 workers would be employed.'[1] In a separate report to the Foreign Ministry, Dirksen supported the economic arguments of the industrialists. In addition, he underlined the political significance of the development:

> At a time when the Naval Disarmament Agreement between France, England and Italy is adding fresh fuel to the suspicion that the great political decisions in Europe are being decided against, or at any rate, without Germany, this tour has demonstrated to the Western Powers the independence and maneuverability of Germany—that area of economic activity which is uncontroversial and difficult to assail.[2]

Despite the precarious financial position of the Reich, the cabinet accepted the arguments of the industrialists and the Ambassador in Moscow, which were supported by the German press[3] and the Foreign Ministry. On March 24, it granted the requested guarantee,[4] and on April 14 the Piatakov Agreement specifying the details of the transaction was signed in Berlin.

The Soviet government took the occasion of the agreement to survey fluctuations in German-Soviet relations during the preceding one and a half years. Molotov's report to the Sixth Soviet Congress on March 8, was symptomatic; he juxtaposed the recent improvement in relations with Berlin to the French-led efforts to

[1] Unsigned memorandum, March 14, 1931, L617/L195975–80.

[2] Dirksen to the Foreign Ministry, March 11, 1931, Trautmann Papers: Russia, Economics, General (not filmed).

[3] *Frankfurter Kurier*, March 10, 1931; *Berliner Tageblatt*, March 11, 1931. Only *Germania* departed from the otherwise favorable commentary of the German press. It spoke of the question of Russo-German trade relations as not being vital for Germany, and concluded that cultural and political considerations dictated 'a certain degree of reserve in economic activity *vis-à-vis* Soviet Russia' (*Germania*, March 10, 1931).

[4] Notes for a conversation between Curtius and Khinchuk, March 25, 1931, L622/L197574–5.

organize an 'economic blockade' of the USSR. In comparing the past with the present he struck a hopeful note. He noted that 'the wave of the anti-Soviet "crusade", which for a time endangered the consolidation and development of Soviet-German relations', had since mid-1930 been replaced by a more positive German attitude: 'The fundamental line in German policy in regard to the USSR has of late been one of friendly collaboration and the further consolidation of relations.' Although Molotov did not give an explanation for the upswing in relations, he mentioned the tour of the German industrialists as further proof of the 'understanding which German leaders have shown of the importance and value of Soviet-German economic collaboration . . .'.[1]

The commentaries of the Soviet press were more analytical. They were in line with the Soviet explanation that the crisis of 1929–30 was the result of an attempt by Germany to trade her relations with Russia for concessions granted in the Young plan and for equality with the western powers. *Izvestiia* of March 13 described recent improvements as a consequence of the realization in Germany that such hopes were vain. Moreover, the reason for the fickleness of Germany's bourgeoisie was that it had not appreciated the potential of the Five-Year Plan for trade relations: 'The German bourgeoisie, which is suffering a great deal from the effects of the unprecedented crisis and the unprecedented levels of unemployment must realize how important the growing Soviet market is.'[2] Repetition had made familiar to readers of the Soviet press the argument that the Soviet market was the key to the German economy's vitality, and that vigorous trade would naturally grow out of close political relations. Now the depression and the revision of Soviet purchasing policies gave the argument some validity for the first time. Implied in it, of course, was the converse, that a continuation of Russia's recently favorable purchasing policy would depend on the maintenance of the existing salubrious political climate in German-Soviet relations.

3. DISCORDANT NOTES

MOUNTING cooperation between the Narkomindel and the Wilhelmstrasse on the diplomatic and military levels and the

[1] Degras, *Soviet Documents on Foreign Policy*, II, 473–9.

[2] *Izvestiia*, March 13, 1931. See also *Izvestiia*, April 21, 1931.

upgrading of economic and trade relations were successful in muting the discordant notes that had crept into the German-Soviet partnership, but they did not silence them. Old problems remained and new ones were added. Despite growing cooperation both governments continued to appraise each other's policies for hints of real or potential shifts. Attention centered on Warsaw and Paris. The Soviets kept a close watch on France's efforts to involve Germany in her anti-dumping measures,[1] while the Germans explored rumors that periodically cropped up of renewed Russo-Polish non-aggression pact negotiations. One could not take chances.

Also, as before, the domestic situations in both countries continued as a disturbing factor. Although the communiqué of June 1930 and Germany's accommodating gestures thereafter had convinced the Narkomindel of the dependability of the Brüning government,[2] the growing instability and unpredictability of German internal politics left in question both the orientation of *future* German governments and the capacity of the Foreign Ministry to hold to any consistent political course. The Narkomindel saw the factors that had occasioned the winter crisis as persisting and realized that a renewed crisis was possible.

Moreover, the success of Right-wing extremism in the election of September 1930, meant that the possibility of German foreign policy becoming more militantly revisionist and of the Nazis entering a government would have to be reckoned with. Maiskii, the Soviet Minister in Helsinki, claimed that the elections had forced the two questions of ending reparations and altering Germany's eastern frontier onto the agenda of European politics. The reparations problem could perhaps be settled peacefully, but it was impossible 'to imagine a peaceful solution' to the problem of the Polish Corridor.[3] *Izvestiia* of September 19, greatly concerned that the Nazis might enter a government coalition, wrote that such a development 'would necessarily result in a worsening of German-Russian relations'.[4] These were contingencies to plan for.

A more immediate phenomenon tending to induce skepticism about maintaining the existing high level of cooperation with

[1] *Izvestiia*, December 12, 27, 1930.

[2] Memorandum by Dirksen concerning a conversation with Kalinin and Krestinskii, November 10, 1930, 1843 (not filmed).

[3] Renner to the Foreign Ministry, October 3, 1930, L622/L197522–5.

[4] *Izvestiia*, September 19, 1930.

Germany was the continuing anti-Soviet tone of part of the German press and public opinion. The Soviets attached much importance to this question. In late November 1930, for example, Krestinskii reproached the Foreign Ministry for failing to control the German press. Why, he asked, were anti-Soviet demonstrations—such as protest rallies against the suppression of religion in the USSR and German press support of the French position in the Ramsin trial (a show trial of a number of Soviet engineers as French agents on charges of sabotaging Russia's industrialization plans at the turn of the year 1929–30)—not being counteracted? Not a single official voice or press commentary had mentioned the advantages of cordial relations; the situation was approaching the depressed level of the previous winter and might easily deteriorate into widespread anti-Soviet feeling in Germany. Such a development, the Deputy Commissar claimed, would be all the more unfortunate since at this moment 'the relations between both governments were very friendly and totally free of incidents'.[1]

The hostile tone of the German press alluded to by Krestinskii grew out of many of the same influences that had led to the press campaign of the previous winter. These were disturbing elements that a friendly speech or vow of good behavior could not remove. First of all, the question of the tie between the KPD and the CPSU continued to stir up the German press even though revolutionary propaganda had decreased somewhat from a year earlier. Furthermore, the persistent domestic battle between all non-Communist parties and the KPD, particularly the internecine war between KPD and SPD, provided numerous incentives for assaults upon the Soviet system. Coupled with the humanitarian revulsion of a part of the German public against the Soviet 'revolution from above', this motive explains the uninterrupted treatment by the German press of the plight of the colonists and the anti-religious war of Moscow.

Thus the Foreign Ministry was put under fairly strong pressure to take up these very subjects with the Soviet government. Indeed, of the many topics that Dirksen raised in Moscow, those of exiled colonists and imprisoned church leaders came up the most frequently. Although a formal *démarche* on their behalf was impossible because of their Soviet citizenship, Dirksen went quite

[1] Memorandum by Dirksen, November 25, 1930, 1843/420366–9.

far in his specific requests of the Narkomindel.[1] He asked for the reunification of families separated in the flight of the colonists in 1929, for the release of imprisoned German pastors, and for the clearing of German relief parcels and money to exiled Germans. All this, he said, was essential to prevent a strong public reaction in Germany.

Krestinskii and Litvinov abandoned their usual defense that the matter was inadmissible to diplomatic treatment because it involved domestic Soviet politics, and promised to do their best. They held out some hope in the subject of relief parcels and the reunification of separated families.[2] Yet when the Soviets had not acted in either of these matters by early 1931, Dirksen warned that 'gradually such a strong current of public opinion would develop in Germany, that the accumulated bitterness might very well lead to outbreaks that could have momentous consequences for the whole of mutual relations'.[3]

Thereafter all Soviet complaints about the hostility of German newspapers were dismissed as a natural reaction to Soviet stubbornness in the colonist question.[4] The matter was regarded as potentially so disturbing for the future of the relationship that it was brought to the attention of Molotov. The influential Chairman of the Council of People's Commissars acknowledged its explosive character; he reported that interior agencies had already been instructed 'to pay the closest attention to the current situation of the exiled colonists; he assumed that an alleviation of the present situation would soon occur, although he was not in a position at the moment to indicate in detail what measures would be applied'.[5] The Foreign Commissariat's handling of German representations

[1] The fate of the colonists and possible relief measures was one of the main questions of discussion in conversations between Dirksen and Litvinov or Krestinskii on the following occasions: October 28, 1930, 1843/420286–90; December 22, 1930, 4620/E198404–17; February 4, 1931, German Embassy in the Soviet Union, Department E, G.M.I., *Geheimakten*, Cultural Content (not filmed); March 24, 1931, 2860/D562062–4; April 13, 1931, German Embassy in the Soviet Union, Department E, G.M.I., op. cit.

[2] Bülow to Dirksen, January 30, 1931, Embassy Moscow, Department E, G.M.I., op. cit.

[3] Dirksen to the Foreign Ministry, February 4, 1931, Embassy Moscow, G.M.I., op. cit.

[4] Dirksen to the Foreign Ministry, March 24, 1931, 2860/D562062–4.

[5] Dirksen to the Foreign Ministry, February 7, 1931, 2860/D562021–2.

—the promise of possible measures in the unspecified future, but the avoidance of a flat rejection because of German sensitivity—demonstrated Soviet officialdom's understanding of the precariousness of the existing good state of relations. Moscow recognized that the fairly secure base of German public support that had once firmly anchored German-Soviet relations was being cut away. Given the instability of domestic German politics, could the stability of German foreign policy be counted on?

4. RENEWAL IN NAME

IN the midst of conflicting developments that either buttressed or threatened the German-Soviet link, the question of renewing the treaty base of the relationship arose. On June 29, 1931, the Berlin treaty, signed on April 24, 1926, and ratified by the Reichstag on June 29, 1926, was due to expire. Unlike similar treaties it contained no provision for an automatic extension in the event of neither party denouncing it; it only stated, in the words of Article Four, that 'the two treaty partners would reach an agreement concerning the form (*Weitergestaltung*) that their relations were to take, in good time before the expiration of the five-year period'.[1]

Negotiations in some form were therefore necessary, and as a first step negotiating positions would have to be defined. There were a number of questions that required consideration. Should a treaty relationship be continued? If so, should the present treaty be extended without change, should it be altered in minor questions only, or should a basically new treaty be negotiated incorporating the lessons learned during the preceding five years of very uneven experience?

Given the recent improvement in relations it was predictable that the treaty partners would quickly agree to continue their association. The Soviet position, expressed by Litvinov at the time the matter was first raised, was that Russia was ready to negotiate a renewal of the existing treaty or a stronger one, depending on German preferences. Dirksen replied that his government had not yet examined the question in detail, but he thought it would favor a simple renewal.[2] This positive attitude was shared in

[1] League of Nations, Secretariat, *Treaty Series* (Lausanne, 1926), LIII, no. 1268, 387–96.

[2] Dirksen to the Foreign Ministry, February 6, 1931, 2860/D562018.

Germany by a surprisingly large part of the press; less astonishing, though, it was expressed with little enthusiasm.

The inclination was to state the case in favor of renewal in largely negative terms, as an unwelcome act made necessary by the inflexibly anti-German alignment of forces in Europe. Grabowsky, the editor of the *Zeitschrift für Politik*, epitomized this view in these words: 'The problem of the renewal of the Berlin treaty signifies for us nothing more than the choice between continued friendship and the beginning of enmity.'[1] The latter choice, he felt, could not be risked because of Allied opposition to Germany and Germany's revisionist ambitions. Even the increasingly anti-Soviet *Germania*, organ of Brüning's Center Party, echoed the Grabowsky thesis. It pointed to the tragic chain of circumstances that compelled Germany to seek allies in her battle for revision, disarmament, and equality among states such as Italy and Russia 'whose extremist rightist and leftist emanations had to be battled domestically in the interests of the general national welfare (*vaterländischen Gemeinwohls*)'.[2]

The Eastern Department welcomed the fairly widespread support for renewal by the German press. But it was opposed to proposals that renewal be made conditional upon Soviet concessions of a political or economic character. Politically it was suggested that a non-intervention pledge more precise and far-reaching than that contained in the joint communiqué of June 13, 1930, be extracted from the Soviets. Economically it was proposed that Moscow be persuaded either to desist from its dumping campaign on the German market or that the bothersome most-favored-nation principle be eliminated from the treaty base.[3]

For some weeks the championing of the economic proposals by groups in the Economic Department (W) of the Foreign Ministry placed a small obstacle in the path of the renewal negotiations. There was no consensus in the Economic Department about which part of the Berlin treaty was most damaging to Germany's foreign economic interests. One group argued that if Soviet dumping came to endanger the German economy, a renewal of the promise in

[1] Quoted in *Izvestiia*, March 13, 1931.

[2] *Germania*, February 24, 1931.

[3] Unsigned memorandum, probably by Trautmann, entitled: 'Aufzeichnung betreffend Erneuerung des Berliner Vertrages', February 5, 1931, L611/L192562–70.

Article Three of the Berlin treaty not to join in a financial or economic boycott of the USSR would cripple Germany in trying to take countermeasures. This group favored an excision of the article before renewal.[1]

Another group, led by Ritter, the powerful Director of the Economic Department, was less concerned about Article Three—in an emergency Germany could evade its provisions by representing her countermeasures as being unilateral. Yet he advanced a more formidable reason against renewing the Berlin treaty *tel quel.* The most-favored-nation principle, he claimed, was the straitjacket that would keep Germany from protecting herself against Soviet dumping. There was the small problem, however, of getting at this principle, which was anchored in the Rapallo treaty. Ritter reasoned that the Rapallo treaty had the same life span as the Berlin treaty because it did not contain a clause about a formal termination procedure; it had only been cited in Article One, Clause One, of the Berlin treaty as the basis of the German-Soviet partnership.

He therefore urged that the Rapallo clause be struck from the Berlin treaty; otherwise, 'we will have tied ourselves to the Rapallo treaty via the Berlin treaty for another two, three, or five years without having any chance to give notice. In that event we will not be in a position to adopt any manner of special measures against Soviet imports'.[2] As an economic expert with responsibilities in a limited area, Ritter admitted that compelling political reasons might outweigh his reservations. But he stressed that in that case, the decision to renew the Berlin treaty should be made in the fullest knowledge that it was economically indefensible.

It was typical of the German approach towards the USSR during the preceding years that political considerations again triumphed. On March 16, 1931, Foreign Minister Curtius formally embraced the political arguments of his advisers; he did so by affixing his signature to a lengthy policy directive to Dirksen, giving the reasons for preserving the connection with Moscow by means of a simple act of renewal.[3] This directive, together with the memoranda and reports that led up to it, are of some interest as a

[1] Memorandum by Ritter, February 25, 1931, L611/L192500–5.

[2] Ibid.

[3] Curtius to Dirksen, March 16, 1931 (IVRu 796/31 Anlg. 1), German Embassy in the Soviet Union, A19a, Berlin treaty, Renewal (not filmed).

systematic statement of the Foreign Ministry's view of relations with the USSR at a moment when they had apparently been stabilized on a fairly high plateau.

The arguments presented were not new. Curtius underlined the need for intimate relations to consolidate what had recently been won in diplomatic cooperation and the even later flowering of trade. Russia's function as a necessary counterweight to the sternly anti-revisionist front in the west was also cited: 'Especially at the present moment of tensions with France and the disappointment of our Locarno hopes, the policy of the Rapallo treaty and the Berlin treaty is a compelling foreign policy necessity.'

Finally the directive explored foreign policy alternatives and the possibility of eliciting compensation from the west for changing political sides. The conclusion was an old one: in view of Germany's objectives, no policy other than one of balance was open to her. Even though the western powers were adamantly anti-Soviet and overtures had been made for cooperation against Russia, 'no side had offered political concessions in any form for an abandonment of our political relations with Russia'.[1] With similar words Stresemann had rejected the idea of a reorientation of German foreign policy four years earlier during the Anglo-Soviet crisis.

While none of these arguments broke fresh ground, what was novel and symptomatic about the directive was the secondary importance attached to all of them. Cooperation at Geneva, parallel interests in opposing France, and even trade relations were all described as peripheral. The central issue was Poland. In the directive, Curtius returned time and again to the one theme — only a simple renewal of the Berlin treaty would foster an anti-Polish attitude on the part of the USSR. The argument was stated in terms of both defensive and offensive German interests:

> Russian power represents so important a factor in those questions of the European east which are of vital interest to us, and, given our militarily weak position *vis-à-vis* Poland, so dangerous a counterweight to Poland even today, that we could afford to give up this advantage only when we were in a position to pursue our interests without Russia or when we were able to trade the abandonment of our Russian partner for such substantial advantages that we would no longer be dependent upon Russia. . . .

---

[1] Dirksen to Posse, February 25, 1931, German Embassy in the Soviet Union, A10, Economic Relations between Russia and Germany (not filmed).

At a time when the German-Polish relationship is more strained than it has been for a long time, we have a twofold reason not to give up our relationship with Russia: Russia forms the natural counterweight against Poland, and Russia would be in a position to veer towards a pro-Polish course if she were not tied to us politically. In addition, there are no visible indications that the French-Polish alliance is loosening up or that England is becoming disinterested in Poland.[1]

This statement may be regarded as the culmination of a tendency noticeable since the winter of 1929–30: to see the value of German-Soviet relations increasingly in terms of the Polish question. This inclination was already evident in some of the press commentaries on the occasion of the Young settlement and the evacuation of the Rhineland. It was given its most explicit form in Trautmann's memorandum of February 15, 1930, advocating a resuscitation of the partnership after the crisis of 1929–30.[2]

The reasons for this development are difficult to sort out. From one perspective, the stress of the Foreign Ministry on the Polish question as the *raison d'être* for relations with the USSR seems to have been less a reflection of changing German foreign policy priorities than of Russia's domestic weakness and international isolation. Both made Soviet support of Germany's objectives in the west seem illusory despite cooperation at Geneva. From this angle the Polish question could be defined as the residual interest that kept the two states together, a view supported to a degree by Trautmann's memorandum of February 15, 1930, and the Foreign Ministry directive of March 16, 1931.[3]

But a fuller explanation requires consideration of changing German foreign policy priorities as well. One interpretation suggests that the evacuation of the Rhineland on June 30, 1930, permitted German policy makers to move on from their western goals to the Polish problem as the next item on their foreign policy agenda.[4] This analysis, while containing some truth, also falls short as a total explanation. It assumes that the Foreign Ministry was at liberty to select its foreign policy objectives with deliberation and to

[1] Curtius to Dirksen, March 16, 1931, op. cit.

[2] Memorandum by Trautmann, February 15, 1930, 4562/E160561–78.

[3] Memorandum by Trautmann, February 15, 1930, 4562/E160561–78; Curtius to Dirksen, March 16, 1931, German Embassy in the Soviet Union, A19a, Berlin treaty, Renewal (not filmed).

[4] RIAA, *Annual Survey*, 1932, 319–20.

pursue them purposefully, according to a conscious plan of action. Yet in the spring of 1931 this situation no longer obtained. By then the Wilhelmstrasse could no longer set the tone of German foreign policy; it was compelled to follow German public opinion, and it did so in a rather confused manner. The mood in Germany had turned uncompromisingly against Poland; in order to survive, the Brüning government had no alternative but to follow in its wake.

The anti-Versailles temper of public opinion that set Germany's policy sharply against Poland in 1931 did not, however, determine the specifics of it. That was still a matter 'of detail' to be worked out by the Foreign Ministry. And when it came to drawing up a blueprint for a change of the German-Polish border, the Eastern Department knew that Germany's political position had not improved to the extent that an early solution was imaginable. France and Britain were considered to be less amenable to Germany's policies than they had been for some years; support from Russia was problematical because of her military weakness and her involvement with the Five-Year Plan. With no hopes for realizing its maximum goal of revision, the Foreign Ministry had therefore to defend its minimal goal of keeping open the border question for a later settlement; in other words, of preventing a consolidation of the *status quo* in eastern Europe. This goal, pursued since 1926–7, was to continue as the guideline of German efforts.

Wilhelmstrasse officials therefore decided to use the negotiations for the extension of the Berlin treaty to have the Soviets reaffirm the conditions regarding Poland that had been attached to the Berlin treaty in 1926. In this manner the 'Polish component' of that agreement was also to be renewed. The directive of March 16 defined this 'component' by quoting from Stresemann's instructions to Rantzau of March 27, 1926. Germany, he had written, wanted firm assurances that the USSR would 'not meet Poland's security needs along her eastern frontier through either a guarantee pact, a non-aggression pact, or even a conciliation treaty'. This condition was to be clearly restated: 'Russia must know that we wish a renewal of the treaty primarily for political reasons arising from our eastern policy and the value of the treaty would vanish for us (*hinfällig wird*) if an agreement with Poland of the kind named in the above instruction should be made.'[1]

[1] Curtius to Dirksen, March 16, 1931, German Embassy in the Soviet Union, A19a, Berlin treaty, Renewal (not filmed).

In deciding to raise this question the Wilhelmstrasse was also trying to meet a current problem. At the time it was being rumored that either Moscow or Warsaw had put out feelers for a Russo-Polish non-aggression pact. The Soviets denied these rumors, but Berlin remained unconvinced. For even before the conclusion of the renewal negotiations, signs multiplied that Russia was beginning to draw conclusions from the deterioration of Germany's international position.

Negotiations for the renewal of the Berlin treaty were begun on March 24 and brought to a successful conclusion three months later with the signature in Moscow of a protocol specifying the terms of the extension.[1] The Berlin treaty which originally had a life of five years (together with the Conciliation Agreement of 1929) were now extended indefinitely. Either party could cancel the treaty at any time after June 30, 1933, by simply giving one year's notice. Thus the treaty in fact had a minimum span of three years, a practical compromise between the original wishes of the Narkomindel for one of five years and of the Wilhelmstrasse for one of only six months.[2]

The conflicting positions of the signatories on the duration question, the only issue in dispute during the negotiations, illustrate the two principal elements of instability in the partnership at the time. The Soviets pressed for a long minimal life for the treaty because they wanted at least a paper guarantee against the fluctuations of Germany's internal politics. These, they felt, could bring to power a government and a Reichstag less favorably disposed toward the USSR than the Brüning government.[3]

Germany, conversely, faced also with the unpredictability of politics at home, was uncertain whether this situation might tempt the CPSU to show its revolutionary prowess; at any rate she wanted the freedom to end the partnership at short notice as a defensive safeguard.[4] 'We need an elastic relationship with Russia,'

[1] Protocol extending the treaty of April 24, 1926, and the Conciliation Agreement of January 25, 1929. July 24, 1926, German Embassy in the Soviet Union, A19a, Berlin treaty, Renewal (not filmed).

[2] Dirksen to the Foreign Ministry regarding conversation with Litvinov, March 25, 1931, 2860/D562067–9.

[3] Dirksen to the Foreign Ministry regarding conversation with Litvinov, March 24, 1931, 2860/D562062–4.

[4] Dirksen to the Foreign Ministry regarding conversation with Litvinov,

Curtius informed Dirksen, 'because we must be in a position to break off this relationship when the tendencies in Russia directed toward world revolution become more active or when the dangerous strengthening of our own revolutionary energies force us to take countermeasures.'[1] Neither the Wilhelmstrasse nor the Narkomindel were viewing the future of their mutual relations with any sense of equanimity.

5. NEW FRIENDS

THE signing of the Protocol for the Renewal of the Berlin treaty on June 24, 1931, after a year of rather close cooperation, was nevertheless not the expected bright signpost along the path of German-Soviet friendship. Rather, it marked the end of a one-year interlude of cooperation and the beginning of a twilight zone in the relations between the two countries which continued until their rapid deterioration less than a year after Hitler's rise to power. During this period, in which political alignments were more fluid than they had been at any time since the early years of the 1920s, the community of interests that had held the Rapallo partners together for almost a decade gradually began to dissolve.

In May 1931, while talks for the renewal of the Berlin treaty were still in progress, it was announced that negotiations between France and Russia would soon begin for a commercial agreement and a non-aggression pact. A period of feverish activity followed, in which Soviet diplomacy concluded a series of non-aggression pacts, thus realizing a diplomatic objective pursued since 1924. The negotiations with France led to the initialing of a non-aggression pact in August. (Because of opposition in France the treaty was not ratified until October 1932.) Negotiations begun in the autumn of 1931 with Poland, Finland, Estonia, and Latvia were concluded early in 1932.

The Franco-Soviet rapprochement represented by the initialing of the non-aggression pact in August, unquestionably paved the way for the later agreements with Poland and the Baltic States. It is also clear that France's modest move toward Russia, which dis-

---

March 25, 1931, 2860/D562067–9; Dirksen to Bülow regarding conversation with Litvinov, April 20, 1931, 2860/D562090–1.

[1] Curtius to Dirksen, March 16, 1931, Embassy Moscow, Renewal (not filmed).

avowed previous French policy, was an admission by the Quai d'Orsay that its efforts to isolate the USSR through a united European anti-dumping front had failed. Paris attributed this failure to German doggedness in staying with Russia despite French blandishments – a plot against France. The Wilhelmstrasse had rejected the arguments advanced by French diplomats that continued cooperation with the Soviet Union entailed for Germany dangers of revolution and economic disaster because they were not accompanied by concessions in the questions of armaments, reparations, and frontier revision.[1]

Not only had Germany refused to dismantle her relations with the USSR, but she had expanded them demonstratively by capturing substantial Soviet orders for Germany's idle factories. The French business community seems to have responded to this upsurge in German-Soviet trade (which was in such marked contrast to the stagnation in Franco-Soviet trade) by demanding an easing of the inflexible line of France's eastern policy.[2]

But perhaps more determining for the French initiative towards Russia than economic considerations was the growing fear of German revanchism. The French had reacted with alarm to the recent electoral shifts in Germany and the sharp rise in the number of vitriolic editorials and speeches about border revision and reparations. A further tightening of the German-Soviet bond along the lines of the previous year, coupled with greater anti-Polish jingoism in Germany, could shake the whole French security system in eastern Europe to its base.

Against this background it took only the jarring news in March 1931 of a plan for a German-Austrian Customs Union to remove the Quai d'Orsay's last inhibitions about the wisdom of a rapprochement with Russia. The Customs Union project was viewed in France as an attempt to undermine plans for the creation of a pan-European union under her aegis and the position of her allies in eastern Europe. For these reasons France moved in May 1931 to shore up her position in the area by edging toward Russia.

The conclusion of non-aggression pacts with as many states as possible coincided with the main thrust of Soviet foreign policy since 1924–5; the Narkomindel therefore welcomed the French

[1] *Supra*, 214–15

[2] Hoesch to the Foreign Ministry regarding conversation with Berthelot, May 31, 1931, 2860/D562115–18.

initiative. Yet, in addition to general security considerations, specific circumstances also dictated this response. In 1927 Russia had offered France a non-aggression treaty to forestall what she regarded as the threat of a massive coalition against her under British leadership; in 1931 the French offer of a similar agreement was accepted for two quite different reasons.

The confusion of Germany's domestic scene had rendered the Rapallo front unstable, making the Soviets eager to reinsure their position against the possibility of Germany's defection. To repeat, the winter crisis of 1929–30 and the persistent anti-Sovietism of large sections of German public and press opinion, had demonstrated that German friendship could not, despite the goodwill of the Brüning government, be simply counted on for the future.

An added incentive to take up the French offer was a hard-headed assessment of the shifting power relations in Europe in the first four months of 1931, which seemed to favor France. To the USSR it appeared that her principal friend, Germany, was becoming infirm in her resolve and unsure of her goals at a time when her chief opponent, France, was moving from one foreign policy success to another. A full month before the Franco-Soviet negotiations began, Dirksen reported that recent developments such as the Naval Agreement between France, England, and Italy; France's vigor in promoting the idea of a pan-European Union; and her seeming ease in checking the Austro-German Customs Union suggested that the European power balance was swinging against Germany.[1] Moscow's conclusion, he wrote, was that France (followed by an obedient Britain) was a stable power with definite and hence predictable goals; Germany and Italy, however, the objects of Litvinov's earlier hopes for a *salon des refusés*, were increasingly becoming 'changeable and unpredictable factors in the great European balance'.[2] Dirksen did not have to make the point: Russia would be glad to liquidate her dispute with the emerging leader in Europe.

German officials reacted predictably to Moscow's negotiations, which until August were conducted only with France; any im-

[1] Report by Dirksen to the Foreign Ministry entitled: 'Die Sowjetunion und die internationalen Kräfteverschiebungen während der letzten Monate', April 13, 1931, L824/L198812–15.

[2] Dirksen to the Foreign Ministry, April 13, 1931, L824/L198812–15.

provement in Franco-Soviet relations might also point to an early Polish-Soviet reconciliation. Since Polish-Soviet enmity had recently been defined as the *raison d'être* of the German-Soviet association such a potential development was a threat. Nurtured by French claims that separate but parallel negotiations were in progress for a non-aggression pact between Moscow and Warsaw,[1] these rumors elicited a variety of German responses.

One extreme reaction was an unsigned article, written in the Wilhelmstrasse,[2] that appeared in *Germania* on June 18. On the Polish question it was as candid as German officials were in their confidential soundings of the Narkomindel.

> Is Russia [it asked], required to give guarantees that the talks with France will not lead to a basis for further, more comprehensive conversations in the East, under Franco-Polish auspices, which would then inevitably lead to the eastern Locarno desired by Poland without Poland fulfilling Germany's conditions for such an eastern Locarno, i.e. the return of Upper Silesia and the Corridor?

Although Russia was said to have given 'binding assurances' regarding this point, the article warned that if these were not meticulously kept the renewal of the Berlin treaty would become a 'song without words'.[3]

On the diplomatic level the objective of the Wilhelmstrasse was to elicit a Narkomindel promise not to bring Poland into the French-Soviet negotiations. But conscious of the German weakness, which had been amply demonstrated by the abortive plan for the Customs Union and the more recent financial crisis of the German banks, Wilhelmstrasse officials were reluctant to put this wish as an ultimatum that they could not back up. Empty threats

[1] Hoesch to the Foreign Ministry regarding conversations with Berthelot, May 31, 1931, 2860/D562115–18; Hoesch to the Foreign Ministry, June 7, 1931, 2860/D562125–6; Hoesch to the Foreign Ministry, June 15, 1931, 2860/D562131; Twardowski to the Foreign Ministry regarding conversation with Krestinskii, June 5, 1931, 2860/D562119–22; Twardowski to the Foreign Ministry, June 11, 1931, 2860/D562129; Dirksen to the Foreign Ministry regarding conversation with Krestinskii, June 19, 1931, 2860/D562136–7.

[2] The unsigned article was written by the Director of the Eastern Department, Trautmann (Meyer to Dirksen, July 1, 1931, 9187/H249510–13).

[3] *Germania*, June 18, 1931, quoted in Kochan, *Russia and the Weimar Republic*, 155–6.

have a habit of backfiring. Conditions regarding Poland for the renewal of the Berlin treaty were therefore not given the explicit form contained in the Foreign Minister's instructions of March 16.

On June 23, the last moment before the signing of the Protocol of Extension, Dirksen asked Krestinskii whether he agreed that the 'guiding principle in this regard [i.e. concerning France and Poland], which the German side had announced to the Soviet government on the occasion of the conclusion of the Berlin treaty, was still in force'. Without seeking an elaboration of these words the Vice-Commissar nodded his assent.[1] In the light of Germany's growing isolation and the variety of attitudes that the Foreign Ministry had in the past taken toward Russo-Polish non-aggression negotiations (extending from a veto on any form of association to toleration of an agreement that did not include an explicit guarantee of the German-Polish border), Krestinskii must have known that his easy agreement might keep intact the line to Berlin without tieing Russia's hands for a *détente* with Poland.

Nevertheless, the recrudescence of German mistrust persuaded the Soviets to offer more than vague assurances. A chronically unstable, but useful and perhaps only temporarily unreliable relationship with Germany was not to be jeopardized for a modest rapprochement with France. Every effort was therefore made to demonstrate Soviet good faith. The standard promises were given concerning Poland, and the Germans were kept informed of the course of the Franco-Soviet negotiations.

At the same time the Narkomindel made a more startling gesture. In a routine conversation dealing with Franco-Soviet negotiations on July 31, Litvinov suddenly revived a theme that had not been seriously discussed since 1926—the continental bloc embracing Germany, France, and Russia. 'Such a treaty between three parties would be worthy of consideration,' the Foreign Commissar observed. 'Poland would naturally not be included in such a grouping; and on the other hand France would be robbed of the opportunity to play off Germany against Russia or Russia against Germany.'[2]

How serious was Litvinov in making this proposal? Did he con-

[1] Dirksen to the Foreign Ministry regarding conversation with Krestinskii, June 23, 1931, 2860/D562136–7.

[2] Political report by Dirksen entitled: 'Sowjetisch-französische Verhandlungen', July 31, 1931, 4620/E199338–41.

sider it a real possibility in the confused international situation of 1931 or was he using it as a mere tactical gesture to lessen German reservations to a Franco-Soviet accord? The continuity of the idea of a continental bloc from Chicherin to Litvinov and its restatement in 1931 would suggest that the Soviets still viewed it as a long-term diplomatic goal. They probably had for some time. In 1929 just after Litvinov had become *de facto* Foreign Commissar he confided to Dirksen that he favored a Russo-French-German combination in principle.[1] But in 1931 the intractable political questions dividing Germany and France suggest that the proposal was premature, to say the least, and should be viewed as a tactical move. Certainly no fundamental importance should be attached to it.

Yet the proposal is interesting because it mirrored the changing international situation. Since 1924, when a continental bloc had first been bruited by Chicherin, the international positions of the USSR and Germany had been reversed. During the negotiations for the Locarno pact the continental plan was proposed by the Soviets as a means of arresting their drift into insularity. In 1931 they revived the plan in order to persuade Germany that she was not slipping into isolation. In the mid-1920s the USSR had faced the threat of Germany's developing association with France; in the early 1930s a Franco-Soviet rapprochement confronted Germany.

The Germans were puzzled and reserved in their reaction to Litvinov's proposal for a continental bloc. Both Bülow and Dirksen were confused about Soviet motives. On the substantive question of whether such a combination was desirable, the Foreign Ministry concluded that, as matters stood, it would mean including Poland. In short, it would be at the price of an eastern Locarno and hence was unacceptable.[2] According to a Wilhelmstrasse directive uncertain relations between France and Germany and intimate relations between France and Poland stood in the way of a three-power agreement. But instead of rejecting Litvinov's proposal, Dirksen suggested that it be put into storage as a future possibility; if Franco-German differences were ever settled Germany might want to use it as an efficient way of breaking France's guardianship of Poland.[3]

On the day of the initialing of the Franco-Soviet non-aggression

[1] Dirksen to Bülow, August 1, 1931, 9187/H249448–53.
[2] Meyer to Dirksen, August 5, 1931, 9187/H249434. [3] Ibid.

pact, Dirksen replied to Litvinov's feeler. Following instructions to eliminate the continental bloc plan as a subject of German-Soviet discussions, he asked Litvinov whether a three-way non-aggression agreement would materially strengthen Moscow's existing treaties with Berlin and Paris. The Foreign Commissar replied that his suggestion had been directed less to an expansion of a non-aggression agreement to the three states than to raising the possibility of a political combination. He was thinking of the future: 'He had only meant that if a clarification of German-French relations should at some time become imminent, it might be desirable and useful to conclude a tripartite agreement.'[1] These words tended to confirm the impression that Litvinov's initiative of July 31 was designed to reassure Berlin and not initiate a new round of political negotiations. An added result was that it kept the proposal on the agenda of German-Soviet relations as a long-term alternative.

6. TWILIGHT

IN the autumn of 1931 it became increasingly clear that after negotiating a non-aggression accord with France Russia was also determined to normalize her relations with Poland, despite German objections. In principle she had been willing to conclude a non-aggression treaty with Warsaw since August 1926; but she had been dissuaded from doing so by German reservations and by what were considered impossible Polish demands—demands that Soviet Russia conclude a collective agreement with a Baltic bloc under Polish leadership (thereby acknowledging Warsaw's hegemony in the area), and recognize the validity of the German-Polish frontier. These old conditions were again put to the Soviet government by the Poles in August 1931, and again they were rejected.[2] Then the Polish Foreign Office softened its demands and in October finally agreed to negotiations for a bilateral agreement on the basis of the Soviet draft treaty of 1926.

This accommodating Polish stance in the autumn of 1931 may be explained by a combination of factors: France was becoming a

[1] Dirksen to the Foreign Ministry, August 12, 1931, 1843/420694–6.

[2] Memorandum by Meyer regarding conversation with Bratman-Brodovskii, August 26, 1931, 2860/D562180–2; Memorandum by Curtius concerning conversation with Litvinov, August 28, 1931, 2860/D562189–96.

less dependable ally and was urging a rapprochement with the Soviet Union, and, more important, there were mounting fears of German revisionism. On the Soviet side, the same general considerations that prompted the agreement with France, coupled with revisionist clamor in Germany, may help to explain Litvinov's eagerness in taking up these negotiations. Although there is no documentary evidence for such an interpretation, it seems in character for the Narkomindel to view an agreement with Warsaw as eloquent notice to Germany that she should not count on Soviet support for early action against Poland. Moreover, the growing reluctance of France to sign and ratify her agreement also generated pressure for the negotiations.

A final development that was probably decisive in getting the negotiations moving, was the deterioration of the political situation along Russia's Asian border in late autumn. The Manchurian crisis, by raising the specter of two vulnerable frontiers, heightened Soviet wishes to avoid foreign complications that could impede industrialization. Events in Manchuria, Boris Shtein admitted to the German Ambassador, had been instrumental in the decision of the Soviet government to hasten a rapprochement with Poland.[1]

Coming scarcely more than half a year after the Wilhelmstrasse had defined the value of further association with Russia in terms of Polish-Soviet antagonism, these negotiations struck at the very heart of Germany's interests and raised some fundamental policy questions. What interests were being threatened and what measures could blunt the threat? Berlin had to decide, for one thing, whether to maintain the inflexible attitude toward any form of Polish-Soviet agreement that it had first adopted in 1926 during the Berlin treaty negotiations, edged away from thereafter, and revived in the directive of March 16 for an extension of the Berlin treaty.

The tenor of German statements occasionally suggested such inflexibility. Dirksen, for instance, at one time told Krestinskii and Voroshilov that 'in the interests of German-Soviet relations, the non-conclusion of the Polish-Soviet treaty was the only possible and desirable course'.[2] But both the Wilhelmstrasse and the

[1] Memorandum by Dirksen regarding conversation with Shtein, January 6, 1932, K1904 (not filmed).

[2] Memorandum by Dirksen regarding conversation with War Commissar Clementi Voroshilov and Krestinskii, November 12, 1931, 9187/H249341–7.

Narkomindel realized that such a demand was meaningless unless clothed as an ultimatum to the Soviets: either break off negotiations with Poland or forfeit Germany's friendship. By 1931 such a policy was beyond Germany's means—the fiasco of the Customs Union plan documented Germany's infirmity,[1] while the runaway nationalism of her public sentiment crippled the Wilhelmstrasse in pursuing any consistent policy.

If a Polish-Soviet rapprochement could not be blocked, one searching question remained: could the Wilhelmstrasse influence the content and political intention of the proposed non-aggression agreement so that German interests, already compromised, would not be hurt beyond repair? This became the goal of German policy in the negotiations from October 1931, until the initialing of the Polish-Soviet non-aggression treaty on January 26, 1932.

Germany's fundamental position was conveyed to the Soviet government by Dirksen in a conversation with Krestinskii on November 10. After expressing regrets that Soviet policy was helping to meet Poland's security needs, Dirksen formally withdrew Germany's objections to a simple non-aggression treaty containing only a prohibition on aggressive wars. But he coupled this gesture with the reminder that a 'direct or indirect guarantee of Polish territory' would violate German interests: 'An open and serious discrepancy between the political lines of both countries *vis-à-vis* Poland would thereby be created and the result would be a shattering (*Erschütterung*) of the bases of the Berlin treaty.'[2]

In subsequent discussions Wilhelmstrasse officials asked for assurances that Russia would retain a free hand in the event that Poland attacked Germany. The most serious differences, however, arose over the issue of what constituted an 'indirect guarantee' of Polish territory. The Foreign Ministry suspected that an 'integrity clause' similar in character to one that had first appeared in the Franco-Soviet non-aggression treaty would be included in the Polish agreement. The draft of the Polish-Soviet treaty rendered

[1] An unsigned memorandum concerning a conversation between a member of the German Embassy in Moscow and an unidentified Soviet official, reported that the official had alluded to the weakening of German prestige as a result of the abortive Customs Union plans. Germany, he had said, would have to become accustomed to the idea 'that Russia and Poland would in the long run make a serious effort to improve their relations' (July 13, 1931, 1843/420665–6).

[2] Memorandum by Dirksen, November 10, 1931, 9187/H249372–8.

the disputed article in these words: 'Both parties declare that they will refrain from an attack on the other side. Every action that violates the territorial integrity and political independence of the other side will be regarded as an act of aggression.'[1]

Circumstantial evidence suggests that a similar clause had first been incorporated by the French in their pact with Russia (where it was quite inoffensive), as a precedent that the Poles could use in their negotiations with Russia. At any rate, Polish insistence that the clause remain and German demands that it be deleted made the issue sharply political and put Moscow in an awkward position. In interminable conversations the Wilhelmstrasse kept alive its claim that the second clause of the article, allegedly of Polish origin, was atypical for a standard non-aggression treaty and disquietingly similar to the *status quo* section of the League Covenant (Article 10).

Warsaw was said to be defending it in order to legitimize the German-Polish border.[2] 'The persistence with which the Poles cling to Clause Two, Article One, is the best evidence that they do not regard it as something self-evident, but that they are using it to pursue far-reaching goals.'[3] The Soviets were also warned that publication of the clause might provoke such a hue and cry in Germany as to make further collaboration psychologically impossible. For these reasons the German side termed the clause an *indirect guarantee* of Polish territory, and claimed that by retaining it the Soviets were letting themselves be manipulated as a French instrument. 'The whole world,' State Secretary Bülow wrote Dirksen, 'would see in it a Russian capitulation and a recognition of the present territory of Poland.'[4]

Given the Soviet goal of bettering relations with Poland and France without jeopardizing the bond with Germany, such intense German reservations were given careful attention in Moscow. Negotiations with Poland were continued, but at the same time the

[1] Dirksen to Bülow, November 29, 1931, 2860/D562261–5.

[2] Memorandum by Dirksen regarding conversation with Litvinov, November 16, 1931, 9187/H249353–7; Memorandum by Bülow regarding conversation with Khinchuk, December 12, 1931, K1904 (not filmed); Memorandum by Dirksen regarding conversation with Litvinov, January 5, 1932, K1904 (not filmed).

[3] Meyer to Dirksen, December 9, 1931, 9187/H249307–12.

[4] Bülow to Dirksen, December 12, 1931, K1904 (not filmed).

Narkomindel tried hard to dispel the view that a Polish-Soviet accord would constitute a belated sanction of the Versailles treaty. Soviet arguments were curiously reminiscent of those Stresemann had adduced in defense of his Locarno policy some six years earlier. The shoe was now on the other foot. It was an argument of necessity. An agreement with Poland, Soviet diplomats explained, was imperative to Soviet security. Since the Poles inflexibly held to the position that they would only sign a treaty including the 'integrity clause', their terms would have to be accepted. Two assurances were given that German interests would not be compromised. The disputed clause was said to be harmless in that it did not specify frontiers or guarantee possessions but merely identified the territory to which the non-aggression undertaking applied. And, in spite of the words of the treaty, Soviet spokesmen asked that it be judged solely for its *political* content, which, they claimed, was not anti-German.

Statements of this kind by Soviet spokesmen were legion. Krestinskii promised that a non-aggression treaty with Poland would alter German-Soviet relations neither in form nor in content.[1] Litvinov asserted repeatedly that his government was determined to continue its friendly relations with Germany and would give proof of this at the forthcoming Disarmament Conference.[2] The influential War Commissar, Clementi Voroshilov, went even further by indicating that conflict regarding the Polish question stemmed less from diverging goals than from differences over *timing*. The Soviet government remained a 'fundamental opponent of the Versailles treaty',[3] and 'would not come to terms with (*nicht abfinden*) the present borders of Poland'.[4] The implication was clear: short run differences about timing should not obscure the shared interests in the revision of Poland's frontiers uniting the two states.

[1] Memorandum by Dirksen regarding conversation with Krestinskii, November 10, 1931, 9187/H249372–8.

[2] Dirksen to Bülow regarding conversations with Litvinov: December 6, 1931, 2860/D562266–8; December 22, 1931, 2860/D562273–5; January 10, 1932, 2860/D562291–2.

[3] Memorandum by Dirksen concerning conversation with Voroshilov, November 12, 1931, 9187/H249341–7.

[4] Memorandum by Dirksen regarding conversation between General Adam (in Russia on an inspection tour of the German military stations), and Voroshilov, on November 10, 1931: written November 14, 1931, 9187/H249348–51.

When these many gestures failed to soothe the Germans, the Soviets tried to document their good faith in a most unusual way. On December 12, 1931, Stalin, in an unprecedented interview with the German author Emil Ludwig, took a public stand on the controversy. Even though it was not mentioned by name, all of his words bore directly on the issue of the 'integrity clause'. He denied that a Soviet agreement with Poland would imply that the 'Soviet Union gives its sanction to, or guarantees, the possessions and frontiers of Poland'. The bilateral undertaking not 'to resort to war in order to violate the independence or the integrity of the frontiers of our respective States', did not, he said, mean 'recognition of the Versailles system', or 'guaranteeing frontiers'. 'We never have been guarantors for Poland,' he concluded, 'and never shall be. . . . Our friendly relations with Germany will remain what they have been hitherto.'[1] As far as they went, these were reassuring words.

As a final gesture to rob the 'integrity clause' of its sting and to demonstrate that it did not recognize frontiers, as the Poles pretended, Narkomindel negotiators included an *explicit* frontier guarantee in their separate non-aggression treaties with Estonia and Finland.[2] The evidence suggests that Russia pressed for conclusion of the Russo-Finnish treaty containing this guarantee (January 21, 1932) prior to the initialing of the Russo-Polish pact (January 26, 1932) in order to dramatize this point and so keep Warsaw from exploiting the 'integrity clause' against Germany.

Faced with the fact of the Polish-Soviet accord, the Wilhelmstrasse tried to interpret it less pessimistically in public. This did not imply that Germany had reconciled herself to the USSR's treaty policy; it meant only that the anti-German alignment of forces in Europe did not offer an alternative policy. Official German statements therefore tended to underline those features of the treaty which were alleged to protect German interests. The Soviet government was said to have retained its freedom to act in the event of a Polish attack on Germany; and the 'integrity clause' was described as less than a border guarantee.[3]

[1] Degras, ed., *Soviet Documents on Foreign Policy*, II, 517–18.

[2] Unsigned, undated, memorandum entitled: 'Sowjet-Russlands Politik der Nichtangriffspakte', 1882/425053–61.

[3] Bülow to Dirksen, January 19, 1932, 1908/429392–5; Dirksen to Bülow, January 22, 1932, 1908/429396–401; Report by Dirksen to

These were the Foreign Ministry's guidelines that were followed by most German press commentaries[1] as well as by Chancellor Brüning in his official defense of German policy to the Reichstag on February 24. In reply to a slashing indictment of Germany's response to Russia's pact policy by a Nationalist deputy, Brüning denied that the development represented a French victory which had freed Poland's hands for action against Germany. He denied too that German political aimlessness and diplomatic incompetence were accountable for Russia's rapprochement with France and Poland. He argued legalistically from the terms of the treaty that Russia had kept her hands free to act if Poland challenged Germany. There was no reason, therefore, to alter Germany's existing ties with the USSR.[2]

Such bland talk about the immutability of German-Soviet relations was little more than the rationalization of a negative development that the Wilhelmstrasse had had neither the skill nor the strength to impede. The 'bluff interpretation' of German-Soviet relations, earlier expounded by Rantzau, was now being revived to show that these relations were still intimate. But it was a 'bluff interpretation' with a new twist. Previously it had been used to strengthen Germany's bargaining position against the western powers; now it was resuscitated to protect the government's shaky domestic position against charges of incompetence by a sensitive public opinion. Statements by German diplomats and government leaders about the viability of the 'Rapallo line' were thus intended primarily for domestic consumption.

This conclusion is buttressed by the realization that Russia's timid rapprochement with France and Poland was at the price of most of the uses that Germany had previously drawn from her partnership with the USSR. Except for military and trade relations, all of these are epitomized by the term 'anti-Versailles'. After all, the intensification of German-Soviet relations in the brief interlude from June 1930 until about May 1931 had been characterized by vocal Soviet support for Germany's revisionist ambi-

---

the Foreign Ministry entitled: 'Paraphierung des sowjetisch-polnischen Nichtangriffspaktes', February 1, 1932, K1904 (not filmed).

[1] *Berliner Tageblatt*, January 27, 1932; *Germania*, January 27, 1932; *Vossische Zeitung*, January 27, 1932.

[2] *Reichstag Debates*, Vol. 446, 2290–1, 2355.

tions regarding reparations and armaments (anti-France), and territory (anti-Poland).

A Soviet Russian rapprochement with France and Poland now required that Moscow jettison or at least mute that support, a development already evident in Stalin's interview of December 1931. At that time Stalin had said that Russia would not become a supporter of the Versailles settlement; yet he had not, as he would have a year earlier, combined this affirmation with a promise of Soviet support *against* Versailles and its principal defenders, France and Poland.[1] In the words of Kochan: 'Russia is not recognizing the Versailles System, but Russia is also not opposing the Versailles System.'[2] The USSR had in no sense come out against Germany, but she was also not taking Germany's side.

The upshot of this devaluation of German-Soviet relations was that Soviet and German policies at the Disarmament Conference were no longer so well coordinated as they had been during the sessions of the Preparatory Commission. Indeed they began to diverge noticeably. Moreover, the term 'Rapallo' was redefined so that instead of being represented as an exclusive relationship with an anti-western point of view it was defined as a model for the USSR's developing relations with third states. The Berlin treaty took its place as one non-aggression accord among many.[3]

7. DUSK

RELATIONS with the USSR during the last year of the Weimar Republic were generally muddled. The disintegration of authority in Berlin had much to do with this, making the definition and maintenance of a clear foreign policy line difficult and sometimes almost impossible. Often the Ambassador in Moscow was either without instructions regarding critical developments or in possession of directives that contradicted statements and rumors emanating from the office of the Chancellor. Such uncertainty was multiplied by the rapid turnover of governments, headed up by men such as von Papen and von Schleicher, whose bases of domestic power were as ephemeral as their views on German-Soviet relations were disparate. The extreme fluctuations to which this

[1] Degras, op. cit., II, 517–18.

[2] Kochan, *Russia and the Weimar Republic*, 159. [3] Ibid.

situation subjected Germany's official policy led the Narkomindel to adopt a reserved attitude bordering on aloofness, which continued until almost a year after Hitler's *Machtergreifung*.

The demise of the Brüning government in June 1932 was genuinely regretted in Moscow. As a member of the Catholic Center, Brüning had found close relations with Russia personally distasteful, but he had been enough of a pragmatist to realize that Germany could not disavow them without first achieving a reconciliation with France. Given the intractability of the problems still separating Berlin and Paris, this attitude had satisfied Soviet requirements. It must be stressed that Soviet leaders concluded non-aggression agreements with France and Poland not because they distrusted the Brüning regime, but because they were skeptical about its longevity.

Franz von Papen, Brüning's successor, was another matter. He came to office with a long record of association with groups that had been most bitter in their criticism of the USSR and of Berlin's entire eastern policy. He identified himself with that wing of the Center Party that was pro-French, pro-Polish and anti-Soviet, and over the years had lent his considerable influence to organizations that carried on anti-Soviet campaigns. It may be recalled that von Papen had summoned and chaired the anti-Soviet Herrenklub gathering of important German politicians and church leaders that had met in March 1930; on that occasion he had been voted a member of the Action Committee that was to stimulate and coordinate anti-Soviet propaganda.[1]

More recently it was reported that he had again confided his thoughts on the Soviet problem to the Herrenklub. Some three months before assuming the Chancellorship, Papen was said to have combined a sharp denunciation of the Wilhelmstrasse's policy toward the Soviet Union with the radical proposal that Germany first renounce her ambitions to the Polish Corridor and then combine with France and Poland in an alliance directed against the USSR. It seems that Papen envisioned such a combination primarily as an economic one, with its point aimed at the Five-Year Plan.[2] Given the political circumstances at the time, this

[1] *Supra*, 193-4.

[2] Minutes of a secret speech by Franz von Papen in the Herrenklub, February 27, 1932, printed in the *Berliner Volkszeitung*, June 4, 1932. The authenticity of these minutes is attested by a memorandum in the files of

particular political grouping was the most far-fetched. Only an authoritarian regime capable of riding rough-shod over the anti-Polish and anti-French sentiments of the German electorate would have been in a position to commence negotiations on such a proposal. (Papen was not Hitler.)

The new government was greeted with unconcealed misgivings by Moscow. Its close ties with the Nazi movement and the disturbing opinions of the Chancellor—which were well known to the Narkomindel[1]—guaranteed such an attitude. But the Soviets did not assume that the views of Papen would be decisive for the long-term future of relations with Germany. His regime was classified as being transitional, and Papen himself was not considered personally strong enough to replace a ten-year tradition of friendship with a chimerical scheme that was bound to find little public sympathy.

Yet the future was regarded as uncertain so long as the domestic German scene remained in flux. For prudential reasons the Foreign Commissariat therefore adopted a wait-and-see attitude; it did not react impulsively to the rumored infidelities of the new regime but tried to preserve the connection with Berlin until Papen fell and Germany's tangled domestic politics were clarified. This policy toward Berlin was doubly necessary because of the failure of relations with Paris and Warsaw to improve as quickly as had been anticipated after the initialing of the non-aggression treaties. It was disturbing for Moscow that Poland did not sign and ratify her agreement until July 1932 and that France did not sign her non-aggression pact with Russia until November 1932.

At first the Soviets expressed their distrust of the Papen regime in their press and in general remarks to the Foreign Ministry.[2] *Pravda*'s first reaction to the new cabinet was to suggest that the French middle class was not about to renounce its claim to reparations, grant Germany the right to rearm, or give up its

---

the Foreign Minister reporting that the editor of the *Führerbriefe* had attended a lecture in the Herrenklub some time previously in which Papen 'sich für die Bildung eines deutsch-französisch-polnischen Militärbündnisses mit der Spitze gegen Russland ausgesprochen hätte' (Memorandum by Völckers, June 23, 1932, 2860/D562329).

[1] Dirksen to Meyer, June 6, 1932, 9187/H249246–9.

[2] Dirksen to the Foreign Ministry, June 7, 1932, 1882/424867–70; Meyer to Dirksen, June 15, 1932, 9187/H249243–6.

alliance with Poland.[1] This outward reserve toward Germany was maintained throughout the half-year of Papen's Chancellorship.[2] Yet in late 1932 the temperature in diplomatic exchanges rose steeply as rumors circulated that during the disarmament and reparations negotiations at Lausanne, Papen had launched his pet foreign project by sounding France about a military alliance against the USSR.[3]

The record of a conversation on June 29, 1932, between von Papen and the French Premier Herriot reveals that there was indeed some substance to the story. According to the Chancellor's own memorandum, he had offered a deal in which Germany would conclude a customs union with France and try to create confidence in matters of security in exchange for France granting her equality in armaments.

> . . . in the field of security we could give no greater proof of our sincerity . . . than that we were thinking of an *entente* between the French and the German armies. This *entente* must have no aggressive tendency ta all directed against anyone, but would simply make possible an exchange of views and information between the General Staffs, and would bring a feeling of security about the present situation.[4]

Whatever Papen may have planned with this offer (Russia was obviously not mentioned), the Foreign Ministry interpreted it as no more than a limited gesture. In reply to Dirksen's impassioned denunciation of any agreement that had the appearance of an

[1] *Pravda*, June 6, 1932.

[2] The Narkomindel gave Dirksen the assurance that the Soviet press had been instructed to refrain from criticizing any members of the new German cabinet (Dirksen to Meyer, July 14, 1932, 9187/H249213–18).

[3] Dirksen to the Foreign Ministry, July 1, 1932, 1882/424896–7; Meyer to Dirksen, July 12, 1932, 9187/H249237–40. Without qualification and without citing sources, Kochan asserts that at Lausanne Papen 'propounded to Herriot his plan for a military alliance against the Soviet Union in return for French concessions to Germany' (Kochan, op. cit., 162–3).

[4] Memorandum by Papen regarding conversation with Herriot at Lausanne, June 29, 1932, 3375/731352–4, cited in *Documents on German Foreign Policy*, Series C, I, number 43, footnote 2. See further a memorandum regarding conversation between Herriot and Ramsay MacDonald, July 5, 1932, *Documents on British Foreign Policy*, Second Series, III, number 175.

anti-Soviet alliance, State Secretary Bülow described German negotiations at Lausanne in these reassuring words:

I fear that you have misinterpreted the alleged initiative of the Reich Chancellor regarding direct negotiations between the German and the French military. There is no intention of fashioning relations between the two armies as closely as those between the German and the Russian. We are negotiating with the French regarding equality in the area of armaments, and we are prepared to initiate them into our plans for the reorganization (*Umgestaltung*) of our armaments. In this connection a discussion between the military leaders of the two sides was suggested.[1]

In brief, knowledge of Papen's general anti-Soviet orientation seems to have nourished Soviet fears, subtly twisting reports concerning an offer for Franco-German military conversations into a German proposal for an anti-Soviet pact of war. Any other conclusion, based on the Soviet view, would have to make the odd assumption that Papen had been approaching the French on other occasions without the knowledge of his key foreign policy advisers, or that the State Secretary was purposely misleading Dirksen. Even Papen was realist enough to know that he was not strong enough to carry through a pro-French, pro-Polish, and anti-Soviet policy against the combined opposition of the Wilhelmstrasse, the Reichswehr, and part of German public opinion.

The Narkomindel was nevertheless convinced that Papen had indeed offered the French an anti-Soviet alliance, German disclaimers notwithstanding.[2] Proceeding from the belief that the German policy was a private initiative on the part of the Chancellor, Moscow adopted the tactic of trying to mobilize German pro-Soviet circles against him. In pursuit of this policy the Foreign Commissariat sought and received assurances from the leading opinion in the Wilhelmstrasse (Dirksen, Bülow, and the new Foreign Minister, von Neurath),[3] that a change in Germany's foreign

[1] Bülow to Dirksen, August 20, 1932, 9446 (not filmed).

[2] *Pravda*, July 8, 1932; Dirksen to Meyer, July 14, 1932, 9187/H249213–18; Dirksen to the Foreign Ministry regarding conversation with Litvinov, November 9, 1932, 1882/425024–7; Dirksen to the Foreign Ministry, December 3, 1932, L622/H045331–8.

[3] Dirksen to the Foreign Ministry regarding conversation with Litvinov, November 9, 1932, 1882/425024–7; Memorandum by Bülow regarding conversation with Khinchuk, August 17, 1932, 2860/D562337–338.

policy was not being contemplated. Under considerable pressure from the Wilhelmstrasse even the reluctant Chancellor was persuaded to receive the Soviet Ambassador and to appear briefly at the Soviet Embassy for the annual celebration of the October Revolution.[1] In addition, the Narkomindel turned to the Reichswehr, that locus of authority that had held the balance in Germany in the first years after the war and whose specific weight in German politics was again rising.

In a conversation with Reichswehr Minister Schleicher on June 29 the Soviet Ambassador expressed his uneasiness 'regarding the rumors of a stronger western orientation of German foreign policy and the concern that this orientation could have a harmful influence upon relations with Russia'. Schleicher replied that the friendly relations between the Red Army and the Reichswehr were some guarantee against a reversal in Germany's foreign policy.[2]

Given the Reichswehr's known pro-Rapallo sentiments, it was with relief and faint hope that Moscow greeted the collapse in December 1932 of the Papen government and Schleicher's entry into the Reich Chancellery. The Russians were also encouraged by far-reaching promises from the new regime that immediate steps would be taken to ratify the Protocol for the Extension of the Berlin treaty, initialed as long ago as June 1931.[3] Even more promising were the words that Schleicher addressed to Litvinov at their first meeting on December 19.

In response to a request by the Soviet Commissar for a statement on German policy, the former Reichswehr Minister and now Chancellor affirmed 'that the fact that he was sitting on this chair was a guarantee of friendly relations toward the Soviet Union, and so it would always remain as long as he occupied this office'.[4]

[1] (1882/425024–7; 2860/D562337–8); various notes by Bülow relating to the difficulties in persuading von Papen of the need for a conciliatory gesture toward the Soviets, November 7 and 8, 1932, 6025/H045320–1.

[2] Memorandum by Schleicher regarding conversation with Khinchuk, June 29, 1932, 1882/424893. In late summer Dirksen noted a growing reserve toward military collaboration by the Soviet government (Dirksen to Bülow, August 13, 1932, German Embassy in the Soviet Union, A3, France [not filmed]).

[3] Meyer to Dirksen, December 17, 1932, 9325/E661376–8.

[4] Memorandum by Dirksen regarding conversation with Litvinov in which he described his meeting with Schleicher, December 27, 1932,

But within six weeks the Chancellor's chair had changed occupants. Within another year the new occupant had revolutionized the foreign policy of Weimar Germany and brought to a decisive end an era in German-Soviet relations.

1908/429453–9; Memorandum by Köpke regarding conversation between Schleicher and Litvinov, December 20, 1932, 1908/429450–2; according to another Memorandum of the conversation, unsigned, Litvinov was reported to have made the interesting and perhaps programmatic statement that 'er würde es durchaus natürlich finden, wenn man die Kommunisten in Deutschland so behandelte, wie man in Russland Staatsfeinde zu behandeln pflege' (Unsigned memorandum, undated, 1908/429461–3).

Bibliography

I. BIBLIOGRAPHICAL AIDS

Anderle, Alfred, and Rosenfeld, Guenther. 'Die Erforschung der deutsch-russichen Beziehungen in der Zeit der Weimarer Republik', *Zeitschrift für Geschichtswissenschaft*, VIII (Sonderheft, 1960), 520–31.

Deuerlein, Ernst. 'Die informatorischen Aufzeichungen des Auswärtigen Amtes 1918 bis 1939'. *Aussenpolitik*, IV (June 1953), 376–84.

Epstein, Fritz T. 'Die Erschliessung von Quellen zur Geschichte der deutschen Aussenpolitik'. *Die Welt als Geschichte*, XXII (1962), 204–19.

Erdmann, Karl Dietrich. 'Die Weimarer Republik als Forschungsproblem', *Vierteljahrshefte für Zeitgeschichte*, III (January 1955), 1–19.

Gatzke, Hans. 'The Stresemann Papers', *Journal of Modern History*, XXVI (1954), 49–59.

Hammond, Thomas T. (ed.). *Soviet Foreign Relations and World Communism.* Princeton: University Press, 1964.

Kent, George O. (ed.). *A Catalog of Files and Microfilms of the German Foreign Ministry Archives 1920–1945*. Stanford: University Press, 1962.

Lötzke H. and Brather, Hans-Stephan. *Übersicht über die Bestände des deutschen Zentralarchivs Potsdam.* (Schriftenreihe der deutschen Zentralarchivs, No. 1.) Berlin: Rütten und Loening, 1957.

Mommsen, Wolfgang. *Die schriftliche Nachlässe in den zentralen deutschen und preussischen Archiven.* (Schriften des Bundesarchivs, No. 1.) Koblenz, 1955. (Printed Manuscript.)

R. P. U. 'Die Deutsch-Sowjetischen Beziehungen 1917–1932 im Spiegel Sowjetzonaler Dissertationen', *Ostbrief*, VI (June 1960), 240–8.

Schwandt, Ernst. *Index of Microfilmed Records of the German Foreign Ministry and the Reich Chancellery Covering the Weimar Period.* Washington: National Archives, 1958. (Mimeographed.)

Slusser, R. M., and Triska, J. F. *A Calendar of Soviet Treaties, 1917–1957*. Stanford: University Press, 1959.

Thomas, Daniel H., and Case, Lyan M. (ed.). *Guide to the Diplomatic Archives of Western Europe*. Philadelphia: University of Pennsylvania, 1958.

Weinberg, Gerhard L. *Guide to Captured German Documents*. Washington: National Archives, 1952. (Mimeographed.)

— *Supplement to the Guide to Captured German Documents*. Washington: National Archives, 1952. (Mimeographed.)

BIBLIOGRAPHY

II. PRIMARY MATERIALS

A. Unpublished Sources

1. *Documents of the German Foreign Ministry (deposited in the Political Archives of the Foreign Ministry, Bonn) and of the Reich Chancellery (deposited in the Archives of the Federal Republic of Germany, Koblenz).*

The documents used in the preparation of this study are of two kinds, which correspond to the two parts of the following list: those microfilmed, which are identified by the microfilm serial numbers given in *a*; and those not microfilmed, which are identified when cited, using abbreviations of the full file titles given below under *b*. All of these files were used in the original. The microfilms are on deposit in the National Archives, Washington, D.C., and the Public Record Office, London.

a. Microfilmed

FILM SERIAL NUMBERS	TITLE OF FILE
354	German Embassy in the Soviet Union: Economic Relations between Russia and Germany
1538	German Embassy in the Soviet Union: General Foreign Policy of the Soviet Union
1841	German Embassy in the Soviet Union: Political Relations between Germany and Russia
1842	German Embassy in the Soviet Union: Political Relations between Germany and Russia
1843	German Embassy in the Soviet Union: Political Relations between Russia and Germany
1882	German Embassy in the Soviet Union: Political Relations between Russia and Germany
1883	German Embassy in the Soviet Union: Political Relations between Russia and Germany
1908	German Embassy in the Soviet Union (secret)
1931	German Embassy in the Soviet Union: Annual Political Reports (1929–1933)
2466	Reich Foreign Minister: Conversation in Thoiry
2860	Reich Foreign Minister: Russia (1924–1933)
3177	Reich Foreign Minister: Military Affairs
3242	Reich Foreign Minister: Relations with Foreign States

FILM SERIAL NUMBERS	TITLE OF FILE
4484	State Secretary: German-Russian Economic Negotiations (1925–1929)
4562	State Secretary: Russia (1924–1930)
4564	State Secretary: Russia; Military Affairs (1923–1930)
4620	State Secretary: Correspondence with Officials of the Foreign Service (1930–1933)
4829	General Consul Schlesinger: Personal Correspondence (1924–1928)
5265	Direktoren: Wallroth Papers – Trade Pact Negotiations, Politics, Economic Relations (1924–1927)
5417	Old Reich Chancellery: Foreign Policy, General (1924–1932)
5462	Direktoren: von Dirksen Papers – Russia, Border States, Political Memoranda, Various Secret Reports and Agents' Reports, Secret Reports of Rantzau (1925–1929)
6698	*Geheimakten*: Russia (1925–1930)
7129	Stresemann Papers, Political
7133	Stresemann Papers, Political
7137	Stresemann Papers, Political
7138	Stresemann Papers, Political
7140	Stresemann Papers, Political
7143	Stresemann Papers, Political
9101	Brockdorff-Rantzau Papers, Political
9187	Direktoren: Meyer Papers – Correspondence with von Dirksen (1931–1932)
9325	Direktoren: Meyer Papers – Correspondence with von Dirksen and Schulenburg
9446	German Embassy in the Soviet Union: Political Relations between the Soviet Union and France
9472	German Embassy in the Soviet Union: Junkers (secret)
9480	Direktoren: von Dirksen Papers – Russian Military Affairs (1928–1931)
9481	Direktoren: von Dirksen Papers – Russo-German Military Cooperation (1926–1928)
9524	Department IV, Russia: Russia, Military Affairs (secret)
K281	Department IV, Russia: Political Relations between Russia and Germany, secret (1927–1928)

FILM SERIAL NUMBERS	TITLE OF FILE
K1904	German Embassy in the Soviet Union: Nonaggression Pact Negotiations between the Soviet Union and Poland
K1905	German Embassy in the Soviet Union: Political Reports
L331	German Embassy in the Soviet Union (secret)
L337	German Embassy in the Soviet Union (secret)
L340	German Embassy in the Soviet Union (secret)
L356	German Embassy in the Soviet Union: Franco-German Economic Collaboration in the Soviet Union
L602	Direktoren: Moltke Papers—Russia, Political
L608	Direktoren: Trautmann Papers—Russia, Political
L609	Direktoren: Trautmann Papers—Russia, Political
L610	Direktoren: Trautmann Papers—Russia, Political
L611	Direktoren: Trautmann Papers—Russia, Extension of Berlin Treaty
L612	Direktoren: Trautmann Papers—Russia, Preparations for the Conciliation Commission
L617 A1	Alte Reichskanzlei: Russia (1924–1933)
L622	Department IV, Political: Political Relations between Russia and Germany (1924–1933)
L824	Department IV, Political: Russia, General Foreign Policy

b. Not Microfilmed

TITLE OF FILE

Department IV: Po 4, Russia—Security Pact—Press

Direktoren: Moltke Papers—Negotiation of Russian-German Complaints

Direktoren: Moltke Papers—Russia, Economics (1929–1930)

Direktoren: Trautmann Papers—Russia, Economics, General

Direktoren: Trautmann Papers—Russia, Economic Relations

Direktoren: Trautmann Papers—Russo-German Economic Negotiations

Direktoren: Trautmann Papers—Russia, Politics, General

German Embassy in the Soviet Union: A3, France, Franco-Soviet Non-aggression Pact and Conciliation Agreement

German Embassy in the Soviet Union: A3, France, Political Relations between Russia and France

TITLE OF FILE

German Embassy in the Soviet Union: A3, Political Relations between Russia and Poland (secret)

German Embassy in the Soviet Union: A9, Political Complaints and Political Clarification

German Embassy in the Soviet Union: A19a, Berlin Treaty Renewal

German Embassy in the Soviet Union: A36, Annual Review in the Areas of Politics, Economics and Culture

German Embassy in the Soviet Union: Department D, *Geheimakten*, Special Folder

German Embassy in the Soviet Union: Department E, G.M.I., *Geheimakten*, Cultural Content

2. *Private Papers Located in the Federal Archives, Koblenz*

Gessler Papers

Groener Papers

Rechberg Papers

Schleicher Papers

3. *Others*

Correspondence between Moritz Schlesinger and Paul Scheffer

B. PUBLISHED SOURCES

1. *Documentary Sources*

Auhagen, Otto. *Die Schicksalswende des Russland-deutschen Bauerntums in den Jahren 1927–1930*. Leipzig: S. Herzel, 1942.

Degras, Jane (ed.). *Soviet Documents on Foreign Policy*. Vol. II, 1925–1932. Oxford: University Press, 1952.

Dobrov, A. F. (ed.). *Lokarnskaia konferentsiia 1925 g.: Dokumenti.* Moscow: Gospolitizdat, 1959.

Eudin, Xenia J. and Fisher, Harold H., in collaboration with Jones, Rosemary Brown. *Soviet Russia and the West, 1920–1927: A Documentary Survey*. Stanford: University Press, 1957.

Germany. Archives of the German Foreign Ministry. *Documents on German Foreign Policy 1918–1945*. Series C. I.

Great Britain. Foreign Office. *Documents on British Foreign Policy, 1919–1939*. Edited by E. L. Woodward and Rohan Butler: (first series), II; (second series), III, VII.

Hohlfeld, Johannes (ed.). *Dokumente der deutschen Politik und Geschichte von 1848 bis zur Gegenwart*. Vol. III: *Die Weimarer Republik 1919–1933*. Berlin: Giersch und Co., 1952.

Michaelis, Herbert. *Dokumente der deutschen Politik und Geschichte von 1848 bis zur Gegenwart*. Vol. IX: *Kommentar*. Berlin: Giersch und Co., 1956.

Schapiro, Leonard (ed.). *Soviet Treaty Series*. Vol. I, 1917–28. Washington: Georgetown University Press, 1950.

2. *Memoirs and Diaries*

Berndorff, Hans Rudolf. *General Zwischen Ost und West*. Hamburg: Hoffmann und Campe, 1951.

Blücher, W. von. *Deutschlands Weg nach Rapallo*. Wiesbaden: Limes Verlag, 1951.

Curtius, Julius. *Sechs Jahre Minister der deutschen Republik*. Heidlberg: C. Winter, 1948.

Dirksen, Herbert von. *Moscow, Tokyo, London: Twenty Years of German Foreign Policy*. Norman: University of Oklahoma Press, 1952.

Ex-insider. 'Moscow–Berlin 1933', *Survey*, No. 44–5 (October 1962). 153–64.

Fischer, Ruth. *Stalin and German Communism*. Cambridge: Harvard University Press, 1948.

François-Poncet, André. *The Fateful Years*. Translated by Jacques LeClercq. New York: Harcourt, Brace and Co., 1949.

Gessler, Otto. *Reichswehrpolitik in der Weimarer Zeit*. Stuttgart: Deutsche Verlags-Anstalt, 1958.

Groener, Wilhelm. *Lebenserinnerungen*. Göttingen: Vandenhoeck und Ruprecht, 1957.

Hencke, Andor. *Darstellung der deutsch-russischen Beziehungen von der Oktoberrevolution bis zum Ausbruch des Krieges im Juni 1941*. (Mimeographed.)

Hilger, Gustav. 'Die deutsch-sowjetischen Beziehungen zwischen den beiden Weltkriegen', *Probleme deutscher Ostpolitik*. Edited by Georg Stadtmüller for Arbeitskreis für Ostfragen. Munich: 1957, (Mimeographed.)

Just, Artur W. *Russland in Europa*. Stuttgart: Union Deutsche Verlag, 1949.

Kühlmann, Richard. *Gedanken über Deutschland*. Leipzig: Paul List Verlag, 1931.

Luther, Hans. *Politiker ohne Partei*. Stuttgart: Deutsche Verlags-Anstalt, 1960.

Meissner, Otto. *Staatssekretär unter Ebert–Hindenburg–Hitler*. Hamburg: Hoffmann und Campe, 1950.

Nadolny, Rudolph. *Mein Beitrag*. Wiesbaden: Limes Verlag, 1955.

Raumer, H. 'Dreissig Jahre nach Rapallo', *Deutsche Rundschau*, Vol. 78 (1952), 321–30.

Rheinbaben, Werner von. 'Deutsche Ostpolitik in Locarno', *Aussenpolitik*, IV (January 1953), 33–40.

— *Viermal Deutschland 1895–1954*. Berlin: Argon Verlag, 1954.

Scheffer, Paul. *Sieben Jahre Sowjetunion.* Leipzig: Bibliographisches Institut, 1930.

Seeckt, Hans von. *Gedanken eines Soldaten.* Berlin: Verlag für Kulturpolitik, 1929.

Spalcke, Karl. 'Begegnungen zwischen Reichswehr und Roter Armee: Ein Rückblick', *Aussenpolitik* (August 1958), 506–13.

Speidel, Helm. 'Reichswehr und Rote Armee', *Vierteljahrshefte für Zeitgeschichte*, I (January 1953), 9–45.

Weizsäcker, Ernst von. *Memoirs of Ernst von Weizsäcker.* Translated by John Andrews. London: Victor Gollancz Ltd., 1951.

3. *Newspapers and Periodicals*

Bayerischer Kurier
Berliner Börsen-Courier
Berliner Börsen-Zeitung
Berliner Tageblatt
Berliner Zeitung
Der Ost-Express
Der Tag
Deutsche Allgemeine Zeitung
Deutsche diplomatisch-politische Korrespondenz
Deutsche Tageszeitung
Deutsche Zeitung
Dresdner Neueste Nachrichten
Düsseldorfer Nachrichten
Ekonomicheskaia Zhizn'
Frankfurter Kurier
Frankfurter Zeitung
Germania
Hamburger Echo
Izvestiia
Kölnische Zeitung
Osteuropa
Pravda
Rabochaia Gazeta
Rote Fahne
Schlesische Volkszeitung
Sozialdemokratischer Pressedienst
Völkischer Beobachter
Vorwärts
Vossische Zeitung

III. SECONDARY SOURCES

Airapetian, M. E., *Etapy vneshnei politiki SSSR.* Moscow: 1961.

Anderle, Alfred. *Die deutsche Rapallo-Politik: Deutsch-sowjetische Beziehungen 1922–1929.* Berlin: Rütten und Loening, 1962.

— 'Die deutsch-sowjetischen Verträge von 1925–1926', *Zeitschrift für Geschichtswissenschaft*, V (1957), 471–502.

Angress, Werner T. *Stillborn Revolution: The Communist Bid for Power in Germany, 1921–1923.* Princeton: University Press, 1963.

Augur [Poliakov, Vladimir]. *Germany and Europe.* London: Selwyn and Blount, 1927.

Becker, Ernst. 'Das Zustandekommen und der Abschluss des deutsch-sowjestischen Freundschafts und Neutralitätsvertrags (Berlin Vertrag) vom 24.4.1926', *Wissenschaftliche Zeitschrift der Universität Rostock*, VI (1956–7), 13–21.

Beloff, Max. *The Foreign Policy of Soviet Russia, 1929–1941*. Vol. I, 1929–36. London: Oxford University Press, 1947.

Bliumental', S. N. 'Peregovory predstavitelei zapadnykh derzhav o perevooruzhenii Germanii v 1932 godu', *Novaia i Noveishaia Istoriia* (1961), 111–13.

Boveri, Margret. 'Rapallo: Geheimnis–Wunschtraum–Gespenst', *Merkur*, VI (September 1952), 872–88.

Bretton, Henry L. *Stresemann and the Revision of Versailles*. Stanford: University Press, 1953.

Breyer, Richard. *Das Deutsche Reich und Polen, 1932–1937*. Würzburg: Holzner, 1955.

Carr, E. H. *The Bolshevik Revolution, 1919–1923*. Vol. III. New York: Macmillan, 1953.

— *German-Soviet Relations Between the Two World Wars, 1919–1939*. Baltimore: Johns Hopkins, 1951.

— *Socialism in One Country, 1924–1926*. Vol. III. London: Macmillan, 1964.

Carsten, Francis L. 'The Reichswehr and the Red Army', *Survey*, No. 44–5 (October 1962), 114–32.

— *Reichswehr und Politik 1918–1933*. Köln: Kiepenheuer und Witsch, 1964.

Castellan, Georges. 'Reichswehr et Armée Rouge 1920–1939', in *Les Relations Germano-Soviètiques de 1933 à 1939*. ed. J. Duroselle. Paris: Armand Colin, 1954.

Cleinow, Georg. 'Sowjetrussland und Europa', *Europäische Gespräche*, VI (1928), 177–93.

Coates, W. P., and Z. K. *A History of Anglo-Soviet Relations 1917–1942*. Vol. I. London: Lawrence and Wishart, 1943.

Craig, Gordon A., and Gilbert, Felix (ed.). *The Diplomats, 1919–1939*. Princeton: University Press, 1953.

Craig, Gordon A. *The Politics of the Prussian Army, 1640–1954*. Oxford: Clarendon Press, 1955.

Dallin, David J. *The Rise of Russia in Asia*. New Haven: Yale University Press, 1949.

Dueck, N. *Die Sekten und der sozialistischer Aufbau*. Kharkov: State Publishing House, 1930.

Ehrt, Adolf. *Das Mennonitentum in Russland von seiner Einwanderung bis zur Gegenwart*. Langensalza: Julius Belz, 1931.

Emma, N. L. *Die Auswanderung ist eine konterrevolutionäre Aktion*. Moscow: State Publishing House, 1930.

Epstein, Julius. 'Der Seeckt Plan', *Der Monat* (November 1948).

Erdmann, Karl Dietrich. 'Das Problem der Ost- oder Westorientierung in der Locarno—Politik Stresemanns', *Geschichte in Wissenschaft und Unterricht*, VI (1955), 133–62.

Erickson, John. *The Soviet High Command: A Military-Political History, 1918–1941*. New York: St. Martin's Press, 1962.

Fensch, Dorothea. 'Das sowjetische neubau Programm in der Rostocker Neptunewerft in den Jahren der Weltwirtschaftskrise', *Wissenschaftliche Zeitschrift der Universität Rostock*, VI (1956–7), 39–46.

Fischer, Louis. *The Soviets in World Affairs, 1917–1929*. 2 vols. London: Jonathan Cape, 1930.

Flechtheim, Ossip K. *Die Kommunistische Partei Deutschlands in der Weimarer Republik*. Offenbach a. M.: Bollwerk Verlag Karl Drott, 1948.

Freund, Gerald. *Unholy Alliance: Russian-German Relations from the Treaty of Brest-Litovsk to the Treaty of Berlin*. London: Chatto and Windus, 1957.

Gasiorowski, Zygmunt. 'Stresemann and Poland Before Locarno', *Journal of Central European Affairs*, XVIII (April 1958), 25–47.

— 'Stresemann and Poland After Locarno', *Journal of Central European Affairs*, XVIII (October 1958), 292–317.

— 'The Russian Overture to Germany of December 1924', *The Journal of Modern History*, XXX (June 1958), 99–117.

Gatzke, Hans W. 'Russo-German Military Collaboration During the Weimar Republic', *American Historical Review*, LXIII (April 1958), 565–97.

— *Stresemann and the Rearmament of Germany*. Baltimore: Johns Hopkins, 1954.

— 'Von Rapallo nach Berlin: Stresemann und die deutsche Russlandpolitik', *Vierteljahrshefte für Zeitgeschichte*, IV (January 1956), 1–29.

Göring, M. *Bismarcks Erben, 1890–1954: Deutschlands Weg von Wilhelm II bis Adolf Hitler*. Wiesbaden: Steiner, 1959.

Goerlitz, Walter. *Der deutsche Generalstab*. Frankfurt: Frankfurter Hefte, 1951.

Hahn, Bruno. 'Die deutsche Ausfallburgschaft für Lieferungen nach Russland', *Osteuropa*, I (1925–6), 554–63.

Halpern, I. P. 'Stalin's Revolution: The Struggle to Collectivize Rural Russia, 1927–1933'. Unpublished dissertation, Columbia University, 1965.

Helbig, Herbert. *Die Träger der Rapallo-Politik*. Göttingen: Vandenhoeck und Ruprecht, 1958.

Helmer, Karl. 'Der Russland-Ausschuss der deutschen Wirtschaft', *Osteuropa*, XII (1951–2), 177–80.

Hilger, Gustav, and Meyer, Alfred G. *The Incompatible Allies: German-Soviet Relations 1918–1941*. New York: Macmillan, 1953.

Hoetzsch, Otto. *Germany's Domestic and Foreign Policies*. New Haven: Yale University Press, 1929.

Höltje, Christian. *Die Weimarer Republik und das Ostlocarno-Problem, 1919–1934*. Würzburg: Holzner Verlag, 1958.

Kennan, George F. *Russia and the West under Lenin and Stalin*. Boston: Little, Brown and Co., 1960.

Kindzorra, Otto. 'Zu den Feierlichkeiten des Zehnten Jahrestages der Grossen Sozialistischen Oktoberrevolution 1927 in Deutschland', *Wissenschaftliche Zeitschrift der Humbold-Universität, zu Berlin*, VII (1957–8), 55–60.

Klein, Fritz. *Die Diplomatischen Beziehungen Deutschlands zur Sowjetunion, 1917–1932*. Berlin: Rütten und Loening, 1952.

Kluke, Paul. 'Deutschland und Russland zwischen den Weltkriegen', *Historische Zeitschrift*, Vol. 171 (May 1951), 519–52.

Kobliakov, I. K. *Ot Bresta do Rapallo*. Moscow: IMO, 1954.

— 'Rapallo-vchera i segodnia', *Novoe Vremia* (1957), 15–16.

Kochan, Lionel. *Russia and the Weimar Republic*. Cambridge: Bowes and Bowes, 1954.

Komarnicki, Titus. 'Polish-German Relations between the Two World Wars I', *Poland and Germany* (autumn 1957), 24–34.

— 'Polish-German Relations between the Two World Wars II', *Poland and Germany* (March 1958), 24–31.

Korbel, Josef. *Poland Between East and West: Soviet and German Diplomacy Toward Poland, 1919–1933*. Princeton: University Press, 1963.

Kornew, W., and Grabowsky, Adolf. 'Um Rapallo', *Zeitschrift für Politik*, XX (January 1931), 619–32.

Krasil'nikov, A. N. *Politika Anglii v otnoshenii SSSR 1929–1932 gg*. Moscow: Gospolitizdat, 1959.

Kretzschmar, Ursula. 'Der Kampf in der deutschen publizistischen und historiographischen Literatur der Jahre 1917–1933 bei der Einschätzung des Aufbaus des Sozialismus in der UdSSR'. Unpublished dissertation, Martin-Luther University, Halle, 1959.

Kruszewski, Charles. 'The German-Polish Tariff War (1925–1934) and its Aftermath', *Journal of Central European Affairs*, III (October 1943), 294–315.

Kuczynski, Juergen, and Wittkowski, Grete. *Die deutsch-russischen Handelsbeziehungen in den letzten 150 Jahren*. Berlin, 1947.

Kul'bakin, V. D. *Militarizatsiia Germaniia v 1928–1930 gg*. Moscow: Gospolitizdat, 1954.

Mann, Golo. 'Rapallo: The Vanishing Dream', *Survey* (October 1962), 74–88.

Martius, G. 'Die rechtlichen Grundzüge der deutsch-russischen Verträge vom 12. Oktober 1925', *Osteuropa*, I (1925–6), 443 ff.

Matthias, Erich. *Die deutsche Sozialdemokratie und der Osten, 1914–1945*. Tübingen: Arbeitsgemeinschaft für Osteuropaforschung, 1954.

Melville, Cecil F. *The Russian Face of Europe*. London: Wishart, 1932.

Menzel, M. 'Die deutsche Aussenpolitik und der Berliner Vertrag vom Jahre 1926', *Wissenschaftliche Zeitschrift der Karl Marx-Universität Leipzig*, VI (1956–7), 113–21.

Morgan, R. P. 'The Political Significance of German-Soviet Trade Negotiations, 1922–5', *The Historical Journal*, VI (1963), 253–71.

Murav'ev, Iu. P. 'Sovetsko-Germanskie kul'turnye sviazi v period Veimarskoi Respubliki', *Vestnik Istorii Morivoi Kul'turi* (1960), 55–63.

Noack, Paul. 'Deutsch-russische Beziehungen von 1922 bis 1933', *Politische Studien*, II (1960), 77–88.

— 'Rapallo—Wunsch und Wirklichkeit', *Politische Studien*, II (1960), 31–43.

Norden, Albert. *Fälscher: Zur Geschichte der deutsch-sowjetischen Beziehungen*. Berlin: Dietz, 1960.

— *Zwischen Berlin und Moskau*. Berlin: Dietz, 1954.

North, Robert C. *Moscow and the Chinese Communists*. Stanford: University Press, 1953.

Pope, Arthur Upham. *Maxim Litvinoff*. New York: L. B. Fischer, 1943.

Posser, Diether. *Die deutsch-sowjetischen Beziehungen seit 1917*. Darmstadt, 1955.

R. P. U. 'Um Rapallo', *Ostbrief*, VI (January 1960), 11–18.

Rosenbaum, Kurt. *Community of Fate: German-Soviet Diplomatic Relations, 1922–1928*. Syracuse: University Press, 1965.

— 'The German Involvement in the Shakhty Trial', *The Russian Review*, XXIII (July 1962), 238–60.

Rosenfeld, Günther. *Sowjetrussland und Deutschland 1917–1922*. Berlin: Akademie Verlag, 1960.

Roth, Paul. *Deutschland und Polen*. Munich: Isar Verlag, 1958.

Schapiro, Leonard. *The Communist Party of the Soviet Union*. New York: Random House, 1960.

Scheffer, Paul. 'Die Lehren von Rapallo', *Merkur*, VII (April 1953), 372–92.

Schieder, Theodor. *Die Probleme des Rapallo-Vertrags: Eine Studie über die deutsch-russische Beziehungen 1922–1926*. Cologne: Westdeutscher Verlag, 1956.

Schleuning, J. *In Kampf und Todesnot: Die Tragödie des Russlanddeutschtums*. Berlin: Bernard und Graefe, 1930.

Schüddekopf, Otto Ernst. *Linke Leute von Rechts*. Stuttgart: W. Kohlhammer, 1960.

Schwertfeger, Bernard. *Deutschland und Russland im Wandel der Europäischen Bündnisse*. Hanover: Adolf Sponholtz, 1939.

Seabury, Paul. *The Wilhelmstrasse: A Study of German Diplomats Under the Nazi Regime*. Berkeley: University of California Press, 1954.

Seeckt, Hans von. *Deutschland zwischen West und Ost.* Hamburg: Hanseatische Verlagsanstalt, 1933.

Seraphim, Ernst. *Deutsch-russische Beziehungen 1918–1925.* Berlin: Hermann Sack, 1925.

Stein, George H. 'Reichswehr and Red Army: The Secret Collaboration, 1921–1933'. Unpublished Master's essay, Columbia University, 1960.

Tarulis, Albert N. *Soviet Policy and the Baltic States, 1918–1940.* Notre Dame: University Press, 1959.

Thimme, Annelise. 'Die Locarnopolitik im Lichte des Stresemann-Nachlasses', *Zeitschrift für Politik,* III (August 1956), 42–63.

— *Gustav Stresemann.* Hanover: Norddeutsche Verlagsanstalt O. Goedel, 1957.

Toynbee, Arnold J. (ed.). *Survey of International Affairs, 1925–1932.* 8 vols. Oxford: University Press, 1927–33.

Trachtenberg, Jakow. *Das Attentat auf den deutschen Botschafter in Moskau.* Berlin: Jakow Trachtenberg, 1932.

Triska, Jan F., and Slusser, Robert M. *The Theory, Law, and Policy of Soviet Treaties.* Stanford: University Press, 1962.

Trukhanovskii, V. G. (ed.). *Istoriia mezhdunarodnykh otnoshenii i vneshnei politiki SSSR 1917–1939 gg.* Vol. I. Moscow: IMO, 1961.

Unruh, B. H. 'The Background and Causes of the Flight of the Mennonites from Russia in 1929', *The Mennonite Quarterly Review* (October 1930), 267–81; (January 1931), 28–41.

Ushakov, V. B. 'Otnosheniia mezhdu Sovetskim Soiuzom i Veimarskoi Germaniei v izobrazhenii zapadnogermanskoi burzhuaznoi istoriografii', *Istoriia SSSR* (1959), 182–90.

— *Vneshniaia politika Germanii v period Veimarskoi Respubliki.* Moscow: IMO, 1958.

Vietsch, Eberhard von. *Arnold Rechberg und das Problem der politischen Westorientierung Deutschlands nach dem 1. Weltkrieg.* Koblenz: Schriften des Bundesarchivs, 1958.

Völker, Karl-Heinz. 'Die Entwicklung der militärischen Luftfahrt in Deutschland, 1920–1933', *Beiträge zur Militär- und Kriegsgeschichte* Vol. III. Stuttgart: Deutsche Verlagsanstalt, 1962.

Volkov, F. O. *Anglo-Sovetskie otnosheniia 1924–1929 gg.* Moscow: Gospolitizdat, 1958.

Wandycz, Piotr S. *France and Her Eastern Allies, 1919–1925: French-Czechoslovak-Polish Relations from the Paris Peace Conference to Locarno.* Minneapolis: University of Minnesota Press, 1962.

Wheeler-Bennett, John. *The Nemesis of Power: The German Army in Politics, 1918–1945.* London: Macmillan, 1953.

— 'Twenty Years of Russo-German Relations, 1918–1939', *Foreign Affairs,* XXV (October 1946), 23–43.

Wiskemann, Elizabeth. 'Germany's Eastern Neighbors', *Survey* (October 1962), 45–53.

Worliczek, Adalbert. 'Rapallo: Drohung und Wirklichkeit', *Die Politische Meinung*, I (October 1956), 22–38.

Zimmerman, Ludwig. *Deutsche Aussenpolitik in der Ära der Weimarer Republik.* Göttingen: Musterschmidt-Verlag, 1958.

INDEX

INDEX

STUDIES OF THE RUSSIAN INSTITUTE

Soviet National Income and Product in 1937 — *Abram Bergson*

Through the Glass of Soviet Literature: Views of Russian Society — *Edited by Ernest J. Simmons*

The Proletarian Episode in Russian Literature, 1928–1932 — *Edward J. Brown*

Management of the Industrial Firm in the USSR: A Study in Soviet Economic Planning — *David Granick*

Soviet Policies in China, 1917–1924 — *Allen S. Whiting*

Polish Postwar Economy — *Thad Paul Alton*

Literary Politics in the Soviet Ukraine, 1917–1934 — *George S. N. Luckyj*

The Emergence of Russian Panslavism, 1856–1870 — *Michael Boro Petrovich*

Bolshevism in Turkestan, 1917–1927 — *Alexander G. Park*

The Last Years of the Georgian Monarchy, 1658–1832 — *David Marshall Lang*

Lenin on Trade Unions and Revolution, 1893–1917 — *Thomas Taylor Hammond*

The Japanese Thrust into Siberia, 1918 — *James William Morley*

Soviet Marxism: A Critical Analysis — *Herbert Marcuse*

The Agrarian Foes of Bolshevism: Promise and Default of the Russian Socialist Revolutionaries, February to October, 1917 — *Oliver H. Radkey*

Soviet Policy and the Chinese Communists, 1931–1946 — *Charles B. McLane*

Pattern for Soviet Youth: A Study of the Congresses of the Komsomol, 1918–1954 — *Ralph Talcott Fisher, Jr*

The Emergence of Modern Lithuania — *Alfred Erich Senn*

The Soviet Design for a World State — *Elliott R. Goodman*

Settling Disputes in Soviet Society: The Formative Years of Legal Institutions — *John N. Hazard*

Soviet Marxism and Natural Science, 1917–1932 — *David Joravsky*

Russian Classics in Soviet Jackets — *Maurice Friedberg*

Stalin and the French Communist Party, 1941–1947 — *Alfred J. Rieber*

The Sickle under the Hammer — *Oliver Henry Radkey*

Ukrainian Nationalism — *John A. Armstrong*

Sergei Witte and the Industrialization of Russia — *Theodore H. Von Laue*

Comintern and World Revolution, 1928–1943 — *Kermit E. McKenzie*

Weimar Germany and Soviet Russia, 1926–1933 — *Harvey L. Dyck*